Keep Smiling

Charlotte Church

Keep Smiling

THE AUTOBIOGRAPHY

with Fanny Blake

Copyright © Charlotte Church 2007

The right of Charlotte Church to be identified as the author
of this work has been asserted by her in accordance with the
Copyright, Designs and Patents Act 1988.

First published in Great Britain in 2007 by
Orion Books
an imprint of the Orion Publishing Group Ltd,
Orion House, 5 Upper St Martin's Lane,
London WC2H 9EA
An Hachette Livre UK Company

10 9 8 7 6 5 4 3 2 1

A CIP catalogue record for this book is available from the British Library.

ISBN: 978 0 7528 7537 8 (hardback)
ISBN: 978 0 7528 9087 6 (export paperback)

Printed in Great Britain by Clays Ltd, St Ives plc

The Orion Publishing Group's policy is to use papers that are natural,
renewable and recyclable and made from wood grown in sustainable
forests. The logging and manufacturing processes are expected to
conform to the environmental regulations of the country of origin.

Every effort has been made to fulfil requirements with regard to
reproducing copyright material. The author and publisher will be
glad to rectify any omissions at the earliest opportunity. Unless speci-
fied otherwise, all photographs are reproduced courtesy of Charlotte
Church's family.

www.orionbooks.co.uk

CONTENTS

'They say hard work never killed anyone, but I say why take the chance?'

Ronald Reagan, fortieth president of the United States, 1981–89

ACKNOWLEDGEMENTS

When I was younger, for every birthday and Christmas, Mum would give me a diary. 'Write it down,' she'd say. 'Write it all down. You'll regret it if you don't.' But I couldn't because she always looked at what I wrote! If I ever caught her, she'd say, 'Oh, I thought you'd have locked it.' All innocent, like. But I know that even if I had locked it, she'd have been there with a penknife! Writing this book would have been so much easier if I'd done what she suggested.

Thanks to Fanny Blake for drawing this story out of me, and for her patience, persistence and skill; to Amanda Harris and Lisa Milton of Orion for convincing me that people were interested in my story; to Mum and Mark for reminding me of things I had long forgotten; to Holly for the behind-the-scenes photos and for organising my life for two years. Finally, thanks to all those who have helped on the way and to the fans who have supported me in everything I've done over the years. This book is for you.

PROLOGUE

One chilly November night in 2005, I was out on the lash with the girls in Cardiff when I spotted the Welsh rugby team across the bar. Like all good Welsh people, I love rugby, so I wanted to congratulate them on that afternoon's winning game, the last of the autumn internationals. Among them, I spotted Gavin Henson, who had been having an excellent season. His spiky hair made him unmistakeable. Although it was something I'd never normally have done, I made a beeline for him.

'Hi. Well done in the game today. Nice to meet you.' Those were my first words to him. He reckons I gave him a kiss, but I never. I shook his hand and that was it.

The other girls had got into house music since we'd spent a week in Ibiza earlier in the year and they wanted to go to Liquid, where there was a hard-house night. I wasn't interested, so I crossed the road to meet my mum and auntie Caroline, who were out together in Braz, a bar brasserie. Earlier in the day we'd been at my cousin Jade's eighteenth-birthday bash so they were all still celebrating. I soon forgot about the rugby team and decided to stick with Mum, who was going on to Charlston's Brasserie, where they serve a mean steak. As far as I know, the steak could be minging but at 2 a.m., covered in garlic cloves, it seems like the best steak in the world. More importantly, they serve alcohol until 6 a.m.

As we were walking down the street, I heard a man's voice

say, 'Charlotte! Come here.' I'm used to being approached in the street, so I ignored him. But he wouldn't give up. 'Hey, Charlotte. You know me.' I turned round to see Mr Henson standing there, looking rather dashing in his suit and holding a pack of chips in one hand. They looked rather attractive too. I smiled and said, 'Hi,' before going over with Jade. As she helped herself to his chips, I chucked them on to the floor. 'Come on, you two. Into Charlston's with me, now!'

It all gets a bit hazy here, but Gavin reckons that he sat at the opposite end of the table to me and that I ignored him all night. I'm sure I was sitting between him and my mum, who was going mad with excitement. 'Oh my God, a rugby player.' She was almost purring. 'Look at you. You're gorgeous. Imagine, if you two got together, how beautiful your kids would be.'

'Oh, Mum. Shut up. Please.' I couldn't believe what she was like.

As for Gavin, he thought he'd walked into the twilight zone. I absolutely fancied the pants off him, mind, because he's just stunning to look at. At one point, I touched his leg, then pulled my hand away. You can't do that, I thought. You're with someone. Get a grip. I was in total turmoil. Ian Shaw, my vocal coach, says I kept banging the table whenever anyone wouldn't listen to me, shouting, 'Listen to me . . .' I'd even forgotten the steak and chips I'd been so looking forward to because I was too busy eyeing up Gavin. Ian, who was on some 'lighter life' diet where you only eat power food, ate almost all my meal without my noticing. As we were getting up to leave, my mum swung into action again. 'Give her your number,' she instructed Gavin. 'Go on.'

'Mum! For fuck's sake!' I was mortified.

She'd always said that she wanted me to move to London so that I could meet other celebrities who would understand my world. But I wanted to stay where I was born and brought up with my friends and family. I knew she was thinking that meeting Gavin was just the opportunity I needed. And it was all happening under her eyes in Cardiff.

None of us could have foreseen that two years later I'd be sitting in our bedroom holding a pregnancy test I'd bought in Tesco, nervously waiting to see whether or not the blue line would appear. Gav and I had just come back from a wicked few days in Chamonix with some friends. While we were there, I felt really weird, nothing I could put my finger on, but I knew something wasn't right. Drink didn't have its usual appeal, so I stayed relatively sober, shepherding the others about the place. We thought we'd been rather well-behaved and had managed not to draw too much attention to ourselves until we saw the headlines back home. Apparently I'd drunk ten sambuccas and six vodka-Red Bulls when I told Gav to, 'Eat the fucking pizza.' If I had managed to down all that alcohol, I wouldn't have been in a fit state to say anything at all.

By the time we got home, it had dawned on me that I might be pregnant. I bought the test without saying anything to anyone. I shoved on some baggy jeans, due to my inexplicably larger midrift, and one of Gavin's hoodies, hoping that no one would recognise me. I hung around Tesco's hay fever section studying the Piriton as I waited for the aisle to clear of people buying condoms and looking at vitamins. The moment I was alone, I snatched a pregnancy test, rushed to the checkout and escaped.

I was so shocked when it came up positive. The half-hour I had to wait until Gav came home from training seemed to last for ever. His mum, Audrey, had come over with a lasagne for Gav. She was completely oblivious to what was going on as she pottered about the kitchen, washing up cups and chatting. I was in a daze, numbly answering 'yes' or 'no' to anything she said while going over and over the implications in my mind.

What difference would my being pregnant make to Gav and me? How would all the people I worked with react? What would the pregnancy mean for my TV show? My head was spinning. At last he came through the door and I broke the good news. We didn't fall into each other's arms, crying and hugging, or anything romantic like that. Gav didn't believe me.

'It's only a £2.99 test,' he said. 'It's bound to be wrong.'

I was pretty confident it was right but agreed to do another. That came up positive, too, but it still wasn't enough for Gav. 'Wait until you've seen a doctor and he's done a proper test,' he said. I think he wanted to believe I was pregnant, but having a baby wasn't exactly something we'd planned, so he was having a hard time getting his head round it. My doctor referred me to BUPA, where I had a scan at seven weeks. Seeing our baby moving about on the grainy black-and-white ultrasound screen was wild. We were both freaked out, but in a really good way, and it was then we got excited for the first time.

We decided to keep the news secret until I was twelve weeks, when the risk of miscarriage was less, but the *Sun* phoned Mum, claiming someone had spotted me in Tesco. I just told her they were lying. Then a journalist phoned my manager, asking if the rumour was true. Apparently someone had contacted one of the papers and spilled the beans. We managed to field that one off, too, by denying everything, but only until I had to have a confidential medical with an insurance company for my TV show. Someone who had seen my insurance form sold the information to the papers.

Although I'm used to stories being leaked about me, I still can't get used to the fact that it happens. Of course I understand that money's money, and if a newspaper's prepared to pay for a story then it's hard for people to resist, but it makes me sick to my stomach that I can't trust anyone, especially after we'd gone to such elaborate measures to keep my pregnancy secret.

The resulting press speculation meant that we had to tell our families and release the news earlier than we wanted. But then, once it was in the open, Gav and I could get on with looking forward to the baby – even if I was feeling as sick as a dog.

So much has happened in my life without being planned, but so far everything's always turned out for the best. I've learned that the unexpected definitely isn't a bad thing. I've come such a long way since I was an eleven-year-old kid who didn't have a clue but who got a totally unexpected break into the music business. I've had an amazing life so far, travelling the world to sing for all kinds of audiences, including the Pope, two American presidents and the Queen, as well as meeting all sorts of cool people. I wouldn't have changed it for the world.

Growing up in the glare of the public spotlight has been weird: I've been praised, criticised and vilified. I've been portrayed as an angel and a child from hell; as a down-to-earth, talented young singer and a drunken, hell-raising chav. There have been times when I haven't been sure who I was myself or which direction I wanted to take. When I'm papped looking a right mess, when stuff is made up about me or when details of my personal life are leaked to the press, there's only one way to deal with it. You've just got to keep smiling.

The one thing that has been constant in my life is my family. They are the people who mean everything to me, and I could never have survived the shit that I've been through without their support. Thanks to them, I've always felt very secure and loved. They are an integral part of who I am, as well as the reason I'm so grounded.

My mother and father were always a strong team who travelled everywhere with me when I was young and kept everything together. It must have been odd for my mother having a daughter who seemed, and certainly sometimes felt, like public property. Living in each other's pockets inevitably created huge tensions between us as I was growing up, but at the same time we were fortunate enough to see the world while I did what I loved best: singing. With the lows came massive highs. Together with my nana, my bampy (grandfather) and Auntie Caroline, Mum and Dad gave me the happiest, most stable childhood I could have had, given the unusual circumstances in which we found ourselves. Now, along with Gavin, the baby and all the rest of our big extended family, they are still the most important part of my life.

CHAPTER 1

Family Business

TIP:

Listen to the opinions of your family and friends. They're the ones who'll keep you grounded by telling you the uncomfortable truth, rather than the people you work with, who tend to tiptoe around the 'talent'.

There isn't a single shrinking violet in our family. If any of us has something to say, we say it. Everyone enjoys our family get-togethers, especially when it comes to stepping up and taking the microphone for a song. We all like to take centre stage, particularly after a few drinks. Even when I was being born, my mum couldn't resist trying to steal my limelight by having an asthma attack after twenty-four hours of labour! As a result, my heart stopped. There was a real *ER* moment as she was rushed into surgery for an emergency Caesarean, double doors clattering behind her as doctors and nurses swarmed around her bed, shouting instructions at one another. I eventually emerged, weighing six pounds twelve ounces, pink and peachy-skinned, at ten o'clock on 21 February 1986.

They say that I was a happy baby and, to my subsequent embarrassment, was breastfed until I was fourteen months old. Mum used to tell everyone that I'd walk over to her and say, 'Titty, Mummy.' She laughs when she tells the story, and although I don't mind people knowing about it now, when I was younger I used to wish she'd shut up. She tells me that she nursed me all the time; we were like a little unit of our own. All I can remember is loving her to bits.

Mum was nineteen when she got pregnant. She was with my biological father for about a month before she got pregnant and about eighteen months later she left him because she was incredibly unhappy. I know that I've got his eyes and that's all. I also know that her version of events may be biased, but it's the one I've grown up with and, whatever he might say in his defence, as far as I'm concerned he stuffed up big time in the way he behaved towards her. I hate the idea of anyone treating my mum badly.

The only thing I regret is that by not contacting him I will never know my two half-brothers, who were born after they split up. They're young and none of this is their fault, any more than it's mine, but that's the choice I've made. Some people feel that their life's only complete when they know their entire family history. Not me. I'm 100 per cent happy with the huge extended family I already have. I don't need to complicate things any more.

Once Mum and he had split up, she and I spent almost two and a half years living happily with her parents, my nana and bampy, and my auntie Caroline in their house in Victoria Avenue in Cardiff. My nana is the rock in our family. She's a tiny woman, only four feet eleven inches tall with size-three feet, and she's very classy. She's always joked that she was born in the wrong class. Her hair's short and neat, and she always looks good, whether she's wearing her best or her everyday black trousers with a loose top. She's a devout Catholic and goes to church every Sunday – it's the one thing I suspect she wishes we'd all do. I really respect her for her belief. After she's got the dinner in the oven, Bampy drops her off for twelve o'clock Mass and picks her up when it's over. I used to go to church with her until I was twelve, then my life turned upside down and it was too difficult to keep it up.

Apart from her religion, Nana has passed on her Welsh pride to the rest of the family. She was born and brought up in Cardiff, although originally her family came from Ireland in the nineteenth century. Jim McKay, Nana's father, and his wife, who I knew as Nana Kay, lived in one of the five streets in Cardiff's New Town that were built for the city's Irish community. Because Jim was unskilled and jobs in the docks tended to be passed from father to son, it was hard for him to find work. They had four children: John, Maureen (my nana), Terry and Frances. John drowned in the docks when he was little. Although she was only four when it happened, Nana remembers that day vividly and believes the tragedy broke her father's spirit. He drifted in and out of jobs, never settling to anything, so that, as Nana says, 'He wasn't a great provider.' Instead, her mother worked hard to provide for them, taking on cleaning jobs and working in a local factory. In those days nothing was easy. The other families in the street were all better off, thanks to the regular money their men brought home from the docks. Nana and her brother and sisters were often dressed in second-hand clothes and didn't have everything their friends had. 'I felt being poor,' she told me. 'And I didn't like it.'

I don't remember Nana Kay, although she was alive until I was about three. All our family remember her sitting knitting, a fag in her mouth, wreathed in smoke because she never inhaled. What's the point in smoking like that? As the column of ash grew longer and longer, her granddaughters, Mum and Caroline, would watch transfixed, waiting for it to drop.

My great-grandfather might not have been much of a provider, but apparently he had a wicked sense of humour, was always cracking jokes and, like Nana Kay, he really loved his children. Nana says he gave them things other fathers never gave their children in those days, things that money couldn't buy. He would take them on long walks where, as they picked bluebells and primroses to take home, he taught them all about nature. Whenever a big ship came into the docks he'd take the kids down to share the excitement and look over it. He also loved musicals and the cinema. Whenever he could, he would take Nana to the Central Cinema, better known then as the Bug House. For threepence (1½p) they'd sit through a Hollywood musical, then go home and re-enact all the dances themselves. Bing Crosby, Gene Kelly, Fred Astaire and Ginger Rogers: they saw them all.

Nana left school at fifteen after the head nun pointed out to Nana Kay that, even if her daughter did pass the scholarship exam to senior school, the family wouldn't be able to afford the uniform. Instead, during her final year of school, she took shorthand and typing lessons for a shilling (5p) a week. She absolutely hated them. Nonetheless, secretarial jobs were ten a penny in those days so she was soon earning a wage. After a couple of false starts, she settled into being a secretary at Roath Furnishing until she got married and had children.

She met my bampy, real name Edward Gary Cooper, though everyone calls him Gary, when she was sixteen and Bampy was eighteen. Nana had noticed him at the St Albans Catholic Youth Club, but she was seeing someone else. Then while she was away on a caravan holiday in Somerset, her boyfriend dated her best friend, so that was the end of him. When Nana makes her mind up about something, that's it: a trait she's handed down to me. The Saturday after she got back to Cardiff, she went to the dance hall in Sophia Gardens, where the band-leader Ted Heath was playing. Bampy was there and asked her to jive. That night he walked her home, and they've been together ever since. They married on 4 August 1962.

Bampy's family originally came from Gloucestershire, just over the border from Wales. His grandfather worked in the Forest of Dean mines until he moved to the Welsh coalfields, and he died when he was only twenty-eight, leaving his widow to bring up their five children alone. Bampy's father started work as a cobbler when he was fourteen. He must have done well for himself because by the time Nana met the family, they lived in a five-bedroom house in Splott, just near Cardiff's docks, with the cobbler's shop in the front room. Before she married, Bampy's mother had worked below stairs as a kitchen maid in a big house somewhere. As a result, her own house was always immaculate. She would never go to bed at night until she had cleaned out the grate, set a new fire for the morning and laid the breakfast.

As the youngest of ten, Bampy was the baby of the family. He left school when he was sixteen to start work in the local steelworks, but the shift work didn't suit him. He's always been a real night bird and was just as bad about getting out of bed then as he is now. He'd stay up all night if he was on a morning shift, but if he was on nights, he'd sleep all day. Eventually, one of his brothers who worked on a building site, came to the rescue and found him a five-year apprenticeship as a plasterer. His five brothers, were furious that the apprenticeship, then a bad knee and the fact that his parents were old-age pensioners, exempted Bampy from National Service. They thought he needed the discipline!

Apart from Nana and his family, Bampy's greatest love has always been music. The skiffle group he started when he was nineteen was the first of many bands he's been involved with. He was still rock 'n' rolling ten years ago with Gerry and the Atrics!

The nearest he got to topping the charts was when he was guitarist and saxophonist in the Solid Six during the early sixties. He always tells us how the band spent seven months roughing it in a van in London, trying to break through. Nana would leave work on Fridays and catch the train to spend the weekend with him. Bampy would book her into a B&B, then park the van, complete with band members, outside for the night. She slept in the B&B and then during the day he'd show her the sights.

While he was in London and on the circuit, he met all the up-and-coming singers. Their single 'If Liszt Could Do the Twist' was a hit in Holland and Australia. The other place they made it big was Israel. They were the first rock band to tour there and spent two months getting their audiences to jive in their seats. When they got back to the UK the band disbanded, but Bampy's never stopped singing and playing the guitar.

Bampy is unique, crazy in the most fabulous way and really entertaining. He's about five foot six and a quarter, although he always says, 'Five foot six and a half, Charlie.' (He's the only one who calls me Charlie.) Drinking a couple of pints every night with the boys has given him a rock-hard beer belly. His brown eyes are always twinkling, and although he's bald on top he's got plenty of grey hair round the sides. Retired now, he still wears his thin, grey working shirts which are completely knackered, covered in bits of plaster, with his old jeans slung below his belly over low, black ankle boots.

He's full of jokes and, thanks to being a lifelong smoker, he's got a deep, gravelly laugh to go with them. He'll often interrupt me, laughing to say, 'I made that one up forty years ago, Charlie.' He's the wisest man in the world and he looks it. His is wisdom that comes with age and experience. He can read people so well and can be very profound. I can't wait to be that wise. He's got so many facets to him that he can talk about lots of things: music, astronomy, politics, you name it. He has loads of catchphrases, too, but the one I always remember comes out when he signs off a phone call. He always says, 'Keep smiling.' His positive attitude to life is infectious and everyone who meets him loves him.

Nana and Bampy settled in Cumrae Street in Splott in a two-up, one-down railway worker's cottage. They might have had an outside toilet but they had a shower in the kitchen, which according to Nana was posh. Everyone else had a tin bath that was covered with a lid when not in use. The house was tiny, but Nana's milkman told her his mother brought up eight children in it. Eventually plans for a hook road that would run right through the street meant Nana and Bampy had to up sticks, and in 1970 they moved to Victoria Avenue, a cul-de-sac just off Victoria Park, where they've been ever since.

This house has always been our family home as far as I'm concerned. I spent so much of my childhood here that however Nana redecorates, I still love everything about it. A short path leads to the front door. I was devastated when Nana changed the old yellow and green wooden door for a white PVC one with little windows. When I told her off, she asked me if I wanted the old one, but it wouldn't be the same without the house!

The front room on the left of the hall is only used for best (so hardly ever) and, when she was living there, as my auntie Caroline's rehearsal room. Nana keeps the colour scheme simple with a brown sofa by the fireplace, an olde-worlde dresser stuffed with her Lladro pottery figurines, a drinks cabinet where they keep all the drink that they never drink and a little glass drinks trolley. There's also a stack of LPs and singles lined up by an old-fashioned record player.

Day to day, we all lived in the big open-plan back room. There's a living area where two red leather sofas sit against the creamy walls on which Nana has always hung family pictures. The TV sits in the corner with her chair right beside it. Through a big archway are the kitchen and dining area, which both look out into the back garden. When Nana and Bampy first moved there, the kitchen was tiny, but they extended it so there's plenty of room for family Sunday lunches or parties. Upstairs there are two double bedrooms, a guest room, a tiny toilet and a bathroom. Nana's changed that too. The bathroom suite used to be that weird-arse Seventies shade of pink, but I preferred that to the white she's got now.

By the time they moved here, Nana and Bampy had two children, Maria (my mum) and Caroline. My mother was born in 1966, with Caroline following in 1968. Mum's an Aquarius and that makes her quite quirky and mercurial with a quick temper. She's always been very smart, but by the time she took her A levels let's just say she had more interests outside school than in, so she didn't concentrate on her work.

Encouraged by Bampy, both she and Caroline loved music. Caroline has a fabulous voice and became a cabaret singer; she still occasionally performs today. Mum was a brilliant classical guitarist and a natural musician. She practised for hours every day and dreamed of playing professionally. Nana and Bampy had high hopes for her passing music A level and going to music college. Instead, she flew through the practical but failed the theory. Nana was furious. The alternative was office work, so she learned to type, then blagged her way into the Cardiff Council's Housing Office, where she worked for eight years, ending up as senior estate management officer.

I was born just as she was starting her career. I may have been a beautiful baby, but I was the ugliest toddler you've ever seen. Needless to say, my mum disagrees, but I've seen the photos. I ate like a pig – everything except bananas – so I was pretty chubby with massive legs. My hair only grew round the sides of my head, leaving me bald on top for the first two or three years. And my big ears stuck out. My teeth didn't come through until I was three, and I had a constantly running red nose – I was minging. However, my mum and Caroline did their best with me. They dressed me up like a doll, always in matching socks, dress and hair bobbles so I looked really girly. Looking at the old photos, some of those outfits shouldn't have been allowed. In one of them, I've got that dodgy hair and am wearing what looks like a little old lady's dress in navy blue with a white lace collar and a big blue bow. Disgusting! My looks aside, I'm told that I was quite a cool, placid little kid who wasn't too much hard work.

Things changed when my stubborn streak emerged. I knew what I wanted and would do what I had to to get it. Once, Mum and Caroline took me into town dressed in a pink dress and petticoat, matching pink and white socks and hair in bunches, as always. When Mum refused to give me some sweets, I hurled myself screaming into the nearest puddle. When I refused to get up, they both waved me goodbye and walked away. That old trick. Most kids would have got up and run after them. Not me. I sat in that puddle until they came back and gave me the sweets I wanted.

The one person in the family I idolised was Caroline. I wanted to be just like her. Our whole family remembers the Christmas when I was three. The day before Christmas Eve, I came downstairs looking radically different. I had found a pair of scissors and cut off one side of my long hair so I'd have short hair just like her. Nana was horrified, although I think she saw the funny side. Caroline had to cut the other side to match before Mum came home, but it wasn't a good look. Then on Boxing Day I struck again. Someone had given Caroline a big bottle of Chanel No. 5 so, because I wanted to smell like her too, I sneaked up to her bedroom and poured the whole bottle all over me. I stank for days no matter how much they washed me.

I may not have been the ideal three-year-old but there was more to my behaviour than just the 'terrible threes'. I blame the fact that Mum had met the man who was to become my proper dad, James Church. She had gone out one night with her friend Mary to a club in Cardiff where everyone used to go for a Sunday singalong, when a guy she knew from work came in with his best mate, James. Both of them were completely

pie-eyed, but James was tall, dark-haired and handsome, or so
Mum says. He worked for Sheffield Insulation, a firm that sold
building materials. They got chatting and Mum ended up
giving him her number. Three days later, he phoned her at
work. All he could remember was her bright red lipstick. He
even asked to speak to Mary! Luckily Mary realised he meant
Maria and transferred him. Mum agreed to meet up with him
that night and it went from there.

Apparently things were a bit strained when he and I first
met, and I'm sure that's because I wouldn't have wanted anything or anyone to come between me and my mum. At the
time he thought I was a brat because I caused lots of trouble
by telling anyone who'd listen how nasty he'd been to me. In
fact, he'd never have been nasty, he's just not the sort. All the
same, I managed to stir up quite a few rows between him and
Nana. I didn't want a stranger in our close-knit, *cwtchy* (affec-
tionate) family and did my best to get him out. My war of
attrition was short-lived, though, and after my initial resent-
ment wore off, I abandoned the campaign and absolutely
accepted him as my dad.

Not that my obstinacy disappeared entirely. My mum
always reminds me of what happened on my fourth birthday
when I played musical statues with my cousins and a couple of
friends. She was watching out for who moved when the music
stopped, but when she picked me I went nuts. Show a bit of
loyalty, Mum. So what if I moved? It's my birthday. I ran
straight to Nana's cupboard under the stairs, shut the door
and refused to come out. In the end, whoever won the game
had to give me the prize – a Galaxy bar – to stop me crying.
As I came out clutching it, right as rain, they all looked at me
as if I was the devil child.

Dad is the one person I've met who's got exactly the same greeny-blue coloured eyes as me. People say he's very good-looking but I don't see him in that way. To me, he's just my dad. None of his features particularly stand out, but they all fit together quite nicely and he wears his dark hair in a stupid quiff. He's always looked after me and I love him to bits, even though for years he teased me about my sticking-out ears and nicknamed me 'Dumbo'. No wonder I had a complex about them.

As far as I was concerned, Dad was my real father until my cousin Nadine told me he wasn't. She broke the news when we were both about five, but as far as I can remember it was a case of, 'Yeah, whatever.' I've always been quite accepting of situations and rarely make a scene – unless I'm drunk! – so I just accepted what she told me and got on with life. No big deal. I think my mother was more upset when she sat me down at the age of nine to break the news. She'd got incredibly nervous about telling me, then I said, 'I know. Nadine told me years ago.' She was so shocked. Knowing had never been a problem for me. I never questioned it.

CHAPTER 2

Happy Days

TIP:

Phoning up record companies and telling them how great you are will get you nowhere. Better to be a star in your local town, because if you're good at what you do, sooner or later someone with contacts in the music industry will hear you and tip them off. Think of it this way, if you're an outstanding schoolboy footballer, you wouldn't call up Sir Alex Ferguson and tell him how great you are, would you? Sooner or later you'll get spotted by a club scout. That's how it should be.

Mum and Dad got married on 9 May 1992, when I was six. The big issue for me was, of course, the bridesmaid's dress. Caroline and my cousin Nadine were bridesmaids too. Caroline had a beautiful pink dress and there were two smaller ones, one pink and one white, for Nadine and me. All I wanted was to look like Caroline, so I had to have the other pink dress, but when I tried it on, it was too big for me, so I was given the white one, while Nadine got to look like Caroline. I was well pissed off. My mum consoled me, saying, 'It's only a colour, you'll still look lovely in your dress.' Yeah, right.

My auntie Margaret had put my hair in rags the night before, so I looked cute with my hair in curls, crowned with flowers and a posy of pink and purple silk roses. I went to the church in a Rolls Royce with Mum and Bampy and followed them down the aisle to Mandelssohn's 'Wedding March'. Mum looked lush in an off-the-shoulder froth of shell-pink tulle with a long veil and a big bouquet. We didn't know until afterwards that Caroline had dragged Dad and his mates out of the pub over the road from the church just moments before we arrived. They'd all arrived early, thought they'd kill half an hour with a pint and then lost track of the time. The service itself was interrupted by us all laughing when Bampy responded to the minister's question of who was giving the bride away with a thunderous, 'I do,' and then again when Dad couldn't get his words out.

Afterwards we all piled off to the reception at the Fairwater Conservative Club, where there was a disco. Caroline kicked off the singing with Shirley Bassey's 'I Am What I Am', my cousin Paul went next with one of his brilliant Elvis impersonations, my godfather, Dominic, sang 'I Used to Know the Bride (When She Used to Rock 'n' Roll)', while Bampy sang 'My Girl', his song for my mum, and Nadine and I sang 'Chick, Chick, Chick, Chick, Chicken (Lay a Little Egg for Me)'.

Afterwards, I stayed at Nana's while Mum and Dad honeymooned in Crete. When they came back home, they brought loads of presents, but nothing quite as special as the crystal heart earrings that Mum had bought Nadine and me for being bridesmaids. They were my first piece of real jewellery and I loved them. Shades of things to come.

Some time after Mum and Dad married, we moved from our house in Glamorgan Street to a bigger, much lighter and airier house in Windway Avenue, just on the other side of Victoria Park from Nana and Bampy. My mum's like a gypsy, always on the move, so this was the second of our five homes together. We moved house almost every two years throughout my childhood. Just as my new bedroom was finished, we'd be off again. Mind you, we never did up my bedroom in Windway Avenue, so it stayed blue with spaceships on the wall. Apart from the usual bed and wardrobe, I had a portable yellow box where my knickers and socks were kept. It looked like a food cooler and opened up into two levels – very odd. I kept my whole dinosaur collection on a table until I grew out of them and into my record player. My very first record was Wham's 'Wake Me Up Before You Go-Go' – I must have half-inched it from my nana's collection.

Windway Avenue was where we had the first of a string of pets. Sybil was a hamster given to me by Mum's friend from work. Sybil ran away, but she was followed by four more hamsters. One bit my dad, then ate a couple of her babies. Another was killed by our white-socked tabby cat, Sophie. I even killed the goldfish I won at the annual Victoria Park Fête. I just wanted to see what would happen if I squeezed him, so I did . . . hard . . . until blood oozed out of his gills. I was so scared about what I'd done that I panicked and put him back in the bowl. Funnily enough, I've never had a goldfish since.

We began to trade up to larger animals but without much success. Dad wouldn't allow Roger the guinea pig into the kitchen for the winter because it was too unhygienic, so poor old Roger froze to death – literally. I went down one morning to find him stiff as a board. That was a horrible moment. Then we moved on to dogs. Bonnie, a Yorkshire terrier, would get so excited when we came home that he'd pee everywhere. Once, he got his leg shut in a door so he was taken to doggie hospital. Or so my parents told me – in fact, they sold him. Bastards! After him came Sam, a massive Border collie who used to dash around all the settees. He was too much for us, especially as nobody was in for most of the day, so he was found a new home on a farm.

Despite all that, I've been an animal lover ever since and now have four Jack Russells, Ike, Tina, Bennie and Frankie, and aspirations to own a farm with as many animals as I can fit – except pigs. I hate pork, although I can't resist bacon.

When the time came for me to go to primary school, I wanted to go to Lansdowne Primary, where Nana was a dinner lady. Instead, I was sent to the same primary school that Mum and Auntie Caroline went to, St Mary's Catholic Primary School in Canton, quite near the centre of Cardiff.

On her way to work, Mum would drop me off with Auntie Frances (Nana's sister), who lived just down the road from St Mary's, then Auntie Frances would walk me round to school with my cousin Nadine (her granddaughter). At the end of the afternoon, Caroline would pick me up and take me round to Nana's, where I would stay until Mum came to take me home.

Nana always seemed to be cooking, even though she claims to hate it. I loved her stew, cottage pie and Sunday roasts, and for Sunday tea she'd put a stick of French bread in the oven and bake it until it crisped up nicely, then we'd have it spread with butter together with a jam sponge, Swiss roll or angel cake. Bread, cake and tea – my favourite meal of the week. She used to make sponge cakes, under pressure from the family, and my job was to lick the inside of the massive cream mixing bowl, so I'd hover on the edge of the kitchen, desperate for her to get the cake in the oven.

It doesn't take much for the women in our family to start shouting. We're all really loud. Gavin says that if I'm not talking, I'm banging and clattering somewhere in the house. Nana's the same. If you mess with her, she'll start shouting. If she's cleaning something she'll double the amount of energy she's using on the job, wiping a surface twice as fast while trying not to shout. Bampy reckons that she loses her rag because she's so unfit and her subconscious is telling her to have a bit of exercise by shouting. 'Have I made her shout recently?' he'll ask with a twinkle. 'I have to give her exercise so she lives longer.'

Nana's house was like no other that I've been in. She organised her week so that she had one cleaning day when everything would be polished to within an inch of its life. The place was always spotless, even though there were so many of us in it. Thursday was shopping day, and when I got home from school the cupboards would be bursting. All the food I ate there tasted wicked. She bought Morning Coffee biscuits, which I still love – they're outstanding when they're dipped in coffee – and custard creams when she was feeling flush. Even a Kit-Kat at my nana's tastes better than a Kit-Kat anywhere else. Friday was her day off, when, ever since I can remember, Bampy would take me to get a fish supper from the chippie down the road, then, sprawled out on the sofas, we'd watch *Frasier* before I had to go to bed.

Christmas has always been a big celebration in our family. I still get as excited about it as I did when I was a kid, and I especially love the lead-up to it. When I was small, everyone, including me when I was old enough, went to Midnight Mass. Then we'd spend Christmas Day at Nana's for dinner and presents. Santa came up trumps more than once. He gave me a desk with a dog's head painted inside the lid and another year a bicycle with stabilisers. I loved them both for years. I also had my brown plastic treasure chest with gold straps that was filled with paper, glue, scissors, rulers and thousands of different coloured felt-tips, pens and pencils. My other treasured toy, but only briefly, was Diana, a lush doll from Hamley's. Caroline must have spent a fortune on her. She had a lovely flowery dress and beautiful thick brown curly hair that you could wash. Or so it said. After I'd given it a good shampoo, her hair went into a hideous frizz. I was *so* uninterested in her after that.

In the evening we'd go to Auntie Frances's, and then we'd go to Auntie Margaret's (Nana's first cousin) on Boxing Day. There were loads of us because Auntie Frances's four children are all married with children of their own and Auntie Margaret's five all came along with their families. But we all squeezed in and the adults got tipsy while all the children played together.

Halloween was another big night. Often I went trick or treating with Nadine, and Caroline would make me costumes. She's very creative and could magic a witch's outfit from a black bin bag or a ghost from a sheet. Being with her was always fun.

For a time, she was with a guy called Andrew who once turned up at Nana's front door driving a van. When he opened the back doors we saw that he'd furnished the inside with his mother's carpet, her settee and a little table with loads of alcohol for the adults and chocolates and toys for the kids. We all stared at it, amazed. 'I'm taking you all to Bristol,' he announced. 'We're going to have a day out.' We all piled in – Nana, Auntie Frances, Mum, Caroline, my cousins Alex, Susan and Nadine, and me. By the time we got to Bristol Zoo all the adults were smashed, so none of them was fit to look after us kids – except for Andrew. All I can remember is them buying monkey masks, putting them on and thinking they were so funny, while us kids wandered off to look at the animals. That's just the kind of crazy thing my family would get up to. There was never any question of us kids not being involved.

I don't think our family is unique by being as close as we are. All the other working-class kids at St Mary's had the same sort of close-knit background. I only found a difference when I eventually left and went to the Cathedral School when I was eleven. That was a much posher school where the other kids didn't seem to see their relations nearly as often as I saw mine. They might see their nan once or twice a month, but I saw mine every day of the week until I was sixteen when I started doing my own thing. But even then I still went down to her house two or three times a week, and I still speak to her every day, just as I do my mum and Caroline. Nana gets really pissed off with me if I don't call her. 'I'm only at the end of a phone,' she says. She's like that with Mum and Caroline too.

As it turned out, I loved almost everything about St Mary's – except for playing the violin and games. I'd always liked the sound of the violin when it was played properly, but after I took lessons, I soon discovered that it could become an instrument of torture when played badly. I finally gave up after I had to play 'Twinkle, Twinkle, Little Star' with two other girls in assembly. I completely fucked it up, and there was no way I was ever going to embarrass myself like that again. As for games? If I could find a way to get out of them I would, and it was Nadine who unwittingly gave me the idea for my best excuse. We were fighting one evening after school when she grabbed a can of deodorant and sprayed it in my face. Somehow it brought on an asthma attack. Our Auntie Alison, who was looking after us, went completely nuts with Nadine; from then on I was sorted. Now I knew the symptoms, all I had to do was learn how to fake an attack at the right moment. A bit of gasping and panting during games and I'd be asked to sit it out. It never failed.

Sometimes I could be such a drama queen that I even managed to convince Mum I was too ill to go to school. Because she and Dad were out at work, I'd get to spend the day at Nana's, wrapped up under a quilt on the sofa, while she made me minestrone soup. Being ill could be quite cool.

One of the teachers we all loved was Mrs Hogan. One day she brought an alien into school called Alfie. Alfie was a stuffed toy who wrote us letters in mirror writing. Like everyone else, I completely believed in him and my best moments were when I was sitting on the steps of the stage in the school hall, excused from games and put in charge of Alfie. I felt so honoured and I knew that everyone else wished they were sitting where I was. But they weren't. How I loved that frigging creature!

The only other two teachers I remember were Mr Jeffries and Mrs Brook. Mr Jeffries was the head who once cracked the whole school up with a pretend striptease one Easter assembly, going right down to a vest covered in yellow ducks.

Manners were top of the agenda, and in many assemblies he would say, 'Manners cost nothing.' Then all together we'd respond, 'But they're worth a fortune.'

Mrs Brook, with her pale skin and black hair, sticks in my mind because she insisted on calling me 'Char-lot', which did my head in. I had to explain to her that everyone except her pronounced it 'Charl'tte'.

I always shared my packed lunch with my first best friend, Sophie Mags, swapping the things we didn't like. Her mum always put in Caramel bars, while mine packed Wagon Wheels: how I hated those things. Sophie was a redhead who had loads of brothers, sisters and dogs. I loved her family because it was so chaotically different from mine. My other best friend was Sam O'Grady. She was mixed race and so small she looked like a tiny bird. She was just beautiful with lovely skin, chubby cheeks and sparkly almond eyes with long black lashes. When a boy in our class called her 'a little black ant', I went nuts. I'm the same today. I won't let anyone disrespect my friends or family. Of course, it goes without saying that I can call them whatever names I want, but it's a completely different story if someone else does it. If I call my mum a nutter, that's OK. If I heard anyone else saying it, I'd strangle them. That's just the way it goes.

When it came to name-calling, my name didn't help. Charlotte Cooper quickly became King Cooper after the big ugly dragon in Mario Bros. Thomas Minto and Christopher Chamberlain used to rip the piss out of me for that. I used to give back as good as I got, mind, often making Thomas cry. Then I'd hug him and say, 'I'm sorry, Thomas. I didn't mean it,' and everything would be OK again. He was a cutey. Fortunately, when Mum and Dad got married, we changed my name to Charlotte Church, after Dad, so that soon put a stop to all that.

One of the big events at St Mary's was our first Holy Communion. Everyone in the class took it at the same time. I found it so hard to remember the prayers and we all mugged up for weeks beforehand. It took ages to get word perfect, but I got there in the end. I had to get it right because having your first Holy Communion was a big deal in our family. Nana is such a devoted Catholic that it meant a lot to her especially. We dusted off my bridesmaid's dress and I wore it again. I felt proud as punch as I walked down the aisle in front of my family and the rest of the school.

Although our first Holy Communion was a huge deal, there was nothing more exciting than Red Nose Day, when we got to go to school in our pyjamas. I've always been a proper pyjama-and-slipper girl, so for me it was the best thing ever. Most schools allow you a day out of uniform if you pay a pound, but this was much better. I got up that morning feeling all excited at the prospect of wearing my Winnie the Pooh pyjamas with matching slippers and Eeyore dressing gown and having lessons in them. What was even better was being taken on a surprise bus trip to see a Roald Dahl play. Everyone was rushing around, made up to be out of their uniform for once.

As we got a bit older, the girls began to give the boys a second look. The boys thought I was a bit weird, because if one of them ever caught me in our endless games of kiss chase, I'd always try to beat him up. They soon stopped including me in the game, which was fair dos. The three boys everyone fancied were Luke Hopkins, Aaron Collie and Gavin Davis. I didn't really want a boyfriend, but because most of the other girls had one, I thought I should too. I thought Gavin might be the one for me, but he wasn't interested, so I went out with David Cross instead, just to be the same as the others, mind. We used to hold hands occasionally, if he was lucky, and one time he cornered me and tried to kiss me. I turned my head away so fast that he licked all the way up my cheek. I was disgusted and went straight to tell his friend Joseph. 'Look, Joseph, he's taking the piss.'

'OK, Charlotte,' he said, really serious. 'I'll tell him. Fair enough, you gave him a chance and he took advantage.'

I still can't believe that we were nine when we had that conversation. I wasn't having any of it, so I finished with David and didn't speak to him again. I never did get to go out with Gavin, though.

Apart from school, I made friends with several kids in Nana and Bampy's street. We played in each other's houses or persuaded an adult to take us over the main road to Victoria Park to play. The pond, the playground, tennis courts and the ice-cream van all exerted a magnetic pull. If there was no one to take us, I played in the street, went to a friend's to play Sonic the Hedgehog, watched TV or chatted with my family. I was a pretty self-sufficient kid on the whole.

Dad used to play rugby for the local side, so early on Saturday evenings, Mum and I would meet him after a game and go to the Electricity Club together. They'd have a couple of drinks and I'd play with all the kids there. The bar was very long and thin, with a dartboard at one end, but the building was surrounded by fields where I loved playing hide and seek. If I got bored with the kids, I'd come in and entertain the adults, making them laugh. I guess I was a bit of a mouthy kid,

29

and even then I liked an audience. If I'd been an adult, I think me as a child might have done my head in, although I hope I was quietly confident rather than precocious. I don't think it was 'me, me, me' all the time.

I never once thought about being an only child. I had plenty of friends and such a close extended family that there was always someone to play with. I did spend a lot of time with adults, but I think that benefited me. They never talked down to me and they included me in most of what they did. I treat my cousin Elliot, Caroline's son, in exactly the same way, and I hope to do the same with my own children. If you talk properly to kids and don't babytalk, they'll talk back to you properly. Elliot's nine years younger than me, but unless we're talking about something emotional, I speak to him as an adult because I think he'll grow more as a result. I think I was quite switched on and understood what was going on when I was a child because I was treated that way. I'm sure that's what gave me the confidence I needed later when facing the press for the first time at the age of twelve.

CHAPTER 3

Finding My Voice

Look after your voice and try to find a
good vocal coach who really understands
it and knows how to bring out the best
in it. It also helps if they can make
you laugh.

Growing up with my family was just about as ordinary as it gets. There was only one thing that marked me out: my voice. I loved singing. I was at one of our usual family get-togethers in our local, the Robin Hood, with Mum, Caroline, Nana and Bampy just a few months before my fourth birthday. The pub was crowded and we were sitting in one of the booths at the side, while the juke-box in the corner played all the recent hits. When Gloria Estefan's 'Anything for You' came on, without any warning I climbed on to the plush, red seat and sang along, word for word with perfect pitch and timing. My family were gobsmacked. The only explanation Mum could think of was that I must have just picked it up off the radio that was always playing at my nursery school. For years, I didn't realise that this was anything special, but the rest of my family had the smallest inkling that there was something unusual about me from when I was very young.

I've loved singing and entertaining ever since I can remember and was never afraid to take the microphone. I was three when I was given my first mic, which came with a karaoke set for Christmas. Most of our family love singing, and Bampy's often plonking away on the guitar so I was always encouraged to join in. Nana's told me how Bampy encouraged Caroline with her singing, then me and now my little cousin Elliot, who's mad for playing the guitar. The one thing he said to all of us was, 'You can have the greatest voice in the world, but you must tell a story. Phrasing is everything.'

Bampy used to sit me on his knee while he taught me songs like 'Chick, Chick, Chick Chicken' or my favourite, 'On a Mountain Stands a Lady', before we moved on to his favourites, 'Cheating Heart' and 'Singing the Blues'. Afterwards, I'd stand in front of the mirror with a hairbrush pretending to be a singer.

The only thing that perhaps made me different from a million other little girls was that I had a knack for picking up lyrics, remembering them and being able to sing them completely in tune. Once I know the lyrics of a song, they stay in my head for ever. My memory must be almost completely taken up with songs – about three thousand of them, I reckon – and that's why I'm so bad at remembering anything else. That's my excuse anyway. I even entertained everyone at my nursery school by singing all the songs I'd heard on the radio.

There are so many talented singers in our family. Caroline used to be a cabaret singer in pubs and clubs around Wales, my Auntie Eileen's party piece was 'One Fine Day', my Auntie Linda has a beautiful Eva Cassidy-ish voice, my Auntie Alison can sing, too, as can my cousins Nadine and Jenna, while Uncle

Paul impersonates Elvis on the cabaret circuit – and that's just seven of them.

I'd often sit in Nana's front room watching Caroline rehearse and copying her. She taught me to use my voice, how to hold a mic and how she timed her stage moves. Sometimes I even went on stage with her. Once she was performing in a club, belting out 'Big Spender' when the audience began to laugh. She was mystified, but kept on singing, then she turned round to see a four-year-old mini-me standing behind her, copying every move. I refused to leave the stage and had to be dragged off!

Mum always encouraged me to do the things I loved and seemed good at, just as any mother would. She never pushed me because she didn't have to. I loved dancing, so she enrolled me in dance lessons down at St Mary's Church Hall. We had a fabulous choreographer, Jill, who had a dancer's tiny little legs and feet. We all loved rehearsing the routines she devised, getting ready for the end-of-term shows. The only thing that mattered was getting a place in the front row. That was all I thought about. Mum remembers having to haul me off the stage after one performance. I had run back on after we'd sung 'A Hard Life' from *Annie* and was far too busy waving at the audience.

Nana and Bampy would take me and Caroline to Haven Holiday Camps when Mum was working. I remember it always raining, with nothing for us to do except huddle in the caravan while the adults played cards. Sometimes I'd play with the Haven Tiger and the other kids and apparently, given half a chance, I'd be on the dance floor, making friends and joining in with the other kids, or getting up on the stage and singing 'Ghostbusters'.

At home, after we'd had Sunday lunch at Nana's, we'd all go down to the Schooner, where all the singers and musicians in South Wales went for a get-together and a sing-song. The Schooner burned down when I was about seven, so after that we went to the Boardwalk, a pub that was made to look like a ship inside, with pinky-orange sofas and tables around a big dance floor. All the oldies were Bampy's friends and they'd get up to play the spoons, or sing Frank Sinatra and the old favourites with the live band. It was an open-mic session, so I'd get up there too. All the songs I knew were Caroline's, simply because we only had the music for those, and when she had the time she'd teach me a new one to try out. I loved those Sundays because I was Bampy's granddaughter and everyone loved me for it, and I also gained a lot of my performing confidence there.

Although I could always hold a tune and remember the words, I didn't really stand out as a singer until I was about eight. By then, I was performing at the socials that Caroline organised in St Mary's Church Hall. I once entered a talent competition at a pub called the Golden Hind. I was the only kid there and was wearing a black and gold taffeta dress that Caroline had made for me. My hair was half up and half down, with the down bits all crimped to make it look thicker. Not a great look! I was competing against adults who were professionals and had their beady eyes on the £250 prize. I sang 'Part of Your World' from *The Little Mermaid*, 'On My Own' from *Les Misérables* and Whitney Houston's 'Run to You'. I came third in the finals and was well chuffed.

Caroline was the first to notice how my voice was developing, at a church-hall social. I thought I was the dead spit of Michael Jackson, dressed in black leggings, a white T-shirt and a black cap and waistcoat we'd bought on holiday in Turkey, singing the disco version of 'The Sun'll Come Out Tomorrow'.

My voice was strong and at least I was in tune, but I was disappointed because I knew I hadn't sung with any vibrato, that tremble you hear in a voice when a singer hits a long note. Vibrato colours the voice, giving individuality to a singer. You can train your voice to produce vibrato, but if you push too hard, you can distort it and lose your natural tone. I'd learned about it from Caroline and longed to have a rich, textured voice like hers, but it wasn't happening.

When we watched my Michael Jackson performance back on video, I kept on telling her it was no good, but she played one bit of the tape back to me again and again where I sang one note, only one, mind, with vibrato. 'Do you see that?' she shrieked with excitement. 'You had the vibrato there. You did it! And now you've done it once, you've got to work on it.' At last I'd heard it. It was so exciting. I had no idea then what a rare gift it is, especially in someone so young.

Having spotted the natural quality to my voice, Caroline also recognised that although I had a belter voice, I was singing from my throat rather than using my abdomen. When she was twenty she suffered from nodules on her vocal chords that had to be surgically removed: all because she was a self-taught singer who controlled her voice not from her abdomen but from her throat. After the operation, she couldn't speak for weeks and then had to learn how to sing properly.

My dad pressed Mum to take me to singing lessons. Once, when he was out of work, he had driven Caroline to her gigs and had seen for himself what cabaret singers have to put up with. She had to lug all her gear around, set it up herself and

35

often sing to an audience of drunk punters, half of whom weren't even listening. How soul-destroying would that be? He thought that if Caroline was right and I did have the makings of a good singing voice, I should be trained properly to see whether I had a future as a singer. He knew how much I loved singing and performing.

Mum was just as keen for me to have lessons but had no idea where to find a good singing teacher. Then Caroline remembered that a few years earlier she had met Louise Ryan. Louise had come to see one of her gigs and had given her number to Caroline, who had kept it. Mum contacted Louise, who said she'd be more than happy to see me. There was just one thing: she was godmother to my two half-brothers! It was an amazing coincidence but, we decided, not one that meant we ever had to meet them. So late one wintery Thursday night, we went to her home.

Louise lived in a terraced house in Bedford Street, Roath. Most people had come home from work by the time we arrived, so there wasn't a parking space in the street. Eventually we found one round the corner and walked back past all the different coloured front doors. I was apprehensive because I had no idea what Louise would make me do or whether she'd like my voice. We stopped at number 89 and knocked the little brass knocker on the blue door. Then we heard someone coming down a hall, and a woman's voice telling her dogs to calm down.

The door opened and, framed in the light behind her, was Louise, soon to be known to me as Lulu, a tall, well-endowed, bubbly woman in her thirties with curly reddish hair piled up on her head (later I'd learn that she called it her 'nest'). She had amazing eyes with long eyelashes brushed thickly with mascara, and she was beautifully made up.

'Helloooo,' she sang at us and asked us in. Slightly intimidated, we followed her into the house, saying 'Hi' to the two dogs who were racing around our feet. I could see the kitchen straight ahead, down the corridor beyond the stairs, but she led us through a door on the right into the living room. It was a very sunny room with yellow and blue walls, brightly framed pictures and a green carpet. At the street end, by the bay window, was a blue sofa, a TV and a phone on a black coffee table. She worked at the other end of the room, where a dark wood upright piano stood by a window that looked out on to a small garden where there was a stone dog howling at the moon. There was a black music stand, a big old stereo, a purple office chair and shelves stacked with pieces of music. It all smelled a bit doggy thanks to Piglet, her West Highland white terrier, and Penny, the white Cairn, so I felt quite at home.

Mum sat nervously in the chair and listened while I sang some scales. Lulu has said in interviews that, to her astonishment, I just kept on going up and up, but I remember her pushing me to go higher.

'I can't get that high,' I objected.

'Of course you can,' she said, 'Don't say you can't. Just try it.'

As I got higher, she winced and pulled a face. She could hear that I was singing from the wrong place.

'Would you like to sing a song for me now?'

Yeah! 'I'll sing "Tomorrow" from *Annie*,' I offered.

She pulled out the sheet music and off we went. I was singing away, quite oblivious to her making a face to Mum behind my back – her jaw dropped in shock. Later she told me she was flabbergasted by my voice. I might have been singing from the wrong part of the chest, but my voice was in tune, well balanced and clear. She knew that if she could get me to breathe properly, from my diaphragm, I would have more air to work with and my voice would improve dramatically.

Next, she asked me if I knew 'Somewhere Out There' from *An American Tale*. I loved that song, so off I went, really loud in my big belter voice. She stopped me and asked me to sing it really quietly instead. I thought it sounded awful, not nearly as impressive – that was all I cared about then – but she reassured me that my voice would grow. At this stage, none of us thought that singing would be my career. I sometimes dreamed of being a cabaret singer like Caroline, or an opera singer, but my family were naturally sceptical. I wasn't the only one in the family to have a great voice, and nothing had happened to any of the others. Why should I be any different?

As a result of our meeting I started going to see Lulu once a week, just for half-hour lessons to start with because it was expensive for my parents. Mum came with me to the first couple, but then she was banned. Lulu felt that having a parent sitting there was too disruptive. As the weeks progressed, my voice grew and grew. Lulu was a fantastic teacher and I owe her so much. She was a soprano like me and had started singing when she was twelve. She was brought up in England but came to Cardiff to study performing arts at the Welsh College of Music and Drama. She fell in love with the city and decided to stay and teach. When it came to music, voices and kids, she was a brilliant teacher. She was patient and kind, knowing what was best for me but never imposing her will. She had a great gift and was able to make everything accessible. I can still remember her favourite phrases: 'Welly from the belly – sing from your abdomen – think about your diction –

think about your breathing – keep focused – think of what you're singing about' – just what Bampy told me.

The first ten minutes of every lesson were taken up with scales. Then we'd practise the songs I was learning, stopping when I did something wrong so she could correct me. 'Try singing this way,' or, 'Try thinking about this when you sing that,' she'd say. As we went through the songs she'd scribble all over my sheet music, putting in an arrow for 'Welly from the belly', a tick for a breath, a line for a stop and so on. I'd make my own marks too, such as an open mouth, to help me with the diction, or to remind me of the sound. Sometimes I'd write a translation if the song was in a different language so that I would know what I was singing about, or a phonetic version to help me with the pronunciation. Lulu would record the backing tracks of my scales and songs on to a cassette tape, so every night I could practise them, and she could always tell if I hadn't.

If there was still time at the end of the lesson, we'd attempt a new song. It was hard choosing songs for me, because although I had a mature voice, the subject matter of the big songs was often inappropriate for someone of my age. They were all about love and loss: emotions I hadn't come close to experiencing. Lulu wanted to get me singing the high notes, so first we added 'Walking in the Air' from *The Snowman* to my repertoire. Then one day she said, 'I think you're ready for "Pie Jesu".' Of course, neither of us had the faintest idea that this was the song that would eventually become my trademark and completely change my life.

I was only nine when I entered my first *eisteddfod* – a traditional Welsh festival where singers and poets compete against one another in different classes – which took place in a school in Bristol. I was wearing a special crystal that some friends of Caroline had given me for my birthday. It hung round my neck on a gold chain and was meant to have healing properties. I'm not really into all that stuff, but I did believe in this crystal, which was probably the most expensive thing I had ever been given. I was wearing a pink satin shirt underneath an awful black leather waistcoat and I had my hair a little bit up and a little bit down, my ears just chilling right out there. I'd rehearsed and rehearsed my songs with Lulu – 'Walking in the Air' and 'Polly Put the Kettle On'. They weren't particularly difficult, just the sort of songs expected from kids my age.

It was a horrible, grey cold day when Dad drove us to Bristol in his yellow Cavalier, with Mum and Lulu. Dad sat quietly behind the wheel, while Mum chattered on excitedly, reminding me what to do. 'Make sure you give it a lot of power, a lot of feeling.' She didn't know about the nitty gritty of singing but she has a brilliant ear for music, my mother. I still trust her judgement more than anyone else's in terms of my voice. She never bullshits me and never has. The trouble is, when I'm nervous I get irritable, so while she was fussing, I was like, 'Shut up. I've got to concentrate.' Eventually we arrived at the school, where the other contestants and their families were gathering, all looking as on edge as we were. The atmosphere was so tense that Mum kept having to run outside for a cigarette.

As in all *eisteddfods*, all the competitors sing in different categories for different ages and songs. Lulu had drummed into me that the key things were to have the right stance, projection, technique, breathing and emotion. That's a lot to remember. I would have felt more confident if she'd been playing the piano with me, but the rules dictated that you had to use the official piano player so no one cheated.

As I stepped up in front of the three stony-faced judges, I could feel the butterflies in my stomach. Behind the judges sat all the parents, giving their kids' rivals the eye. God, it was daunting. I totally messed up 'Polly Put the Kettle On' by not taking a big enough breath, so I ran out on one of the notes. I wasn't at all happy. My dad videoed the whole thing, but his hands were shaking so badly with nerves you can hardly see me. Towards the end of the tape, you can eventually see me singing 'Walking in the Air', looking as if I'm with Leonardo di Caprio on *Titanic*: my little fists are all scrunched up and my arms are stuck straight out behind me, as if I was heading into a gale-force wind ready to take off. This time, though, I didn't make any mistakes and sang particularly well. And I won!

All the way home we talked about how well it had gone, dissing the other kids who had been my main rivals – I know they'd have been doing the same about me. I was dying to get back and tell Nana and Bampy. Other than them, I didn't tell anyone, except perhaps my best friend, Sam. None of my friends were into singing, so they weren't particularly interested. Like all kids that age, I didn't want to stand out from the crowd, so I didn't tell them about my lessons with Lulu.

Once Lulu started teaching me and my voice began to develop, I was often asked to sing locally. Mum sometimes arranged for me to sing at local charity dinners, at old people's homes or at hospices. She thought I should wear something suitably classical, so Nana's friend Rose made two long satin dresses for me: one in turquoise and one in white, both with puffed sleeves. Instead of petticoats, which I wanted, they had big hoops to hold the skirts out, but I refused to wear them. Stubborn to the last!

One night I was invited somewhere really posh, about twenty minutes outside Cardiff, to a beautiful private house where I was to sing three or four songs for a private dinner party. I was to be paid an unimaginable £500. My parents were told that I would have my meal in the kitchen and that they couldn't stay while I sang but should pick me up later. Suffice to say, I didn't sing at that posh house after all: there was no way my parents were going to leave me there alone.

All Mum did was steadily encourage me. She certainly wasn't trying to live her dreams through her daughter. She didn't need to because I loved what I was doing.

When people heard me sing, they were usually quite shocked, because my voice was unexpectedly mature and I sounded quite different. When people listen to children singing, they usually say something like, 'That's nice.' But when I sang, they'd go, 'Wow!' Saying that sounds narcissistic, but it's just the way it was. I was completely aware of my talent and how different I was, but for me it was just an everyday thing. I was aware of people's reaction, but for some reason I was always pretty level-headed about it. I never got above my station or had crazy, over-ambitious ideas. I think that's because I was brought up a working-class girl. I think that really matters. I saw the people around me work hard for what they had, so that's what I expected to do, too.

CHAPTER 4

Starting Out

Turbulence tossed the small plane all over the sky. We'd suddenly drop through the air like a stone, then bump along as if we were on a rutted farm track. This was nothing like the large commercial planes in which we'd flown to Turkey on family holidays. Mum and I squeezed each other's hands, petrified. Never have I been so happy as when that plane made a safe landing at a gloomy, wet Glasgow Airport. We made our way to an equally gloomy hotel room, where we were staying so I could appear on a children's TV programme called *Bright Sparks*, a series featuring talented kids and presented by Toby Anstis and Diane-Louise Jordan on children's BBC.

It's funny how word travels. Somehow a researcher for the programme had heard of me and phoned my mum to ask whether I would like to appear on the show. She and Lulu seemed to think it was a good idea, so off we went. For some reason, it was in that Glasgow hotel room that Mum decided I should know that Dad wasn't my biological father, so she sat me on the bed to tell me and I stunned her by saying I already knew. Perhaps this colours my grey memories of the city.

The BBC studios were just as bad – cold and unfriendly. Also appearing on the show was an amazing young violinist. I was awestruck by the way she played Rimsky-Korsakov's 'Flight of the Bumblebee', especially when I remembered my own worse than useless efforts with 'Twinkle, Twinkle, Little Star'.

I'd chosen to wear a pair of really tight, brown Lycra trousers with an orange roll-neck short-sleeved jumper. Yet another fashion disaster. I've always been the most unstylish person ever. You just have to look at old photos of me to see that. I try really hard but it never comes together naturally. Me and fashion just don't get along, most of the time.

Mum and I sat quietly, slightly shell-shocked that we were there, and just doing what we were told, watching the violinist's mother make sure the music stand was in the right place for her daughter and waiting for the moment when I was due to sing 'Pie Jesu'. I don't remember anything about my performance at all; both Mum and I were far too overwhelmed by the whole business.

Apart from my singing, I was still going to dance lessons with my friends. By the time I was eight I'd joined the Meggitt Dancers in Penarth. The classes were on Saturdays from ten till two, and we did everything from ballet and tap to modern jazz. I enjoyed it all, except the ballet. I was a shit ballerina, partly because I was too heavy and partly because I was flat-footed. I wasn't at all graceful and I sounded – and probably looked – like an elephant. At lunchtimes we'd go down to the corner shop, buy shitloads of sweets, then eat them all after-noon, especially during the hour when we watched the older girls dance. I loved those classes and went to them for as long as I could. When I became famous, my schedule meant I couldn't really go any more, but our teacher, Lisa, agreed to go on teaching me in a little attic room in her house for a while.

Mum saw a piece in the local newspaper saying that a local drama group were auditioning for *Annie*, so she took me along to St Peter's Hall in Roath, where I sang my heart out. The director said he wanted to give me the part of Annie but I was too young, so instead he gave me the part of Molly, another orphan girl. I got such a buzz from being in that show. It was the first proper showbiz production I'd been in. The whole thing seemed huge, with a big cast, lighting and sound people. Looking back, it was as amateur as you can get, but there were some really talented kids in it. There must have been some-thing in the Cardiff water around that time!

We've still got a video of the production and you can hear that already my voice is more powerful than anyone else's. While the camera pans along the full cast as we belt out the last number, 'New Deal for Christmas', all you can hear is my voice. At last the camera stops on me and there I am, my little face scarlet with the effort of holding the last note really loud and long. After that performance, I got some bit parts in their production of *The King and I*, including the role of Tuptim, who did a fancy little dance that I loved.

My performance as Molly was enough to persuade Vic Atkins, the director of the Rhiwbina Youth Theatre, to let me audition for them, despite the fact that they had never taken on anyone as young as me before. We met every Saturday from ten till four in the afternoon, but more often if we were rehearsing one of the annual shows or the showcases where all the members had a turn at whatever they were best at, music, drama or dance. I began in the chorus line, but eventually they started to write parts especially for me because I was too young for any of the main roles.

None of this was about being groomed for stardom. All I was interested in was finding more opportunities to sing, as it was the one thing I loved doing more than anything else. I wasn't interested in going to theatre school. I was happy being at home, doing my singing and dancing lessons and acting when I could. Like most kids, I just lived in the moment, never thinking seriously about what I might do with my life.

After one of the *eisteddfods*, Mum and Dad were approached by Mr Gray, the head of the Cathedral School in Llandaff, which had a brilliant academic reputation as well as an excellent music department. His daughter Suzannah had a beautiful voice and was competing in the same age group as me, which is how he'd heard me sing. He asked my parents whether they had thought of putting me forward for a scholarship to the school. They had assumed the scholarships were only open to boys as the school hadn't always been open to girls, and besides, even if I were awarded one, they'd be hard pushed to make up the extra as well as pay the fees for my dancing and singing lessons. Mum has always been genius at spotting an opportunity and taking advantage of it, so once Mr Gray had made the suggestion, she decided to put me in for the scholarship exam and to cross the financial bridge when they came to it.

When I won a scholarship at the age of ten, Mum wasn't going to let a small thing like not being able to pay the short-fall stand in her way. Mr Gray agreed to put our case to the board of governors, who gave us an additional £1,000 on the basis of my singing audition. Mum was undaunted by the fact that she and Dad still couldn't afford the rest. Her determination to get the best for me was amazing. That might make her sound pushy, but remember that morning, noon and night, she had a ten-year-old whining on about how she wanted to go to the posh school and sing.

Mum wrote to every company and businessman she could think of, explaining our situation and asking if they would sponsor me. Eventually Lyn Jones, a friend of hers, approached a local businessman, Stanley Thomas, who generously agreed to sponsor my first year. At the end of that year, Luke Evans, another pupil of Lulu's who had become a family friend, introduced us to Terry Kenny, Director of the Rufford Foundation, an organisation that gives money to worthwhile charitable causes. Terry agreed to come to one of my singing lessons, where Mum explained the situation. Once he'd heard my voice, he asked her to write a letter that he could pass on to his trustees. Thanks to him, they agreed to pay for my second and final year at the Cathedral School.

The Cathedral School was a total culture shock after St Mary's. We had to stand up whenever a teacher entered the room, pupils were called by their surname – a hangover from it being a boys' school – and academically we were really pushed. Mr Gray, the head, was in his forties with big, bushy eyebrows, kind eyes and a strong nose. He had an abnormally long body for his legs so his suit jackets looked a little too short as he flapped down the corridors like a big crow in his black academic gown.

Originally founded in the nineteenth century to provide an education for the boy choristers at Llandaff Cathedral next door, the Cathedral School has continued its strong musical tradition. Every morning there was choir practice in the chapel, and on Monday evenings the girls' choir sang evensong in the cathedral. Mr Gray took the choir, but although he encouraged me, he didn't like the way Lulu was teaching me to sing and wanted me to drop the vibrato from my voice. He felt it made me stand out in the choir when all the others sang straight. Of course Lulu was adamant that I should keep it, because that's what makes a singer, and besides, it came naturally to me. I was caught between the two of them, but then I found that I could sing straight if I wanted to. It was as if I had three different voices to switch between, depending on what was wanted: my natural one with the vibrato, a straight voice that blended in with the choir and my belter voice for the show tunes.

The one teacher I had a problem with was Mr Hoeg, the music teacher. Or rather it wasn't so much me as my mum. I don't think she will ever forget the night she turned up to the parent-teacher evening and Mr Hoeg told her, 'Ninety-nine per cent of singers never make it and Charlotte is part of that ninety-nine per cent.'

Mum hit the roof. By now she thought I had some kind of future as a singer, although she didn't know exactly what. 'You know what? I believe my daughter is one of the one per cent and she will prove you so very wrong.'

She's never been one to mince her words! Mr Hoeg must have been a bit taken aback, but to give him his due, he wrote to her some years later, apologising for what he had said.

Whatever he thought of my voice, Mr Hoeg did give me parts in the two big musicals we put on: *Bugsy Malone* and *Oklahoma!* I adored playing Blousey, a shy but go-getting gal with her eye on Hollywood, and Ado Annie, the ditzy gal who's caught between two fellas and 'cain't say no'. Both of them had great show-stopping songs that I could make the most of.

Bugsy was played by a boy I fancied called Marco. I used to stand in the corner, looking all shy and staring at him, willing him to look at me. I was gutted when I had to miss the school disco for one of Lisa's dance shows because I knew Carly with the bleached hair would get her claws into him. And sure enough . . . Then, by the time *Oklahoma!* came round a year later, he was going out with Helena Ryan. Worst luck. He only played the pedlar while Gwylym Evans took the leading role. Gwylym and I didn't get on too well. We were really competitive, particularly after we discovered he had a higher IQ than me, which I was more than a bit pissed off about.

I enjoyed my two years at the Cathedral School, although now that I was growing up, I sometimes felt uncomfortable in the presence of some of the boys. There weren't many girls there, but I mostly hung out with girls in the year above, particularly Gemma Hawkins and Helena Ryan. They were always getting into trouble. Gemma was the leader, while Helena and I would skulk around after her, watching her admiringly when she smoked at the back of the school buildings. I acted like their little runaround.

When I was eleven, I was put in the Year Seven scholarship class. There were just thirteen of us and the pressure was on. No Common Entrance for us. We were going to be groomed to pass scholarship exams into private secondary schools, probably Monmouth in my case. We were expected to work hard and were given at least two hours' homework every night. But I didn't mind that. I took a real pride in my work and wanted to get good results. There were eleven boys and two girls: just me and Christie Maynard, an American. We sat together but we didn't really hit it off. My real friends were Sam Furness and Anish Patel, but they'd go off with the other lads at break, leaving me to my own devices, which made me feel quite lonely.

Several of the boys used to wind me up by calling me names, trying to trip me up or pulling my chair away just as I was sitting down. They were always giving out because I had blue-striped crisps and Wagon Wheels, when everyone else had Walkers crisps and Kit-Kats. I was the only one who wore shoes from Peacocks, a store that was even cheaper than Primark. Our family car, Betsy, a rusty, burgundy-coloured Ford Fiesta was another target for ridicule. Quite a steep hill leads up to the school, so every morning it was touch and go whether or not Betsy would make it to the top. The posh kids would whizz past looking preened to the hilt in their Mercedes 4x4s. How unnecessary. They'd really take the piss when we finally arrived outside the school because I'd have to climb in and out through the boot and out of the rear window because none of the doors opened from the inside!

The teasing got more and more unpleasant until one day Mum caught me in my bedroom, crying my eyes out, sobbing that I didn't want to go to school any more. She already knew something was up because I'd been so sullen and preoccupied for the previous few days. I didn't want to tell her what was wrong or dob anyone in. Nobody likes a sneak. But in the end, she wormed it out of me and I told her how the boys had started to push me about or pick me up and put me in a corner. Mum had always thought of me as a strong kid, so to her, my breaking down in tears was a sign that something was seriously wrong.

'I don't advocate violence, Charlotte, but,' she said, 'the next time one of those boys picks on you, pull your hand right back and whack him as hard as you can.'

So that's exactly what I did, and I laid the boy out!

Mr Gray was on the phone to Mum immediately and she came up to the school, guns blazing. 'Now before you start, Mr Gray, Charlotte has been picked on and I . . .' She was certain that he was going to have a go at her and then suspend me, but Mr Gray was a very fair man who always tried to keep things level. He knew she would never have advised me to hit anyone without good reason, and he knew that I would never behave like that off my own bat. He listened to all sides and suspended all three of the boys, who, from then on, had a new-found respect for me. I was let off with a warning. As far as I'm concerned, she definitely did the right thing. If I had a kid in a similar situation, I'd do the same, and I'd certainly be secretly proud of my kid for standing up for themself.

Although we didn't realise it at the time, my career was already beginning to bubble. One morning, a month before my eleventh birthday, Caroline and I were sitting in Nana's living room, having breakfast on our knees and watching *This Morning* on TV as usual. I was still on Christmas holidays and was just about to go back for my second term at the Cathedral School. Richard and Judy were running a phone-in called 'Talented Kids', asking for kids with any kind of special talent to phone in and appear on the show. Why not?

I jumped up and went over to the phone in the kitchen. 'I'm going to call them, Car.'

To my amazement, I got through, but the researcher said they had to speak to my mother.

'I'm with my Auntie Caroline,' I explained.

'Can you put your Auntie Caroline on the phone? We need to speak to an adult.'

'Car, Car. I've got through. Come here. Take it. Take it.' I practically threw the phone at Caroline, who explained who she was and that her niece could sing. They didn't seem overly impressed, but they got her to pass the phone back to me. I sang a snatch of 'Pie Jesu' to three different researchers and we were told to hang on. The silence seemed to stretch on forever. Caroline and I were wild with excitement, breakfast forgotten for once. When one of the researchers came back on the line, they said, 'We're going to put you live on air to Richard and Judy. Just speak to them.'

I couldn't see the TV from the kitchen, but I knew they had Zoë Ball's dad as a studio guest and I could imagine the three of them sitting there. All I heard was one of them say, 'Hello, sweetheart. What's your name?'

'Hiya. Charlotte Church.' When I hear the tape now, I can't believe how cute I sounded. Unbelievable.

When they asked me to sing, I gave them a burst of 'Pie Jesu'. When I'd finished, one of them told me to stay on the line because they'd love to have me live on the show. I passed the phone to Caroline as if it was on fire. She was about to hang up when I yelled, 'No, no, no! Stay on the phone and speak to them.' I was so gobsmacked that I couldn't say a word. She was almost as bad, but managed to hold it together and make the arrangements for us to go up three days later on Monday 9 January.

When she put the phone down we just looked at each other and screamed. We did everything we could to get hold of Mum, but she was out of the office on a visit. Eventually, when she got back, one of her colleagues broke the news, 'Charlotte's been singing on the phone to *This Morning*.' When she'd recovered from the shock, she was on the phone to us immediately to find out what had happened. By then, everything was arranged. The three of us were to get the train to London and stay the night in a hotel so we could get to ITV's South Bank studios early the next morning. We were so nervous on the journey. Mum was talk, talk, talk, while I got more and more het up inside.

For me, the highlight of the day was having my make-up done. I thought that sitting in make-up with all those lights around the mirror and having your own make-up artist was amazing, although I was a bit pissed off that instead of the full works, all I was given was a bit of concealer under my eyes and some lip balm. I mean, come on!

After that it was on with the show. I was wearing Rose's turquoise satin dress, so I looked lush. First I had a little chat with Richard and Judy, who were really lovely to me and made me feel quite relaxed, and then I sang 'Somewhere'. It doesn't sound like much, but we were all on a real high from the excitement. What's more, I met Sharleen Spiteri from Texas – I had no idea who she was, but I did know that she was famous, so that was fabulous. The actor John Hannah was on, too, which made me come home wondering why they were all Scottish.

Mum's since told me that she half-hoped we'd be inundated with phone calls on our return, but there was nothing. At least not immediately. I suppose we all thought something might come of it. After all, you go on TV, you get famous, don't you? Not this time. Oddly, not every TV executive is glued to the TV at all hours of the day and night, talent-spotting.

Mum was disappointed, but she made her mind up that the show was just a one-off thing. As for me? I didn't care. I just enjoyed entertaining and I didn't mind where. The world then wasn't nearly as fame crazy as it is now. The cult of celebrity didn't exist in the same way as it does today. There weren't all the magazines devoted to it and none of the TV reality shows had taken off in a big way. Being famous happened to other people, and those it did happen to had real talent. Few people of my age thought seriously about being famous, and if they did, it was far ahead in the future. I certainly had no ambition for it.

Because of my singing and my success with the Rhiwbina Youth, Mum wanted me to audition for the Sylvia Young Theatre School. We went up to London, but as soon as I walked through the doors, I knew it wasn't for me. It was way too scary. The parents all seemed so pushy as they fussed over their children and looked daggers at everyone else. The kids all wore make-up and looked completely stressed out.

I've always had quite a sensible head on me and I knew that sort of crazy environment might bring out the best in lots of people but it wasn't going to do it for me. I think Mum knew that, too. All of my family and me were beginning to hope that I might become a classical singer one day, maybe even with the Welsh National Opera (WNO), and the small successes I'd had just confirmed to us that I had a good voice and that perhaps our ambitions weren't entirely misplaced.

CHAPTER 5

The Big Break

TIP:

*Choose your management with care. Your
relationship with them is like a business
marriage. You'll probably spend a helluva
lot more time on the phone with them
than you will with your boy or girlfriend.*

At last Caroline got the break she'd been waiting for. She'd
sent a couple of demo discs around the record companies in
the past, but they'd all come to nothing. Now she had audi-
tioned and was booked to appear on ITV's *Big Big Talent Show*
with Jonathan Ross. This was her big chance.

Before the show was recorded, a researcher came to Cardiff
to see who from our family should introduce her live on the
show. My nana wouldn't have done it if they'd paid her, my
bampy would have loved to have done it but no one can understand his strong, throaty Cardiff accent, and Mum's never
been easy in front of a camera. So who was left? Me! I was
busting to do it, but the researcher obviously didn't think I
was capable until Nana played him the video of me appearing
on Richard and Judy's *This Morning*. He saw that I was artic-
ulate and confident, and he liked the fact that Caroline had

initially introduced me to *This Morning*. Perhaps I could introduce her and sing a bar or two of 'Pie Jesu'? So this was payback.

On 17 July 1997 we all travelled to London on the train. Poor Caroline was so nervous she was sick, while I was transfixed by the amount of make-up the make-up girls slapped on her – and then she put her own on top! Her nerves were making her so agitated that we were trying not to say anything to upset her. She looked very rock chick in black leather trousers with a black bra under a black see-through shirt. I, on the other hand, was a vision in brown. I wore a short skirt made with big pieces of patchwork and a dark brown T-shirt with an open light brown short-sleeved shirt. My hair was part pulled back to show my crystal earrings and I had my lucky crystal on a ribbon round my neck. Worst of all were my shoes, which were also a patchwork of browns – burnt orange, chocolate and caramel – with a strap around the back: another retail triumph from Turkey. Why did my mother insist on buying all my clothes from Turkey? We sat together through the first few acts, which included a female comic who went way over her allotted three minutes. The crew were signalling and mouthing at her to stop, but she kept going as Caroline got more and more anxious.

At last it was her turn. I went on first and sat opposite Jonathan in a deep brown chair that I thought would swallow me if I sat too far back. He didn't intimidate me, because although he was famous, I'd never seen him on TV. We'd rehearsed that I would sing a snatch of 'Pie Jesu' before Caroline came on.

'I've been told that you have a terrific voice. It's a very different style to your aunt, is that right?' asked Jonathan.

Introducing my family. From left: Nana, Dad, Mum, Elliot's father Mark, Auntie Caroline, cousin Elliot, me and Bampy. Taken in 1999.

Me at five months.

None of my family is afraid to get up and sing. I was three (I'm on the right) when I was given a karaoke machine for Christmas.

Preparing for the real thing. I've now got four Jack Russells that are a lot more trouble!

Life's a beach!

The day Dad made an honest woman of Mum, 9 May 1992.

All dressed up for my first Holy Communion, aged seven.

With my new cousin, Elliot.

A new haircut, a dead serious business.

With Mum and Dad — note my ears chilling out there!

Singing at a church social. Eat your heart out, Michael Jackson!

With Richard and Judy after my appearance on the show.

ITV plc

ITV plc

My big break —
appearing on
*The Big Big
Talent Show*
with Jonathan
Ross.

With my
wonderful
voice coach,
Lulu.

Louise Ryan

Feeding the ducks with Elliot, aged 12 (Elliot was four).

Shirley Bassey, signing her autograph, one of the first in my collection.

Posing for my first publicity shot in the gardens of Llandaff's Insole Court.

The man who signed me up. With Paul Burger, Sony UK President, after I'd clinched a five-album record deal in 1998.

With Mum after signing the record deal. Smiles all round!

'Very different,' I replied. 'I'm a soprano and I'm into opera and she's not!'

'So you're eleven years old and you're into opera.' He obviously didn't believe me.

'Yeah.'

'I've been told you have a beautiful voice, will you give us a little burst?'

'Of course. Please can I get a "C" off the orchestra?' Hearing this back now, I sound so posh.

'A "C" off the orchestra? Well, you can try, they haven't been hitting them this evening!' Jonathan mocked.

'"C", please.'

The orchestra played the note and off I went. When I finished, there was an audible gasp from the audience, then lots of clapping. Jonathan said, 'Wow! Listen to that.' Then he introduced Caroline, 'Ladies and gentlemen, Caroline Cooper.'

As the band struck up, she must have been thinking, I wish I'd never brought the little bitch! If she ever did, mind, she has never said so or even suggested it. So all power to her. She's a real pro, mind, and as she stood there, you would never have guessed how nervous she'd been all day. She sang an original and beautiful song called 'Roberta' by John David, and she sounded fabulous, although I was on the edge of my seat because I knew she'd been having trouble with one part, where the song had been shortened to fit the time slot. In rehearsal she'd kept missing a phrase because she was expecting four beats before it instead of two.

My lessons with Lulu meant that by this time I knew how music worked and was good with my rhythm and timing, so I was listening out, willing Caroline to do well. In fact, the only problem she had was when one camera angle was feeding into another and, as she lowered her hands, one of her eyes didn't open properly because she'd overdone the mascara! As for her performance, she was spot on.

The TV critic Gary Bushell, who was on the show, said she was the strongest singer to appear during the whole series, but the studio audience still voted for the comic. We were gutted and really begrudged her victory. Caroline should have walked away with it. She must have been bitterly disappointed, but she's a typical Cancerian and quite a private person, so she crawled back into her shell and didn't really talk about it.

To make matters worse, when we were backstage after the show, loads of people came up to Mum and said, 'Can I talk to you about your daughter?' 'Has she got an agent?' 'Has she got a manager?' Mum was completely overwhelmed, but also excited as she explained that no, I hadn't and I only sang socially at home in Wales. She had always known what a good voice I had and believed I was something special, but what mother doesn't believe that of her child? Something like this might have happened in her wildest dreams, but the reality was very different. It was as if the floodgates had opened, and of course she hadn't a clue how to deal with it all. I had gone there thinking it was Caroline's big break, so I was glued to my mother's side, not quite believing what my oversized ears were hearing.

A very gracious, elegant woman introduced herself as Jan Kennedy, a theatrical agent who'd been in the audience. She must have been in her mid-fifties but looked at least fifteen years younger, wearing high heels with a trouser suit and a big shawl around her shoulders. She reminded me of Honor Blackman. 'I'm very sorry it's not about your sister. I want to speak to you about that little girl. Is she your daughter?' She was very keen to represent me. Mum gave her our phone number and agreed to talk to her later in the week. If it hadn't been for Caroline's disappointment, we would have gone home on cloud nine.

What we didn't know was that the next day the show's producer, Nigel Lythgoe, bumped into a friend of his, Jonathan Shalit, in the Ivy, a posh restaurant in London. A small, pugnacious man, Jonathan was a showbusiness manager who had had some success making a record with Larry Adler, bringing in Elton John and Sting on his album *Glory of Gershwin*. The story goes that Jonathan asked Nigel if there had been any talent on the previous night's show. Nigel must have enthused about 'a little eleven-year-old girl with an opera voice', and the next thing we knew, Jonathan had got hold of Mum's number and phoned her at work. His first words were, 'How would you like me to make you rich and famous?' He explained that he was a manager and that he'd heard all about me and wanted to come to Cardiff to meet us all.

I've said before that Mum has a sharp eye for the main chance, and she knew immediately that this was an important turning point for us. She knew that to have such a mature voice at my age was what made me special, and that once I hit puberty, my voice might change and I'd be in competition with other singers. This was one of those defining moments in my life and she recognised it. She might not have foreseen what was going to happen, but she knew that to let an opportunity like this pass would be nuts. We might never get another, so she agreed to Jonathan coming to meet us in Cardiff.

A few days later, he was on our doorstep. Sharp-suited with brightly coloured braces and socks, he reminded me of a Womble. He talked to Mum and Dad before coming with us to one of my singing lessons, where he sat sprawled in an arm-chair, with one leg hooked over the chair arm, watching and listening. I didn't really take to him, but I never said a word because the rest of my family were so excited about his prom-ises of record deals, concerts and a future in singing. Anyway, what did I know? I supposed everyone in the music business was like him.

Jan had also phoned my mum several times, and what my family loved about her was that she didn't want me to be famous too young. She knew that Jonathan, as well as a couple of other potential managers, had been in touch, but she had her own ideas of what I should be doing. She knew they were talking record contracts, but in her eyes the music industry wasn't a place for a young girl. She wanted to groom me for the future, letting me carry on at school and putting me in for the odd theatrical audition until I got older. Mum appreciated her advice, so we agreed that she would be my agent.

Jonathan wasn't happy that we'd appointed Jan, but he let that go for the time being. As far as he was concerned, the next step was to make a demo tape that he would send around the various recording companies. To be honest, at the time I didn't have a clue what he was going to do with it, but I was more than happy to go along with the flow. I was happy what-ever happened, provided I could sing.

In the end I went up to London to record the demo with Shirley Bassey's producer, but Jonathan wasn't pleased with the result, because he felt it was too bland and didn't show off my voice, so he asked me to record another. One of Bampy's old friends, Richard Dunn, had a recording studio in the basement of a house he was doing up in Palace Road, Cardiff, so Mum, Louise, Caroline and I headed down there, through a load of overflowing black bin bags by the front gate. I felt a bit doubt-ful, but once we got inside, the studio was fine. A technician played the backing tracks and I sang a variety of songs that showed off my range, including 'Imagine', 'Somewhere Over the Rainbow', 'Pie Jesu' and 'Somewhere'.

Jan asked Mum to organise a photoshoot in the gardens of Llandaff's Insole Court so I would have some publicity shots. I wore a gorgeous black dress with flowers on it, and I was allowed a bit of mascara and lip balm, although afterwards Jan said she thought I had lipstick on and that I looked too old. But my lips are naturally red and I couldn't do anything about that. Jonathan used the photos, sending one with the demo tape he was finally happy with to Warner, EMI, Decca and Sony.

Jonathan began pressing Mum to sign some contracts appointing him as both my manager and my record company. He would organise my professional life, and if he wasn't able to get me a record deal, he said he would put a record out him-self. What overcame any doubts I might originally have had about him was my bampy saying, 'Oh, I liked him. He shook my hand with two hands. A good firm handshake.' Before we knew where we were, he had, unlike Jan, produced a couple of contracts for me to sign, clarifying the terms under which he was to be my manager and record company. He also firmly suggested that there would be no room for Jan in any agree-ment we might come to. Of course Mum knew nothing about nothing when it came to all this, although she did her best to find out.

We needed a lawyer's advice to help us with the contracts, so Jonathan recommended Mum go to the Musicians' Union. One of the lawyers who acted on their behalf, Mark Melton from P. Russell & Co., offered his first hour free so, ever the skinflint, Mum picked him. We visited him together in his office and liked him immediately. He's very calm, quite direct and has a way of getting straight to the nub of a problem. Although we didn't know it then, he was to become an invaluable member of the close-knit team that has looked after me over the years.

At that stage, Jonathan still wasn't sure if he could find me a record deal or whether he was going to have to put out a record himself. I remember sitting on the stairs in our house in Fairwater Road East – yes, we'd moved again! – while Mum went through the contracts with him, clause by clause, trying to get to grips with it all. Mum and Mark both remember feeling that perhaps this wasn't the greatest deal in the world, but over-riding it was an even stronger sense of urgency and a feeling that this was a once-in-a-lifetime chance. Everyone felt that my age was a massive selling point, and that if I was going to stand out from the crowd we should get a move on before I got any older. Mum was also worried that Jonathan might walk away if we caused any trouble over the contracts. It was now or never. So despite our reservations, I signed a management deal and a record deal with him, my mother counter-signing because I was a minor.

While we waited to see what would happen, Lulu and I were also preparing for my first *big* concert. After *This Morning*, Mum had been contacted by John Peleg Williams, the music director of the Festival of Welsh Mixed Voices, which was taking place at the Royal Albert Hall in early October. The soprano Sian Cothi, the mezzo soprano Sian Meinir and the baritone Jason Howard were appearing and John wanted me to join them.

When Mum and I arrived at the Royal Albert Hall we were really spooked. One of Mum's colleagues at the council was a

woman who was a psychic. Mel never did anything professionally, she just passed on whatever messages she received. When
I was about nine she had said to Mum, 'I can see Charlotte.
She's about fourteen. She's wearing a white dress and she's
singing in a hall. But the hall's weird. It's completely round on
the outside and completely round on the inside. The only
colours I can see are red and gold.' We'd laughed about it at
the time, but here we were. She had described the Royal Albert
Hall exactly, as well as the dress I was going to wear, which
Mum had had made in Cardiff and brought with us to London.
The only difference was that I was eleven, not fourteen. I've
never really believed in psychics, but that was weird.

I was completely in awe of the two Sians. I was sharing a
dressing room with Sian Cothi, who had lovely curly hair and
did her best to put me at ease, encouraging me to drink water,
to breathe deeply and not to think too much about the seem-
ingly gargantuan task ahead. I was intuitively professional. I
didn't have strops or complain, but waited quietly until my
moment, then got up there and gave my performance in what
I hoped was a professional way, just like being back on a
Sunday afternoon in the Boardwalk with Bampy.

I sang 'Somewhere' and 'Pie Jesu' well, but completely bug-
gered up 'Ave Maria' by repeating a verse. The conductor
realised what I'd done, and by keeping desperate eye contact
with each other, we managed to keep it going. I don't think
anyone really noticed except for Mum and maybe Dad, Nana
and Bampy, who were in the audience. Performing to an audience that big for the first time was awesome. I was so focused
on what I was singing that I was like a machine, almost
unaware of anything else around me. It was only the sound of
the applause that brought me back into the hall, then I took

my bow, relieved that it had all gone well.

Jan got me a spot on *Sterren Voor Kinder*, a Dutch TV phone-in talent show that was raising money for charity, like Children in Need. I was unhappy that the organisers had asked if I would sing 'Amazing Grace' – *so* not my showiest song. The other competitors came from all over the world and we were all put up in a hotel outside Amsterdam, about forty-five minutes away from the studio. For three days, we were picked up in a minibus at nine in the morning and dropped off at the studio, where we stayed until seven in the evening, even though we were only needed for half an hour each. That would never happen in the UK because of the strict child employment laws that limit the amount of time a minor can work.

Those three days were grim, freezing cold, and no one seemed to speak English or want to give us the time of day. It was so hard and tiring, partly because I didn't have a clue what I was meant to be doing and partly, I learned later, because everyone was smoking spliffs! The mothers were up in arms because a lot of the competitors were singers and needed to look after their throats. Instead we were all stoned and starving.

There was a little Russian girl with a blonde bob who screamed out 'New York, New York' in a thick accent. Her mother wouldn't let anyone direct her, 'Come here, my daughter,' she'd order. Then, 'Leave her alone.' The one act I'll never forget was the Chinese acrobats. About fourteen of them performed incredible aerial stunts on two long, slightly bendy poles. I was absolutely taken with them and during our three days of rehearsals I watched everything they did.

At last the day of the competition dawned. I had brought a ball gown with me that was completely inappropriate for singing 'Amazing Grace', so the wardrobe ladies had made me a little black velvet dress, which I wore with black tights and boots. I felt slightly uncomfortable because the dress made me look as if I had boobs. The song went all right, nothing special, and Mum and I waited with the others as the votes came in. I was glad when the acrobats won. At least it wasn't the Russian girl, although the cute factor put her above me on the scoreboard. Rats!

Jonathan had also arranged for me to sing with Shirley Bassey, who was appearing at the Diamonds Awards Festival in Antwerp. I was filmed meeting her in make-up, where she was wearing a big, white fluffy dressing gown. She signed two autographs – one for me and one for the Kings Cross, a gay pub where Caroline sang. She asked if the Kings Cross was a hospital and seemed a bit taken aback when I told her it was a pub. 'I like my wine,' I said, laughing. She seemed to think that was even funnier. Then we hugged for the cameras. On stage, we had to sing the Welsh anthem together and we both forgot the words. It was reassuring to learn that even a true pro can have their bad moments.

The day Mum and I got back to London, we had to go straight to Pinewood Studios, where I was going to film the part of a singing nun for an American TV series called *Merlin*, which starred Sam Neill. I nearly went mad learning a Latin chant to a bunch of random notes in two days. We'd only had about two hours' sleep and I was bored stiff. Every time I moaned that I wanted to go home, Mum would shut me up with, 'Shhh. This is a real big deal.' She only thought that because she was star-struck by Sam Neill. When we met him in his trailer and she took a photo of him and me together, her hands were trembling so much that our precious souvenir was a blur. As for my singing nun? She got left on the cutting-room floor.

As my singing commitments increased, I began to struggle with my schoolwork and wanted to be moved out of the scholarship class. My teachers were keen for me to continue, but Mum suggested that we thought about my moving to Howell's, a brilliant girls' school in Llandaff. We decided that I'd stay in the same class but would try for a place at Howell's instead. Everything was happening so fast that we didn't have time to plan anything. All we could do was react to events as they occurred, hoping it would all turn out for the best.

Meanwhile, Jonathan was setting up meetings with various record companies. Several expressed interest in me, but before we went to see any of them, Jonathan wanted me to look the part, so Mum and I were sent shopping in Oxford Street with an astronomical £500 to blow on clothes. We chose a big tan fake-fur coat with a hood from Gap that wrapped around me. I absolutely loved that coat and wore it for about three years. Then we bought a brown velvet suit with a beige top to go underneath, brown tights and little brown boots. I thought I looked the business. It was the lushest, best put-together outfit I'd ever put on.

Jonathan took us to the meetings he had set up with Decca and EMI. I took it all in my stride, but Mum had to keep pinching herself. For her, the whole thing was completely surreal. Jonathan made us walk out of the meeting with EMI because they kept us waiting for two hours. Mum and I were mortified. Whoever we were due to see should really have got his secretary to rearrange another time that was more suitable. Walking out seemed so rude, but Jonathan's view was that it was their loss. Although we didn't believe it at the time, as it turned out, I guess he was right. Finally, three weeks before my twelfth birthday, we were invited to a meeting with Paul Burger, the chairman and CEO of Sony UK.

Mum and Dad were way out of their depth and didn't know what else to do but listen to Jonathan, believe in what he said and take his advice. My whole family were excited by what was going on, but none of us thought it would result in anything more than an album that might sell a few copies and set me off on the path to being a professional classical singer. Perhaps our dreams of my becoming a singer with the Welsh National Opera were going to come true.

Going up to London on the train on the morning of the meeting with Paul Burger, I spilled tea all over my lap. Mum went nuts, spitting on her hand and rubbing it really hard over my brown skirt and tights. I didn't think it mattered as you couldn't really see the mark.

We met Jonathan, who took us, all excited and nervous, to the Sony office. We only learned later that Paul was busy that day and had wanted to cancel the appointment. When Becky, his PA, reminded him that we were travelling up from Cardiff especially to see him, he felt bad so decided to keep it, but make it short. We sat on two little sofas in the waiting room outside his office, too nervous to look at any of the magazines lying neatly on the table. Besides, I was much more interested in the neon juke-box and the Coca-Cola machine where you put in 10¢ for a proper bottle of Coke. Fabulous!

Running through my head was everything Jonathan and my mother had drilled into me. 'If he says this, say that.' 'Explain that you have singing lessons.' 'Explain that you sing properly.' 'If you get a chance to sing, sing.' That last one was the one they kept on about until I felt like shouting, 'Shut up. I know.' Mum knew that the demo tape was one thing, but hearing me sing live was quite another – I was such a tiny thing with this massive voice. Although I was as excited about the meeting as her, I wasn't thinking much beyond it – it was just one step at a time.

We were eventually summoned in. Paul was sitting behind his desk in a large plush office. Tall with short, dark hair, he seemed stern but charming. He got up and joined us as we sat down, Mum and Jonathan on the sofa and me on a swing chair that I couldn't stop spinning round. The meeting seemed to go well. We talked about my training, my singing, where I went to school and what my interests were, and I remembered everything I was meant to say. The one thing Paul didn't do was ask me to sing. Mum and Jonathan's instructions were still whirling round my head, so as we were standing up to leave, I piped up, 'Don't you want me to sing?'

'No,' he replied.

I ignored him and launched into 'Pie Jesu'. I kept on singing, and Mum says they couldn't shut me up for twenty minutes! Afterwards Paul said that hearing me sing was what made up his mind to sign me.

Our final choice of recording companies was between Sony and Decca, but we left it to Jonathan to play them off against each other. In the end our decision boiled down to two factors. Paul was the first to spot the possibilities in what was later called classical crossover. Although I would be recording classical and religious music that showed off my soprano voice, it would be in a pop style. Popera! I wasn't going to be some mini classical diva but an ordinary kid in jeans and trendy trainers: a classical artist with a pop style. Someone even coined the phrase 'Opera Spice'. That was the thinking that persuaded us to go with him.

The other thing that impressed me happened when we arrived at the last of the meetings in which Sony were pitching to us. As we walked into the conference room, I was looking at the wall covered in photographs of Sony artists and there among them, smack between the Manic Street Preachers and Céline Dion, was me! A smart move on Paul's part and one that finally persuaded me I wanted to be part of the Sony brand.

At that meeting, I even tried to outwit Paul by asking, 'What will happen if I don't want to go on singing like this for the rest of my life?' Paul didn't flinch, he just said, 'Well, we'll just have to turn you into Alanis Morissette.' That was my insurance policy. I would have made him keep his word if that had happened.

In April 1998, the waiting game for the first album was over. I was signed to Sony in a five-album deal worth £100,000 – that was a lot for a first-time artist. My parents knew nothing about what we were getting into, but they both recognised that this was a once-in-a-lifetime opportunity for me. I think their excitement probably overcame their anxieties about the unknown.

I didn't tell many people at school about what was happening, although I suppose they might have seen it in the papers. I was never that forceful at school and didn't push it in their faces. I wasn't the most popular or the least popular kid in the class, so no one was that interested. Kids are so egocentric at that age that everyone else was into who was going out with who and that sort of thing. The only unpleasantness I remember came from one of the few boys who used to take the piss out of me for being poor. We were in the school playground when he bragged to me that his dad was going to give him £100,000 when he turned sixteen. That was my moment! I was like, 'Well, I don't need Daddy to give me £100,000 because I've earned it myself and I can have it *now*.' I felt absolutely triumphant.

Lulu, Mum and I went back and forth to London for various meetings with Paul to discuss which songs should be included on my first album, *Voice of an Angel*. What on earth does an angel sound like? I thought the title was a tad unoriginal but it seemed to stick, and that was how I would be known for the next five years. Lulu went through the songs that we'd been singing for a while and we picked our old favourites, such as 'Pie Jesu' of course, and 'Ave Maria', some popular classics such as 'Danny Boy' and 'My Lagan Love' as well as some Celtic folk songs, 'Suo-Gan' and 'Three Welsh Birdsongs'. Jonathan was keen for me to sing 'Jerusalem'. 'Jerusalem'? Virtually England's second anthem! Why? But in the end we agreed on that, too.

We went to other meetings to decide how Sony were going to market me: Nicky Chapman was responsible for arranging all my TV appearances; Nick Goddard covered the radio work; and Chris Griffin was my project manager. Having all these people looking after twelve-year-old me was reassuring but rather odd. Were they really going to be able to come through with what they were promising? They were talking about my first album, putting marketing money behind me, a world tour. What made things even stranger was that the BBC was already involved in making a documentary about me for simultaneous transmission with the album release, so we often had a film crew in tow.

Once the seventeen songs had been chosen, the Welsh National Opera, conducted by Sian Edwards, recorded all the music with the chorus of the Welsh National Opera and Meinir Heulyn on harp and Celtic harp. We went to the recording to meet the orchestra and Sian, who was to become one of my favourite conductors.

A conductor is so important when you're singing with a live orchestra because it's their responsibility to make everything fit together. They have to know all the different instrumental parts and use eye contact to bring in each section of the orchestra. Different conductors work different ways, but they usually take their lead from the singer, watching them the whole time and using eye contact to communicate.

Sian was brilliant, and was always very sensitive towards what I wanted to do, allowing me a lot of artistic freedom. She had to listen so that if I deliberately changed something in the performance, perhaps taking longer over a breath or a phrase than I had in rehearsal, she would slow down the orchestra. If I wanted to build up the drama of a song by singing louder or softer, she would raise or lower their volume. It's a really hard and an incredibly skilled profession.

All I had to do was turn up at the BBC studios in Cardiff for two weeks in August and sing to the backing tracks. It was really hard work but a brilliant experience. Because my voice wouldn't have coped with singing all the songs flat out, the sessions were spaced over two weeks.

As I sang, earphones clamped to my head, I could see my producer, Grace Row, an American-Korean woman with a wicked sense of humour, sitting in the control booth as she talked me through what she wanted me to do. She had a very soothing way with me. She knew what I was capable of and never patronised me. Jeremy Caulton, the executive producer, was there too. He was in his fifties, skeletally thin, always in a suit and primed to correct my French and Italian pronunciation. He was the ultimate gentleman, a sincere, interesting and cultured man. He, Grace and Lulu still stick out as three of the people I have especially liked working with during my career. Some producers just do their job, but these two cared about me and about what we were doing together, just as Lulu did. Even though we came from such different worlds, we all gelled, and they got on brilliantly with my family, too. You don't meet many such genuine people in this business. They made the whole experience as relaxing as possible, right down to letting me wear my bunny slippers. Lulu was always the only one in the studio with me, Diet Coke in hand, giving me moral support. There was so much to remember, although everything was gradually becoming second nature to me: the pronunciation of another language, my diction, breathing, keeping in tune and controlling my voice from my abdomen, not pushing anything out too harshly.

Grace was so good at her job and knew exactly how to handle me. She'd say, 'This next take, try it this way,' or, 'She's getting tired now. We're going to have to leave it.' The whole recording took us five and a half days altogether – an unbelievably short time in which to record a whole album, but we did it. The experience was typical of that first year of my career, when everything was new and exciting, nothing was too scary or too hard. There would be a lot of work and a lot of travelling, but it was never dull.

CHAPTER 6

Bubbling Under

TIP:

*Don't give up on your education too
easily. Even if you leave school early,
you're in a job where you have time to do
some self-education. It will always come
in handy, even if it just means you can
read a contract.*

Just as I'd got used to the boys at the Cathedral School, I was flung into the all-girls environment of Howell's. Surrounded by acres of playing fields, the gothicky grey stone building looks just what it is: a traditional school with high academic standards. That suited me because by then I had my sights fixed firmly on going to university before I hoped to join the Welsh National Opera. I quickly discovered that the Cathedral School had prepared me so well that I was streets ahead in most of the classes. That made life much easier for me to begin with, since I had so much going on outside school during that first term. Although I had to keep taking days off here and there, it didn't stop me from making some really good friends.

Abi was a very pretty girl in a bitchy pretty way, with sharp

73

features and mischievous eyes. She was the fountain of gossip because she knew everything about everybody. She was quite a tough cookie and could sometimes seem a bit cool, but scratch the surface and you'd find a sweet and lovely person. Jo was clever but quite shy and unassuming with a wicked sense of humour. She ended up studying Japanese at university: we always knew that she'd work her life out. Kim was highly emotional and nuts about shoes, fashion and boys. Charlie was more of a tomboy, who loved all sports and was obsessed with *Friends*. I loved all of them and together we made a loyal, tight-knit group.

Between August and November 1998, when I wasn't at school or singing, I was kept busy with pre-publicity for my album. I had to give magazine interviews and I recorded TV shows and photoshoots galore. I loved the constant dressing up and being made up for the cameras. Initially, whenever we came to London we stayed in hotels at Sony's expense, but then Terry Kenny, who had helped raise the money to get me through school and had since become a close friend of my family asked us to stay with him in his flat. Before he moved to the South Bank right by the London Eye, he lived in Covent Garden, so it couldn't have been more convenient and it was much nicer than all those impersonal hotel rooms.

Terry is a lush man: sensitive, strong and straight as a die. He's always shown me unbelievable kindness, and has been a bit like a second father to me, but without all the paternalistic shit. He gave me a lot of his time, often taking me out when my parents were busy doing something else. We'd go rollerblading along the South Bank, where we'd eat crêpes: mine were Nutella while he had weight-watching fruit on his. We'd go for meals in Covent Garden or trawl the girly shops together. Most adults' worst nightmare would be going to an amusement arcade with a twelve-year-old, but he never complained. I loved being with him and had so much respect for him that I never took the piss. I've been able to confide in him about anything, from a performance I didn't want to do to my innermost secrets, knowing that he would never repeat a word to my parents. I could always rely on him to talk sense, and I still do.

Even though I was unheard of, Paul Burger somehow managed to swing my appearance as part of the cabaret at the Royal Variety Club's annual charity bash at London's Dorchester Hotel. It was the first black tie affair that Mum, Dad and I had ever been to, so we were incredibly excited but also apprehensive, especially when we learned how many big celebrities were going to be there. I'd glammed up in a lush black Dolce & Gabbana number with flowers on the skirt, but I was most excited that George Michael was going to be there and Paul was determined to introduce me to him. Mum was dying to get a look in, but Paul, always with an eye for publicity, was adamant that I should go with him alone.

In the end, George Michael was sweet to me, asking me about my singing, and even had me sit on his knee as the *Hello!* cameras snapped away. We didn't notice Mum grabbing one of the disposable cameras on the table so that she could take some photos for us. When he noticed the flashes, Paul went absolutely nuts at her, telling her not to embarrass him like that and how her behaviour wouldn't help my career. Mum doesn't take criticism lying down, but this time even she was intimidated. We knew nothing about magazine exclusivity deals or how publicity worked, so we didn't realise she was doing anything wrong. However, a couple of hours later, the tables were turned.

Paul wanted one of the photos to use as a publicity shot – it had been his plan from the beginning – but because *Hello!* wanted the exclusive, they refused to give him one. He was livid. So who did he come running to? Mum, of course. 'Where's that fucking camera?' were his first words. As soon as she handed it over, he sent the film off with someone to be processed. By morning, the print was on his desk, and that photo was subsequently seen all over the world. The people at *Hello!* were well pissed off, but there was nothing they could do.

Before the album was released, Sony had held an October showcase in the Red Rooms in London's Park Lane. Paul was so on edge. He had obviously taken a huge risk in signing me and the results of the showcase would give him a good idea of whether or not his hunch had been right. We watched all the media people arriving, as well as the PR people and the big Sony representatives, all of them went to sit down at the tables, looking as if they were expecting something special when all they were going to get was me.

But if Paul was nervous, I was a thousand times worse. Showcases are the hardest shows to do because they're in front of all the industry cynics and critics who go to them week in, week out. They're nothing like a theatre audience who come for a good night out, wanting nothing more than to be entertained.

I had to stand on a small platform and sing six songs from the album, wearing jeans, a grey Kookaï top with a fur collar and platform trainers to reinforce my 'popera' image. I had the harpist Rhodri Davies to accompany me. Jonathan had been adamant that a male harpist should accompany me because he felt a woman would take away from any impact I made. Rhodri was in his twenties, tall, pale with a kind, open face and smiley eyes. He was an unusual musician, a brilliant jazz harpist and a jovial, easy-going man. Having him there really steadied me. I stepped on to the platform and sang the very best I could. When I finished there was thunderous applause and some loud whooping from my family, who were sitting at the front, before I was faced with various interviews with TV, radio and music journalists.

When it was all over, Paul took us and the Sony staff who were working with us out to dinner at San Lorenzo, a high-profile Italian restaurant and celebrity hang-out in London's Knightsbridge. All my family were there, dressed up to the nines. There were about twenty of us altogether and I was the only one underage. As the evening went on, the adults lost all decorum and I got caught up in the atmosphere, probably showing off and telling stories as I always did. There was a TV in the corner where we were allowed to watch the BBC evening news because Paul hoped I would get a mention. Would they show me or not? Right at the end of the major bulletins, they announced, 'A young girl, Charlotte Church, has been signed by Sony,' and showed a short piece about me. Our table went mad with excitement and Paul looked both ecstatic and massively relieved.

The evening was spoilt, however, when Nana missed a step down on her way to the loo. She came back to the table in agony, helped by Michael Flatley's girlfriend. She'd fallen straight on to her shoulder and couldn't get up because she was in so much pain. Michael Flatley was sat by there and did nothing while his girlfriend came to the rescue. I thought he behaved disgracefully.

On the drive home, Nana tried to pretend it wasn't as bad as all that although we could see she was lying. When she went to the hospital the next day, they confirmed that she had broken her shoulder. She was in a terrible state for weeks, unable to move her arm or do anything for herself. One good thing to come out of it was that she finally resigned from her job as a dinner lady after twenty-eight years. Bampy had been begging her to pack it in for ages because he knew how tired she got, but she was determined to keep going until her retirement. This time she gave in.

I was convinced that no one would buy *Voice of an Angel*. On 8 November, the day before the album was released, I thought we had a great big flop on our hands. That feeling of imminent disaster has dogged me throughout my career. I never get my hopes up for anything and always err on the side of caution to avoid disappointment. Lots of people would say that's no way to be, that you've got to have dreams and ambitions. I agree, but in terms of my work life, I can't help it. I don't know why I'm like that when in the rest of my life I tend to throw caution to the wind. My mum's the complete opposite and is always optimistic for me. My family tried to keep my spirits up, insisting, 'Let's just see what happens.' I don't think anyone except perhaps Mum and Paul had any idea that it would do as well as it did. After 9 November, everything went mental.

In the first week the album went to number twenty-four in the pop charts. We were on cloud nine. Mum visited every record shop in Cardiff to see how many copies they had left in stock and to move them to a spot where they'd be more visible. What we were most excited about was that I was on the sides of the Cardiff buses. Forget hoardings in Piccadilly Circus, those Cardiff buses were something else. When I saw that, I knew I'd made it. We even took a photo of one of them, which Nana had framed.

Nobody told me the 'midweeks' – the predicted week's sales and the probable position in the coming weekend's charts – so I was completely unprepared for Paul's call. It came on Sunday afternoon when we were at the pub in the middle of a big family lunch. Someone passed me their phone so that I could hear him say, 'You're number one in the classical charts.' I immediately told the family, who started getting in more drinks to celebrate. But Paul hadn't finished, 'And you're number four in the pop charts.'

Sony had put out 50,000 albums in the first week, but they sold so fast they had to press another 150,000 for the second. None of us had been expecting that. Mum says it was then that it dawned on her that I was going to be famous. No – that I *was* famous. She had started the ball rolling and there was no stopping it now. As for me, I was just really excited and pleased. Being so young, I didn't stop to think of any of the implications, and neither did my family. We were all on a massive high.

That evening we celebrated with a party at Caroline's. Everyone we knew came. There was a big banner hung outside the house, loads of balloons everywhere and my voice was blasting from the stereo through all the open windows into the street. The album's success was such a shock to everyone because classical records never sold in those sorts of numbers. Today there are plenty of crossover artists, such as Il Divo,

G4 or Katherine Jenkins, who all have to compete in a massive marketplace, but then classical crossover was a new thing, so we were tapping into something only Aled Jones and Vanessa-Mae had tried before.

Come Monday, it was school as usual. Jonathan had warned us that there might be one or two paparazzi outside, but we arrived to find about fifty of them, as well as TV outside-broadcast vans with satellite dishes on their roofs, all lined up opposite the school. We couldn't believe our eyes. Mrs Fitz, the head teacher, was waiting for us with her deputy, Miss Davis. Jonathan wasn't there to advise and neither was anyone from Sony, so the teachers had to make it up as they went along. They had no experience of anything like this and agreed with Mum that they had to let the journalists speak to me. Mrs Fitz took charge and let Mum ferry one TV crew at a time into the first lesson – maths. They were each allowed to film for five minutes. I don't suppose our maths teacher was too happy about it, but no one else minded having the class interrupted. The kids were happy to be on TV and not to have to do maths, although I was a little embarrassed by all the fuss.

Shortly afterwards, I was due to perform my first show, a PBS special for American TV at Brixton Academy in London. Sony had only gone and spent a massive £500,000 on it, decorating the place so it looked like La Scala opera house. Paul was shitting himself and said to me, 'You've got to sing well on this, otherwise you're finished. It's being broadcast in America and we've spent a lot of money. You've got to get it right.' Thanks, Paul. No pressure then.

We had three days of intense rehearsal, by the end of which Mum was jumping from the rafters. She was on a steep learning curve herself, becoming familiar with the draconian child employment laws and the ways of the music business. She was also anxious that my voice might crack and that I shouldn't be working that hard. There were often stories in the press of pop stars collapsing with exhaustion and she wasn't going to let me be one of them.

People forget how hard you're working and keep on pushing for more. These things are always bloody hard work. You may not have to sing for long on the night, but you still have to prepare for the performance, rehearsing in the afternoons, waiting around, doing lighting and sound checks, thinking about the songs and about what you're going to say in between them. In those early days I was rehearsing with Lulu for an hour every evening as well to make sure everything was perfect. Even when I had a song off pat, there was always room for improvement, however small. During the performance, you have to put in every ounce of emotion you've got, which can be intensely draining. I was just a kid, unable to say no without it sounding rude, but Mum was always ready to jump in on my behalf.

Sony gave me a stylist who brought along a selection of clothes that I could pick from. For this evening, I chose a red Moschino suit that was tailored to fit me and a Dolce & Gabbana top that had a built-in bra and corset, though I was too tiny for any of that, so it was taken out. It was the most expensive thing I'd ever worn and I loved it. Moschino *and* Dolce & Gabbana – I was well impressed.

Mum's interest had quickly bypassed what I was wearing and was totally taken by Flavian, who did my hair. I might as well not have been there as he tweaked and twirled, chatting away to her about how he loved people. We hadn't met anyone like him before: beautiful and sexually liberated. 'I just love people,' he enthused. 'If I fall in love with someone, I fall in love with them as a person and it doesn't matter whether they're a man or a woman.' We were mesmerised.

When it came to the show, I gave it everything. I didn't want to let anyone down, least of all Paul. In the end, nothing went wrong. Boy, did he look relieved when it was all over and everyone said what a success it had been.

For me, the highlight of that year was in November, singing at Prince Charles's fiftieth-birthday celebration at the Lyceum Theatre in London. We were a bit overwhelmed by the idea that I'd be performing alongside Robbie Williams, Geri Halliwell, Boyzone and Martine McCutcheon. I didn't feel that I belonged on the same stage as all those big names, but I was over the moon about having the chance to appear with them. I was asked to present the programme to Prince Charles before the show started, then I changed out of my velvet suit into my lush black Dolce & Gabbana dress. We didn't realise until afterwards that wardrobe had burned a bloody great hole in it with an iron. They covered it up brilliantly, and wisely kept quiet until after I'd sung. I had my hair half up and half down, as I had for most of my performances that year, and was wearing a pair of strappy shoes that made my feet looked like stringed pork.

I tried not to dwell on the idea of standing alone centre stage with the red-jacketed Welsh Male Voice Choir ranked behind me, otherwise I'd never have got out there. Knowing Rhodri was there on the harp helped. As the curtain rose, I walked out, took a deep breath and sang as if my life depended on it. I sang the first verse and a chorus of 'Men of Harlech' alone in Welsh and then the choir took over. As they sang, I stood, arms by my sides, making sure I had my proudest face on before I joined in for the final verse in English. I was terrified I wasn't going to reach the final B flat, but I needn't have worried.

After the show, I stood in line with the big stars to wish the Prince a happy birthday. From then on, I have been his biggest fan. He is such a down-to-earth, charming man who always remembers my name and has even noticed the changes in my voice as I've grown up. It was definitely a night to remember.

Looking back, it seems amazing that I sang in front of all those people, including Prince Charles, as a twelve-year-old girl, but I just went ahead and did it because that's what you do. I look back at all the things I did and think, How the hell was I so cool, calm and collected? How did I get through it, like? If I had to do the same thing now . . . there's no chance. I couldn't deal with the workload or the emotional pressure. I know that when I say it was hard, people think I'm just another celebrity having a good old moan, but for a young girl, it was unbelievably difficult. The more I think about it, the more I think I must have been pretty strong and clever to be able to deal with it all. I've lost a lot of that as I've got older – all those good attributes have gone right out of the window! Perhaps because I'd grown up in a performing family, these things came naturally. If someone's listening to you sing, it doesn't make any difference if there's one or ten thousand.

Within four weeks, *Voice of an Angel* went double platinum, selling 600,000 copies. I was the youngest singer ever to have a number-one classical album. It was a sensation. Mum always says that I captured the imagination of the British public. All I know is that Paul was a brilliant business and marketing man. It all seemed unreal to me.

My real life didn't stop just because I was an overnight success, though. I had earned a lot of money from the album deal, but much of it went to my manager and the tax man. Even though the album was successful, royalties take a long, long time to filter through, so none of this made any immediate financial difference to us.

Although I was appearing on TV and doing interviews, I was still trying to settle into my new school. Mum used to say, 'You're in a very fortunate position, having a career that's made you famous, but now it's back to school.' Hard though it may be to believe, going back to school felt quite normal after a few days off. My friends mostly came from the same sort of background as me and we were interested in the same sorts of things. They couldn't have cared less about what I'd been doing, and I was much more interested in finding out what they'd been doing, talking about shopping, boys, our favourite TV shows and the music we all liked – the Corrs, Puff Daddy and Gloria Estefan. Aside from that, I had to catch up on all the work I'd missed.

When *Voice of an Angel* became such a success, Mum, Sony and Mrs Fitz soon realised this wasn't going to be a flash in a pan and something had to be done about my education. Mum was adamant that my schooling shouldn't be affected, but those first four months were tough. Sometimes I'd have to take a whole week off and at others just the odd day or two, but it was obvious I couldn't go on like that and keep up with my studies.

Sony were talking about cracking the international market, and in the first instance that was going to involve travelling to America and Europe, sometimes for weeks at a time. Mum would have to leave her job so she could chaperone me, but we needed someone else to travel with us to stop me slipping behind with my schoolwork. Then she had a brainwave.

As my career started bubbling, Mum was working in the housing department opposite Richard Leyshon, who was an out-of-work geography teacher who had ended up there on a six-month contract. Mum had no idea what was going to happen to us, but she used to joke with him, 'When Charlotte's famous, you can be her tutor.' Nobody took her seriously, least of all herself, so they'd all have a good laugh, but she still kept his phone number, just in case.

He was gobsmacked to eventually get a call from her. 'It's Maria here from Housing,' she said. 'Remember me?'

Of course he did.

She went on, 'Remember that joke I used to make about you being Charlotte's tutor when she became famous? Well, now it's happened and we need you.'

'You're joking!'

As luck would have it, he was looking for work and was only too happy to accept a teacher's salary in exchange for travelling the world with us and tutoring me in maths, geography and science. He was a good teacher and took his role very seriously, getting quite stern with me when it came to my lessons. If I arrived ten minutes early, we'd have a laugh for ten minutes while we set up, but the moment the hour struck he'd stop. If I tried to carry on laughing, he'd say, 'No. Work now. We've got a lot to get through.' If, which was more likely, I was late, Richard would ring our hotel room saying, 'She's ten minutes late. Get her over here now.' He even came with us to some of the TV shows, so that he could tutor me in the long breaks when you just wait around between having your make-up done and going on air.

Richard was in his twenties and had big almost black eyes with thinning (sorry, Richard) brown hair. He always wore a named T-shirt and was very fit and active. He introduced me to the only sport I play, squash, and we used to play together. I couldn't imagine Mum or any of the girls playing.

When we weren't in lessons, he and I got on really well. He was really into his comedy and was always talking about *The 11 O'Clock Show*, Ali G, Eddie Izzard or the latest new comedian he'd discovered. I soaked it all up and was happy to watch whatever he thought would make me laugh. He was usually right, too. I'd always watched shows like *Friends, Frasier* and the rest, but he introduced me to stand-up comedy. By the time he'd finished being my tutor, I had Eddie Izzard's *Dress to Kill* almost off by heart, even the French bit, and that's saying something.

It wasn't long before everyone realised I needed help with my other subjects, too, so Richard introduced us to Catherine Aubury, a college friend of his. She was lush: tiny with the most fabulous legs I've ever seen. She had long, thick blonde hair, amazing skin and lovely big blue eyes under dark eyebrows. She and Richard split the load between them, so she taught me French, history and English. She had to relearn French to teach me, so our first few lessons were pretty basic.

Catherine was very easy to talk to and I had my first proper intellectual conversations with her. She'd explain Darwinian theory, or we'd talk about philosophy, poetry or whatever her opinion was about something in the news. I found analysing literature enjoyable but pointless, so I said so. We'd argue for ages about that, too.

Richard and Catherine soon became part of my new 'family'.

They travelled everywhere with us, and while we were away they were substitutes for my friends. I'd speak to Catherine about everything and was always laughing with her, as I would with a close girlfriend. I loved them both, and when they weren't tutoring me, they were free to go sightseeing, so it wasn't such a bad job for them.

The other regular member of our team, apart from Lulu, was Rhodri. He was brilliant to have around because he was such an easy-going, witty person and he got on with everyone. I was already learning how important it is to work with people you like.

The travelling began with more Sony showcases as the album was released across the world. First stop was Rome. All the European press and Sony executives came to see me, and wherever we went, we were looked after by Sony's PR people. In Italy, it was Fausto and Susan who made sure I was in the right places at the right times, as well as showing us the city. I instantly took to Rome, impressed by the Spanish Steps, the boutiques and cafés and how stylish all the people were. Sony made use of every second they had with us, so we often had a TV crew or journalist in tow when we went out. I couldn't stand doing that today, but then I just accepted it. I suppose it's a bit like being on a reality TV show where, after a bit, the cameras' presence becomes quite natural and you stop noticing them.

Susan and Fausto were full of life and kept things as much fun as possible without patronising me. One night we ate pizza in a beautiful old square and it was the best pizza I've ever had. I've always loved my carbohydrates, but this pepperoni pizza was way ahead of everything else. Not too much cheese – I hate them when they're overflowing with cheese and tomato –

and as big as the table top. We had one each! Afterwards, I learned my first words of Italian: *'Voglio un gelato cioccolato'* (I want a chocolate ice cream), so that I could get a chocolate cone from a fabulous little shop beside the restaurant.

The showcase was in Villa Wolkonsky, a beautiful nineteenth-century palazzo that is the British ambassador's residence. The coloured marble floor and elaborate furnishing all took second place to the biggest flower arrangement I have ever seen in my life, containing my favourite lilies and all sorts of other flowers and towering at least four feet in the air. It was a warm evening and the gardens of the palazzo were beautiful, with fountains playing and elegant statues standing discreetly among the plants.

I was introduced by the British ambassador and sang in the ballroom, where four chandeliers glittered above us. Having done the London showcase, I knew what Paul expected of me. After singing four songs I had to meet everyone – 'Hello, nice to meet you' – and remember where they were from. Paul had drummed into me that 'It's really important that you give the Sony people your time. You've got to motivate them. If they like you, they'll understand the whole marketing concept and will want to make you work in their territory.' That meant I was interested in where everyone came from and said how much I was looking forward to visiting their country. I must have said the same thing about a hundred times.

The interviews were just as exhausting. I had to sit in a hotel room with Mum and the PR person outside while a succession of TV crews and journalists came in. I did at least thirty or forty interviews in a day, answering the same questions with the same answers over and over again. Everybody wanted to know where I came from, where I went to school, when did I start singing, what music did I like, how was I finding being famous, what did I like doing with my friends at home and so on. Being the object of all this attention was really exciting, but for some reason I took it in my stride, just like everything else. Besides, my mum was there to make sure that I was always polite and never got above myself.

I was starting to learn that musical success isn't just about recording an album, then sitting back and watching people buy it. The world of marketing and promotion was opening its doors, showing me that the business was all about getting the artist as much exposure as possible. Sony saw me as a commodity they could sell worldwide. Their aim was to turn me into a household name, and to do this I had to be kept in the public eye through press interviews, TV and radio appearances and personal appearances. It wasn't just about getting my voice heard, but about getting my story told and my face recognised.

I was singing on *Blue Peter* when the call came inviting me to sing at the Vatican Christmas Concert. Mum, Dad and Nana came with me. Nana was so excited at the thought that she might see, never mind meet, Pope John Paul II. This was also the first time she'd been abroad since she went to Israel with Bampy all those years ago.

We arrived three days before the show so that we could rehearse with Sarah Brightman, Shola Ama and the girl band Cleopatra. In between rehearsals, I was asked to do interview after interview with the press, so Mum and I saw very little of the city while Dad and Nana had time to explore.

The concert was traditionally in the Paul IV auditorium and starred a host of European artists. I had no idea who they were, beyond being the very best of Europop and rock. I felt very special standing on the all-white stage in front of a stone crucifix and a lush arrangement of roses. The atmosphere was magical. I was wearing a long, red velvet empire-line dress with embroidered flowers and sang 'Hark the Herald Angels Sing' and 'The Lord's Prayer' to the accompaniment of a sixty-piece orchestra.

With so many people performing, the concert was long and tiring with a lot of hanging around. Sadly, the Pope was too ill to attend, but I was given a papal scroll, which Nana proudly took home and had framed to help make up for our disappointment.

That night we went to a huge Christmas banquet some-where in the Vatican. I had never seen opulence like it: the walls were lined with white chiffon, there were flowers every-where and the tables were beautifully decorated with enough knives, forks, golden plates and gold-rimmed glasses for at least seven courses. The centrepiece of each table was made up of candles and flowers. Women with huge coiffeured hair-dos swanned about, shoulder blades poking out of their dresses – a common feature at all these fashionable dos. The whole place stank like Harrods' perfume hall. People swarmed around, chattering in every language, as we found our way to our seats. We were sitting with Jonathan, his PA, Cerys, and the girls from Cleopatra (comin' at ya). The lighting dimmed and candles flickered, making everyone look their best – although it meant we couldn't see what we were eating!

One elaborate dish followed another, all of them beautifully presented. Unfortunately the food was too rich for us, though, so we hardly ate a thing. As one course came and another went, we became more and more hungry, longing for the main meat course, which according to the menu was pheasant. There wouldn't be anything wrong with that, surely. But when the birds were brought in on silver trays, their feathered heads still bobbing on their roasted bodies, it was a step too far. Staunch meat-eaters that we are, we couldn't bring ourselves to touch them, especially when we saw how rare the meat was. When the meal was eventually over, we left absolutely starving. Never has a burger bar looked as welcoming as the one we stopped at on the way home.

That evening summed up all the contradictions that became a regular part of our lives. For one surreal moment we were part of an unfamiliar world of glamour and extravagance that had nothing to do with where we came from, and the next we were thrown back to the reality of our normal lives in Cardiff, where nothing had changed. Would we ever get used to it?

CHAPTER 7

Globe Trekker

Early in the new year, we found ourselves back in Rome. This time Jonathan, Mum and I were standing in a long queue of hundreds of people which snaked around the vast modern audience hall in the Vatican. We had been invited to return to meet the Pope, who had recovered from his illness. I had imagined that there would be only a few of us there. Wrong! We were part of a general audience and surrounded by newlyweds, couples with screaming babies, stern-looking nuns and old people with walking sticks, all hoping to be blessed.

Ahead of us, the Pope sat on his throne with priests and minders on either side of him. Although he looked really old and frail, enveloped in his white cassock, scapular and skull-cap, there was a definite luminosity about him. As I waited, I couldn't help but think how much this would have meant to my nan. She was so disappointed not to have seen him the last time. I had stopped going to church with her only a few months earlier because of all the travelling I'd been doing, but this was one of the biggest honours I could imagine. We had been sent three tickets. When I asked Jonathan if I could give one of them to Nana, he had insisted on taking it himself. I was really angry with him. Even when Mum and I explained to him how important it was to my nan, he still refused to give up the ticket. Nana had to make do with giving us her mother's crystal rosary beads, in the hope the Pope would bless them.

Eventually we got to the front of the queue. One of the minders whispered something in the Pope's ear as he watched me take his right hand and bend to kiss his large ring. I was quite overcome, but then my hair fell forward and got stuck in my mouth. All that I could think about was that I wished I'd tied it back. Then the minder said something else in Italian and the Pope touched my face and murmured, '*Ah, la cantante.*' (Ah, the singer.)

'Yeah,' I muttered hopelessly, too overawed to speak.

Then he noticed me fiddling with Nana's rosary and blessed it, and that was it. Fifteen momentous seconds. Mum went after me, but she was so overwhelmed by the Pope actually speaking to me that she forgot to kiss his ring while he made an enormous sign of the cross over her. Then it was Jonathan's turn. I seem to remember Jonathan talking and being moved on – he was probably trying to get a business deal! It was rather like Bono giving the Pope his dark glasses. Yeah, the

Pope really wants your glasses. Well done there, Bono.

The year 1999 was important to me because it was the year I became a teenager at last. I celebrated my thirteenth birthday at the Llandaff Rowing Club with lots of friends, and Paul came down with his wife, Ossi. Whereas he was always quite paternal towards me, she was a fabulous crazy woman who was very kind, but never maternal. Terry Kenny was there, our friend Luke Evans, Mark Melton and his wife, Sarah, and all my family of course. Terry gave me a Vivienne Westwood bag that was constantly on my shoulder for months, I loved it so much. It only came off when I swapped it for the silvery duffel bag that Sarah gave me. She always comes up with the best presents. Inside it was lots of Lancôme make-up, including some Lancôme teardrops, which I'd stick on my cheeks – very artistic, I thought. We had a great party: everyone got up and sang, including Caroline, who sang Céline Dion's 'My Heart Will Go On' from *Titanic*, which was ironic since Paul had discovered and signed Céline. Caroline was nervous but I thought her version was every bit as good as the original. I suspect that she may have had her own hopes about singing in front of Paul that day, but she never said anything to me and, like any thirteen-year-old, I wasn't really sensitive to what was going on in the adults' minds.

That whole year would be nothing like anything we had ever experienced or expected. By the end of it, Mum and I would have travelled the world promoting my albums and I would have sung in front of the Pope, the Queen and President Clinton. Seeing so many different countries was fabulous and educational too. We were brilliantly looked after almost everywhere and met so many interesting people.

In between my travels, I went back to Howell's, where my friends made sure I didn't get too big for my boots. If there was any danger of that, they soon brought me back down to earth with a bump. I suppose the great thing about thirteen-year-old girls is that they're much more interested in what's happening to themselves and I was only too happy to drop back into whatever was going on. I never had a problem with that. I just inhabited two separate worlds that didn't often meet. I did sometimes feel a bit out of the loop, but I had my contacts and I kept in touch as much as I could by phone, so I knew most of the gossip. Abi was especially good for that. I'd ask her a question and still be on the phone half an hour later!

The first six months were taken up by doing more show-cases around the world and then promotional tours as *Voice of an Angel* was released in different countries. I was quietly confident about making all these appearances. I suppose some people saw me as precocious, but inside I felt the same as always, calm and collected. That quiet confidence is some-thing inherent in me. I think I'm an old soul, and always have been.

Of course, Mum always came with me, fiercely protective, making sure I was never exploited or overworked. We always travelled with our tight-knit team. Louise was there, making sure I got everything right, as well as Rhodri, Richard and Catherine. We tried to have lessons at regular times, but often ended up having to grab a couple of hours on a plane, in a stu-dio waiting between make-up and a TV appearance, or in a hotel room between interviews.

Our first stop was New York. That's when we discovered the Parker Meridien Hotel: forty-two floors of luxury with an enormous public lobby where they sold the best hot chocolate I'd ever tasted. In rehearsals, I met J-Lo and marvelled over the size of her arse and the symmetry of her face. She was wearing a pink satin skirt that didn't help her derrière. Because she knew Paul, she agreed to be photographed with me, though she obviously didn't want to give me the time of day.

Paul had flown over to introduce me at the showcase that was being held in the Sony Studios building and to present me with my platinum disk.

After the presentations I sang four songs from *Voice of an Angel*, accompanied by Rhodri. Mum was as nervous as Paul, and because she knew my songs so well, what she did, and still does to this day, is breathe through her nose with me. Just before a high note or a particularly big breath, she'd take an extra big breath herself. She was so loud you could have heard her in another room. Other than that, though, I loved the whole evening.

The TV chat shows had sent their talent bookers but, most importantly for me, Tommy Mottola, the then president of Sony Music Entertainment, was there, which was a huge compliment. Peter Grosslight, the worldwide head of music and senior vice-president of the William Morris Agency, was there too, and shortly afterwards he agreed to represent me in the States.

John Vernile was also there: one of Sony's PR people who became another member of our close team and for years went everywhere with us in America. To my mind, my success in America was absolutely down to him. John was a highly sensitive, biggish Italian New Yorker with thick salt-and-pepper hair. He was a hard taskmaster who would arrange loads of interviews in Manhattan, but relented enough to let me do them in Serendipity, a chilled little midtown restaurant where you can get the best frozen hot chocolate in the world: a mix of ice cream, hot chocolate and milkshake that's the most delicious thing I've ever put in my mouth.

From America we flew to Canada. Toronto was freezing. We were taken to Niagara Falls where we walked along pathways cleared through snow that was six feet high on either side. I say 'we', but Mum had got out of the car, decided the ice was too much for her high heels and said, 'Right, I've seen the Falls,' and got straight back in. Up close, the swirly black railings were thick with ice and the Falls themselves were spectacular, one of the most amazing natural wonders of the world.

The showcase I gave there stays with me because it was when Richard and I began our obsession with Eddie Izzard's video *Dress to Kill*. I watched it immediately before the showcase so came on to the stage on a roll. I was coming up with one-liners just like a stand-up and everyone was laughing. Having an appreciative audience always helps me sing well too.

When the album was released in the States in March, we returned for our first promotional tour. The first chat show I did was *The Rosie O'Donnell Show*, quickly followed up by *Today*, *Good Morning America*, *Donny & Marie*, *Entertainment Tonight* and the *Late Show with David Letterman*. We then went on to LA, where the *Tonight Show with Jay Leno* is made and where Peter Grosslight lived.

Apart from being a godsend in my professional life, Peter also became a good family friend. Tall and as impeccable as an

English gentleman, he stood out from the generic sharp-suited American men. He had a fabulous way about him and was very laid-back, with a real drawl that made him sound as if he didn't care, when in fact he was the ultimate professional. Whenever we went to Los Angeles, we'd see him and his family. His wife, Carolyn, was a typical English rose, petite, freckly and, like her husband, impeccably dressed. She introduced me to loads of books, from Margaret George's *The Memoirs of Cleopatra* to Ann Rice's *Vampire Chronicles*, and they helped me pass the endless hours spent waiting for things to happen when I wasn't wailing along to my Walkman, doing my mum's head in, sightseeing or having lessons.

Peter and Carolyn had two children, Sammi and Charlie, and lived in a fabulous Bel Air mansion where we'd be invited for barbecues and to swim in the pool. We became very close to them.

Peter's assistant, Germaine Lathouwers, was another brilliant person, a great friend and completely nuts. She looked like an older Maggie Gyllenhaal, and was permanently tanned with a reddish bob. She was a real party girl, great fun to be around and always had somewhere up her sleeve to take us to, whether it was a show, a theme park or a restaurant. Nothing was out of her grasp. If someone said, 'No, you won't be able to get tickets for that.' She'd say, 'Watch this!' And before you knew it, you'd be in the best seats. She was the same age as my mother and they soon became good friends as Germaine gave Mum advice and took her shopping and out at night. During my time off on that first visit, we managed to fit in a tour of Universal Studios and the newest ride, *Terminator 2*. That was just the kind of thing my friends back home wanted to hear about.

To this day, one of the coolest people I've ever met is Julie Colbert, one of the top film agents at William Morris. She's about my mum's age, with thick honey-coloured hair and high cheekbones and she looks just like Helen Hunt. Wise, clever and always interesting, she lived with her dog in a great condo on Venice Beach. She came from a family of high achievers and the older I get, the more I appreciate the bond I formed with her.

William Morris were always nudging me towards acting, so later on, I went to various castings with Julie and she'd always brief me brilliantly beforehand. 'This executive loves dogs; that one's an egotistical prick, so appeal to his ego.' There was no bullshit. She'd say exactly what she thought and we could talk about anything and everything. These were the people who made our trips to LA so fabulous every time.

We were never in one place for long as my first promotional trip rolled on, taking us to different cities across America, all of them merging together in my memory with one notable exception: Las Vegas. We had a blast. I was due to sing in another showcase in front of a huge convention of top radio executives from all over the country. Mum and I were driven to our hotel in a stretch limo, our eyes on stalks at all the neon lights, casinos and people. It was just like we'd seen in the films. I had a little camera with me and stood up in the car, head out of the roof, taking photographs. Everything was bigger, bolder and brighter than anywhere I'd been before. The Hilton hotel, where we were staying, was so large that we got totally lost trying to find our room. Downstairs, I could hear the crashing of coins and the sounds of the one-armed bandits in the casino, but I was never allowed to walk through it. Las Vegas aside, the pressure during the trip was horrendous, so by the time we got home, let's just say I was tired and emotional.

I was never under any illusions. I knew that my age was what made me special. If I'd been thirty-five with the same voice, I would probably have been earning a living as a mediocre soprano somewhere. As it was, I was becoming incredibly successful all over the world. I hadn't even visited Australia, New Zealand and Hong Kong, but *Voice of an Angel* went gold immediately in all those countries. The closest we got to them that first year was when we visited Japan for a showcase and a promotional tour that went brilliantly.

Japan was lush. I absolutely loved Tokyo and its chaos: hundreds of people rushing about their business; the glare of neon lights everywhere; the roar of traffic; women in kimonos tottering past department-store windows stuffed with designer clothes and the latest fashions; funky teenagers with spiky, coloured hairstyles, white mascara and lipstick. The Japanese culture is so different to our Western world; it's such a wild combination of old and new, beautiful and ugly. Everyone was unfailingly polite and courteous: all the shop assistants and restaurant workers greet you as you come in and wish you well as you leave. And everywhere is so clean, not a speck of litter anywhere. I was fascinated by all the latest technology, from the heated loo seats and the range of sprays, jets and driers that came with them to the lifelike robotic dogs and phones no bigger than credit cards.

After the showcase, I was booked on to TV shows and did loads of interviews. I was even used for a Japanese chocolate advert, where I was made up and had my eyes 'stretched' to make me look vaguely oriental. Odd! I can still remember the song I had to learn phonetically. We were even taken to

Disneyland, where I had to have three minders to deal with the screaming crowd. How weird that they were there for me. Half of Japan's media seemed to have come with us and were snapping away while I said hello to Mickey and Minnie. I enjoyed the rides, but Mickey and Minnie!? I wasn't into them at all.

All the time we were there, it was work, work, work, then out every night. One evening we were taken to a teppanyaki restaurant that was really more of a shack. We sat at a huge square table that seated about twenty-five people, and in its centre was a griddle the size of a family dining table with a chef standing at it, cooking. Flames shot up from under the grill as he juggled his knives and utensils without chopping off his fingers. I was open-mouthed, watching raw fish being sliced into sashimi before being beautifully arranged on a plate. The art of presentation is everything in Japan.

As our starters arrived, I could see my dad swallow hard as he was offered a cold raw snail to try. It would have been impolite for him not to eat it, but Mum and I were killing ourselves as we watched him trying not gag as he washed the grey slime down with saké. Thank God, this seemed to be a male-only delicacy. I tucked into the teriyaki chicken with rice and soy sauce just as adventurously as I did wherever we went.

A Japanese tradition I loved was the giving of presents. Gifts seemed to be a way of saying thank you, welcome, congratulations, you name it. After a week, I came home laden down with them: an electric guitar, a Seiko watch, a pearl and gold bracelet, twelve lush stuffed toys, a Furbie and a kimono. No surprise that I liked it so much.

Travelling with Mum was fun. I don't remember missing the company of other children because everything was like being on a massive adventure as we experienced different cultures, stayed in fabulous hotels and met so many people who looked after us and showed us amazing sights. The Sony bosses and their representatives were always lovely to me. Mind you, after a bit, all hotels tend to blend into one. Once you've seen a few you've seen them all and it stops being such a big deal. Besides, as far I was concerned, this was work. I got used to the routine, and although there were times when I wished I could be at home, I just got on with whatever was asked of me. When I could, I kept in touch with my friends by phone and was always pleased to see them when I got back home again.

The one person I did miss was Dad, who often wasn't able to come with us. And of course Mum missed him, too. Jonathan and Sony agreed that I only needed Mum and Cerys, Jonathan's Welsh PA, to travel with me. If Sony had offered to pay for Dad, too, he would have given up his job in a heartbeat. As it was, Sony was paying for my tutors, as well as all our costs, hotels, food, drink and so on. Of course, that's what every company should do when their artists are away from home, working to sell more records for them, but we were realistic about the situation. My family didn't have all our hopes and dreams riding on my success, so Dad needed to hang on to his job in case the whole thing came crashing down around our ears.

I was a proper daddy's girl and didn't like being away from him, even though, with so many new and exciting things happening, we hardly had time to think. Sometimes we'd be away on the road for as long as a month, and Dad would miss us badly. He'd be doing his humdrum job, then we'd get back full of where we'd been and what we'd seen. It was very hard for my parents during that first year and our absences must have put a lot of pressure on their relationship. Of course I wasn't privy to what went on between them, but in retrospect I can imagine how hard it must have been. We were such a close-knit family that not seeing each other every day put a strain on everyone. What was happening was all so unexpected and so fabulous in many ways, but it was breaking the family apart. All we could do was include Dad whenever he could get time off and make the most of the times when we were together in Wales.

One of those times was the opening of the Welsh Assembly on 25 May 1999, when I was picked to sing alone in front of the Queen. It would be one of my biggest performances that year. My nan wouldn't stop nagging me about my shoes: 'You just don't wear open-toed sandals in front of the Queen, Charlotte,' she said. 'You just don't.' Of course I took absolutely no notice of her and wore them anyway. They looked great with the blue satin Karen Millen suit I was going to wear during the day when I sang in front of the Queen in the debating chamber. A beautiful Welsh song had been written specially for me which, obviously, I understood fully!

I was planning to wear a beautiful white Grecian dress for the evening concert. I thought it was stunning and loved the diamanté beads that hung right down to the floor, but there was absolute murder at Sony about it being too sophisticated for me. Jonathan ranted and raved about it being unsuitable, so Mum and I ran away and hid between the trailers. I wasn't happy about him criticising what I wore. Needless to say, I went ahead and wore it anyway, leaving Mum to cop the blame!

As the concert was outdoors, all the performers had their dressing rooms in different trailers. When I went into the make-up trailer, Shirley Bassey was sitting next to me. As we'd sung together in Antwerp the year before and had had our photo taken together, I said, 'Hello, Miss Bassey. Nice to see you again.' But she didn't reply. Perhaps someone had warned her about performing with children and animals. Anyway I wasn't impressed. Tom Jones, on the other hand, was very friendly. He'd heard my album, or said he had, and thought I had an amazing voice. He also thought it was good that I'd sung the specially written Welsh song in the afternoon.

The atmosphere that evening was great, with an enthusiastic audience who seemed to love everything they heard. Afterwards I was in the line-up for the Queen. I was struck by how small she is and watched as she moved down the line, shaking hands and saying something appropriate to everyone. When she got to me, she said, 'Have you been singing long?' Her handshake was ridiculous, though, as if she was frightened of catching something. Come on, go the whole way!

Before I had a chance to say anything more than a mumbled 'Yes', Prince Philip chipped in, 'Elizabeth, don't you know who this young girl is? We listen to her all the time on the radio. It's Charlotte Church.'

She then muttered something inaudible and moved on. To be honest, I felt a bit sorry for her because she looked a little lost to me. It must be so hard thinking of something to say to a line of people that you've never met or know nothing about, with only the briefest bit of information whispered in your ear by an aide. She's probably really nice, but she looks so uncomfortable, as if she's racking her brains for a sentence, whereas Prince Philip's much more relaxed and funny and just chats about anything.

The after-show party was in St David's Hotel, where everyone had a great time. I was so shocked because one of the TV newsreaders was hammered. She reads the news, I thought. Look at the state of her. I was at that age when kids get incredibly sanctimonious about adults drinking and smoking – not that it lasted long, mind – and I hated anyone, especially my mother, smoking. I stood there soberly looking round, thinking, You bunch of idiots. What are you doing? You all look ridiculous. I wasn't to know how the tables would turn in a few years' time!

I made a lot of TV appearances in the UK that year, but one of the first and most memorable ones was on *The Des O'Connor Show* – for all the wrong reasons. Richard was really excited because his brother loved James Bond and Pierce Brosnan was going to be on the show. Richard felt too stupid asking for his autograph, and as I was another guest, he thought it would be better if I asked. I was very polite, but Mr Brosnan signed the book as briskly as he could while talking to someone else. He seemed very dismissive, even if he was otherwise occupied, and I swore to myself there and then that I would never be like that with anyone.

I got my revenge, though, when Des O'Connor said, 'Welcome Charlotte Church, the new singing sensation,' and I walked through the doors. Brosnan's face was a picture. Mum swears he was thinking, Oh, shit, she's not just some bloody little kid. She's on the show. Then he had to kiss me. He must have been gutted! The other lesson I learned on that show came from Paul Burger. When the interview was over, I said, 'In short: go watch his movie and buy my album.' The audience laughed, but it did sound cocky, and afterwards Paul said, 'You don't need to sell yourself. Don't plug yourself like that again. Let your work speak for you. Remember that.' And I have.

Dad was able to come with us to America in June where I had been invited to sing at a gala performance raising money for Ford's Theatre in Washington DC. I loved it when he could come along and see for himself, instead of us coming home and telling him about it. Ford's was the historic theatre where President Lincoln was shot in 1865 and which only re-opened as a theatre in 1968. Washington reminded me of two other American cities I love: Baltimore and Boston. Nice people, lovely scenery, nothing too new and nothing too pretentious.

The real excitement was being invited to the White House for tea on the afternoon of the concert. On the way there in the limo, Mum snagged her brown crochet dress with one of her false nails, making a really noticeable hole at her shoulder. Her three-quarter-length matching coat didn't hide it so she had to walk around for the whole afternoon with her hand covering it. We met the actor Beau Bridges, who was very friendly and even invited us to his house – unfortunately we weren't staying long enough to take him up on the invitation.

Eventually President and Mrs Clinton joined us. President Clinton has that gift of making you feel like you're the only person in the room when he talks to you by giving you his full attention. He asked me about my album sales and told me I was singing his favourite song, 'Amazing Grace', at the concert. I couldn't help noticing how big his nose was, though. Once I had, I couldn't take my eyes off it, however hard I tried. Hillary Clinton spoke to me as well, telling me all about her Welsh ancestors.

Whenever I spoke to someone famous, I was concentrating

so hard on what they were saying, while thinking, Wow! I'm actually speaking to so-and-so, that immediately afterwards, I could never remember a word of the conversation. Whatever we'd talked about only came back to me hours later. Mum and Dad were dying to know what the Clintons had said, but as usual, they had to wait.

The White House was clinically clean. I was much too disturbed by the secret service men lurking everywhere to notice anything else. They looked super-menacing and their faces were completely deadpan, like the faces of the soldiers in front of Buckingham Palace, to the point that you think, Just crack a smile. Yeah, it's a job and yeah, you have to be professional, but you don't have to look like a fucking hit man. I wasn't so disturbed that I couldn't slip a napkin into my bag as a souvenir, though. Stupidly I said I'd taken it when I appeared on a chat show back in the UK, joking that I would have taken a teaspoon but I couldn't fit it into my dress, so I took the napkin instead. The press leaped on it and the next day the headlines read, FALLEN ANGEL, as if I'd sinned. That was my first lesson in how the press are always waiting to trip you up and how careful you have to be about what you say in public. For God's sake, don't be ironic. Jokes like that aren't allowed.

Not all the concerts I did were to such large audiences. In June, Mum and I were flown from Los Angeles to New York in Rupert Murdoch's private jet so that I could sing at his marriage to Wendi Deng. Jonathan convinced me that being part of the event would stand me in good stead with Murdoch's newspapers in the future, so instead of accepting the offered fee of £100,000, he agreed that I would perform for nothing in exchange for the loan of Mr Murdoch's helicopter and the good will of his press men. A fat lot of good it did me!

The wedding was a twilight ceremony aboard the *Morning Glory*, a yacht that set sail from Manhattan's Chelsea Harbour. All of the eighty or so guests had to take off their shoes as they boarded so they didn't damage the antique deck. I sang three songs, including 'Pie Jesu', which seemed a bit odd to me because it's a funeral song, but Elizabeth Murdoch especially asked me to sing it as a present from her to her father. As usual, Lulu and I chose the other songs I would sing. The only hitch in the service came when Murdoch dropped the wedding ring and everyone had to help him hunt for it.

The yacht itself was lush. I'd never seen such luxury before: gold taps and bottles of Chanel for anyone to use and amazing flower arrangements everywhere. As for the food, there was more lobster, crab and caviar than you could shake a stick at as well as gallons of champagne to wash it all down. As night fell, we could see the New York skyline twinkling against the darkness. The city looked so beautiful and for the first time I began to love it.

As for the helicopter ride? Jonathan used it to fly us out to see some record executive and his family in the Hamptons, where I spent the whole day babysitting their two young children! I know who got the better end of that particular deal!

By this time, I was making serious money, and Mum needed professional financial advice about how to manage it on my behalf. Fortunately we had Terry Kenny on side to advise us. The fact that he managed the Rufford Foundation and some trust funds belonging to the other trustees meant we had total confidence in him. We asked for his help and he's organised my affairs brilliantly ever since. He advised us to set up a trust, which we did, with himself, my lawyer Mark Melton, and my mum and dad as trustees. I would receive a modest allowance from it each week, and if I needed more, I could ask the trustees.

My mother was on a salary from Sony and my dad had his own job, so what I earned was squirrelled away into the trust fund. My parents never took any of my money, so our lifestyle didn't change dramatically because my mother was so careful. When I reached eighteen, I would have the option to dissolve the trust, but in the event, I decided to leave everything as it was until I was twenty-one – but that was a long way off yet.

At the time, having all that money was almost irrelevant to me. I didn't particularly want to have more cash than any of my friends, so I was more than happy with the arrangement and have been ever since. Of course having money has made a difference to me. Having earned so much puts me in a great position. First and foremost, I've tried to look after my family. I've bought Nana and Bampy's house for them and gave them some money so they didn't have to keep on working. I've been able to help Caroline and my parents buy their houses, and one of the hotels my parents now run in Cardiff, and now that my cousin Elliot's old enough, I pay his fees at the Cathedral School. But when I was thirteen, I hadn't thought of any of this. I was wrapped up in the present and whatever adventure was happening next.

The Minack Theatre must be one of the most stunning landmarks in the world. It stands on the southern tip of Cornwall, its auditorium looking beyond the stage out to sea. This was where Ford Motors decided they wanted to film me singing 'Just Wave Hello' for their millennium advert. I loved the song because it had a bit of a beat and a sort of Brazilian drum breakdown, although the words were ridiculously stupid, but there you go. The production was massive for such a short advert. Crew members swarmed all over the theatre, setting up the huge cranes and cameras that were needed for the wide-angle and aerial shots. The filming was to take place as the sun rose over the sea behind the theatre, so there was only a short window in which to do it. The weather was beautifully clear but cold, and although I was wearing a white poncho for the recording, I had to keep warm between takes by wrapping myself in a blanket. While we were rehearsing, I played tennis with Louise, which was a first for me because I hate games, but it had unexpected results. Running about helped open up my lungs, so I sang better and clearer than I ever had before.

We re-recorded 'Just Wave Hello' for *Charlotte Church*, my second album, which I recorded during the school summer holidays that year. Making it was much harder than *Voice of an Angel* had been because I had to learn so many new songs and even get my voice round a couple of arias, which were more technically demanding than I was used to. Through the months leading up to the recording, I was learning a new song every two weeks with Lulu, challenging myself a little more every time. My voice was changing and becoming more powerful as I got older. The songs we chose were less religious than those on *Voice of an Angel*, ranging from 'Summertime' from *Porgy and Bess* to more traditional songs such as 'She Moved Through the Fair' and 'Lullaby'; two French songs 'Plaisir d'Amour' and 'The Jewel Song'; a couple of Italian ones, 'La Pastorella' and 'O Mio Babbino Caro', and one Welsh, 'Men of Harlech'. Everyone agreed that we had the selection I sang best and which was appropriate for me, as well as having a broader appeal than the first album.

Once again I was working with the same people: Grace, who had had a baby since the last album, her husband, Charles, who was my engineer, and Jeremy the executive producer. I was much more relaxed working with them second time round, and this time I also had an Italian and a French coach to help me with the unfamiliar pronunciation. The atmosphere was so easy and everyone in the studios was really friendly, even letting me run around without shoes on. As the summer sun streamed through the windows, I felt relaxed and happy as I kept challenging myself to get each song perfect. Working with those great people made the whole thing fun. This time we took a little longer – a grand total of six and a half days, interrupted by two-day breaks to rest my voice.

Now that I was quite well known, I was beginning to be offered the odd film and TV part on both sides of the Atlantic. I didn't have any ambitions to be an actress, but appearing in something might be fun and would get me more exposure. In America, Julie Colbert came to all the castings and didn't hold back in telling me how I'd done. In one, I had to be a New Yorker, but the only Americans I could imitate convincingly were Al Pacino and Robert De Niro. I thought I'd done rather well, but when we emerged from the casting, Julie looked at me in amazement: 'What was that, *Scarface*?' Needless to say, I didn't get the part.

The first part I did get was a guest role in an American soap, *Touched by an Angel*. I played an ungrateful teenager with a great singing voice that an angel wanted for itself. Justin Timberlake and N Sync were playing street singers in the same episode, so it was wicked meeting them. I was also chuffed to be offered a part in the *Heartbeat* Christmas special. I was playing a Welsh girl whose parents had split up and who liked to sing. No typecasting there, then! Mum and I went up to spend five nights in a creepy hotel near Goathland, up in the

Esk Valley. It was a bit odd filming Christmas in the middle of August and the Sixties clothes I had to wear were rank, but the cast and crew were fabulous, especially Phyllis Logan, who played my mum. They all helped me as much as they could and made me feel as if I was part of a big happy family. My acting was absolutely shit. I hadn't been much better in *Touched by an Angel*, but I loved every moment of filming. It was such a change.

Although my new life offered me many different experiences, the big downside was how much I continued to miss my family, especially my little cousin, Elliot. When I was back in the UK, I took him with me whenever I could, to the TV studios and out filming. Once we were filmed together looking at a nativity scene in an edition of *Songs of Praise*. You can quite clearly hear him asking, 'Charlotte, why's that man got such a long beard?' He was so cute.

However much I missed home, I never got to the point of crying from homesickness. I never cry. Even today, when I'm on my own and I feel down, my usual reaction is, 'Oh, fuck off, Charlotte.' It's not that I'm too strong a person to cry, it's more that I haven't got time for self-pity in anyone, least of all myself. If I ever feel sad, I remind myself that there are so many people who are going through experiences that are at least ten times worse than mine. 'Get a grip of yourself, girl. You're fine.'

One exception to this I can remember was at a Sony conference in Bournemouth. I had reached a point where I didn't want to work with Jonathan any more. Over that first year, I had felt increasingly uncomfortable with him, particularly when he commented that a pink cashmere polo neck I was wearing showed off my boobs too much. I was a young girl who felt self-conscious about my body changing and I loathed the idea that some people might be looking at me in that way. I felt he could have handled the situation more sensitively. Worst of all, I felt as if he was trying to oust my family by stirring things up between us, telling us each something with a slightly different spin so we'd end up arguing. We are such a tight-knit bunch that I would never let anyone split us up. Besides, I needed their support in this mad world we'd entered.

Mum and I both realised by now that we were dealing with a difficult individual. Imagine our amazement when a picture appeared in *Music Week* showing Jonathan shaking hands with President Clinton and me looking on admiringly. The photo had been cropped, with my parents no longer visible! We were also worried that some of his negotiating tactics might sour our relationships with some of the people he was trying to win over for us.

After my initial success, Jonathan showed some encouraging signs that he would be willing to negotiate a fairer deal between us. Shortly after I'd signed the management and recording contracts with him, we realised that Sony were going to sign me and that Jonathan's role would be restricted to that of a manager. We entered into negotiations for him to release me from the record deal and act solely as my manager, otherwise he would be effectively earning more commission than he would normally be due as a manager. That would have been fine if he had shouldered the financial risk of putting the record out himself, but now it was Sony speculating with their cash rather than Jonathan with his. However, his refusal to sort things out quickly and amicably caused friction between him and my mother, and when he did finally agree to release me from the record deal, after months of stressful negotiation, it was only from the second album onwards. He continued to take a larger than usual commission from *Voice of an Angel*, my first and most successful album.

By this time, I had a clear idea of how the business worked. I was a reasonably intelligent kid and was really interested in what was going on. I read a lot and could read a contract by the time I was fourteen. Although there was a lot of legal lingo, I could get the general drift of what was being said. I was also interested in how my trust worked and what was happening with my money. I wanted to meet my accountant and my stockbrokers. Even though I'd get bored about twenty minutes into an hour-long meeting, the initial interest was there, so I had a pretty well-formed idea of everything that was going on in my life.

I felt that Jonathan had taken advantage of my family's ignorance of the music business. Certainly he introduced me to Paul Burger at Sony and secured that contract for me, and I will always credit him with that, but after that, Paul and his team were 100 per cent responsible for putting hundreds of thousands of pounds worth of resources behind me and building my career. From that stage, both Paul and Jonathan wanted to control my career, and I was perhaps caught up in the politics.

The growing tension between Jonathan and Sony led Sony to confide in us that dealing with Jonathan wasn't always easy. We were aware that the responsibility for any decision lay on our shoulders. Mum freely admitted she was out of her depth and had to rely on others for advice.

I was probably exhausted from all the touring, but it was at that conference that I burst into tears and refused to work with him again. I don't remember anything specific happening

– another petty row was probably the trigger – but I told Mum, 'If it means that I have to work with him, I'm not singing another note.'

'This will cost you so much, Charl,' she warned. 'You'll have to pay him off.'

'I don't care,' I replied. And I didn't.

I had made a lot of money by then, all of which was stashed away in my trust fund, and I was widely reported as being worth 10 million – sadly not true – but I was aware that I'd have more than enough to cover our costs.

Mum and Mark agreed that they would try to persuade Jonathan to do whatever was necessary to ensure a smooth relationship between us and Sony. Mark had dinner with him later in the year and tried to warn him that the relationship was in danger of collapsing. However, nothing changed and everything spiralled downwards until the decision was eventually made to let him go.

Although my mum was later accused of getting rid of Jonathan because she wanted to take over my management, this was absolutely not the case. Because I was a minor, she was an integral part of my career, but she never took on the role of manager. The final decision to sack him came from me. That may sound a bit much, given that I was only coming up to fourteen, but you have to remember that I had an old head on me and Mum and Terry constantly talked to me about what was happening, explaining anything I didn't understand. I had spent a huge chunk of my life with adults and I'd learned a lot about the business. I had never got on with Jonathan. I knew that other managers generally took a 20 per cent commission from their artists, and that Jonathan had taken much more than that from my most successful album.

The one good thing that came out of all this was that Dad, who was dying to give up his job so that he could see more of us, offered to tour with us and to see whether Mum's and my complaints about Jonathan were unfair. We were thrilled that we were all going to be together, although we had little idea of the chaos we were about to unleash.

CHAPTER 8

The Calm Before the Storm

TIP:

Introduce yourself to reading to kill the hours you'll have to spend waiting around during promotion. Otherwise when your three minutes on TV comes, you'll be bored and jaded and possibly blow your big chance.

Standing on the stage at the Hollywood Bowl, staring out at a crowd of 18,000 people, was awesome. Singing in this huge auditorium where so many amazing performers had been before me was wicked. The audience sat under a beautiful starry sky in deckchairs, picnicking from their hampers in the terrace boxes, or on the benches that stretched to the back of the auditorium. All around us, trees reached up to meet the night. Thinking about it, I suppose it was astonishing for a twelve-year-old girl to perform there, but it's hard for me to look at it like that. As far as I was concerned, it was just another gig, albeit a pretty special one because all my family were there.

I began the concert with 'Pie Jesu' and as I finished the song, the audience fell completely silent, apart from a piercing whistle that I knew all too well. Bampy! When I asked him to stop, the audience roared with laughter. This time, my whole family and Terry Kenny had come to America with me and I knew they were sitting in the audience somewhere near the front. That concert was one of the best I've ever given. My voice was crystal clear and I hit every note bang on. I included 'Papa, Can You Hear Me?' from *Yentl* that night especially for my dad because I felt he was always so underappreciated by everyone. Whenever I sang anything with such an emotive melody, the audience was so respectful, and this time was no exception. You could have heard a pin drop. I was aware that everyone was watching me as I simply stood there singing. I had even worked in a couple of big arm movements – quite unusual for me. Caroline was always very Shirley Bassey in her performance, using her arms all the time, but I was more reserved. This time, though, the huge auditorium demanded something more.

For the first time in my life, I'd been lent jewellery especially for the occasion. Asprey had loaned me a simple diamond choker and a bracelet that were worth a cool three-quarters of a million. That kind of jewellery does a hell of a lot for your confidence, let me tell you. Never mind a nice dress or good shoes, something that expensive makes you feel invincible. Once I came off stage, Germaine, Peter Grosslight's assistant, took them straight off me. She was meant to give them back to the man from Asprey, but she'd had a drink or two and decided to wear them out. There she was with £750,000 of diamonds dripping off her as the man from Asprey anxiously followed her wherever she went.

After the show, we went on to Le Dôme, a fabulous restaurant that looked a bit like the inside of an old Italian villa and was right round the corner from our hotel. I was looking after Elliot at a corner of the table while all the rest of them enjoyed themselves. Don't think that because I wasn't an adult and wasn't drinking I didn't have a good time. For me, it was enough just to enjoy the atmosphere. I didn't mind when the adults were tipsy: everything seemed more exciting and fun when they were.

That whole trip was a huge thing for our family. First of all we'd had to get Nana on to an aeroplane, where the ten-hour flight was made even more traumatic by being non-smoking. She and Caroline were gasping for a cigarette all the way, even though Nana was covered in nicotine patches while Caroline had brought enough nicotine inhalers to go round the whole plane. When we eventually turned up at the Bowl for rehearsal, we were so impressed to find my name up outside that Dad took photos to prove it. He always had a camera with him and would take pictures wherever we went. If I objected, he'd say, 'You'll really want this when you're older.'

'Oh, leave me alone, Dad. I'm not interested.' Of course, I wish I'd let him now.

We stayed at the Sunset Marquis Hotel in West Hollywood. We had stayed in many fabulous hotels all over the world, but this has always been one of my favourites, with its understated décor and the individual villas in lush, tropical gardens. With two bedrooms, a huge kitchen and dining room and an amazing marble bathroom, it's a bit like having your own home – a bit posher than ours was, mind. Near the main building, there's a brilliant swimming pool where we'd have breakfast, and there's even a recording studio. Loads of famous people stay there. I remember seeing Eminem and Mariah Carey, and Nana was so excited to see John Mahoney, who played Martin Crane in *Frasier*. She and I had watched him every Friday night for years and suddenly there he was in the flesh. I met Robbie Williams there, too. He was with some friends in the jacuzzi, wearing his pants – not even proper swimwear. I was shocked. Mum kept telling me to go over and introduce myself.

'No, Mum. No way.' I was far too embarrassed. Then he called me over. It would have been rude not to go, but I was mortified because of his pants and made sure I kept looking away. If I'd been older, I'd have had a good old look, but not then. I reluctantly went over, but he was funny and kind as he asked me what music I liked and what I'd been doing, then chatted away about LA and how he wanted to break into the American market as effortlessly as I had. Despite him being so cool, I found it hard talking to famous people then, so I quickly tore myself away. As I walked away, he called after me, 'Don't work too hard.' Thanks, Robbie. Sound advice.

The whole place was so laid-back with celebrities dropping in all the time. Most of the staff, like everyone in LA, were waiting for their break into the film business. I got really excited when one of the waiters, Dietrich, told me that he knew Angelina Jolie. Ever since I'd seen her in *Girl, Interrupted* earlier that year, I'd thought she was the best thing since sliced bread. I was dying to meet her, so Dietrich said he'd be sure to tell me when she and Billy Bob Thornton were next in.

A couple of days later, I was in tuition with Richard when Dad rang through. 'Dietrich's just called to say that Angelina

With George Michael at the Royal Variety Club's charity bash in November 1998.

Get the girl a new pair of shoes! Singing for Prince Charles's 50th birthday celebrations.

Meeting the Pope, one of the most momentous occasions in my life. I wished I'd tied my hair back.

In my Howell's school uniform.

On London's South Bank after a hard day's shopping, with John Vernile, Dad, Mum and Terry Kenny.

Visiting Japan for the first time was wild.

Me and Mum sharing a joke with Minnie and Mickie.

Ken McKay/Rex Features

Meeting the Queen at the Royal Variety Performance at Birmingham Hippodrome in 1999.

No one ever came up with a better idea so I was always singing surrounded by thousands of candles — to hell with the fire risk!

Meeting Bill Clinton at the White House, 1999. When he spoke to me, he made me feel as if I was the only one in the room.

Backstage at the 1999 MTV awards — getting carried away with Richard Branson.

My first album
— my first
platinum disc.
Fabulous.

Sharing my 14th birthday with Dad, Jo and a kangaroo in Sydney's Taronga Zoo.

Swimming with dolphins in Hawaii was an unforgettable experience.

With the artist Amanda Dunbar and Oprah Winfrey, 2000, after appearing on Oprah's show.

Clutching my trophy for Best British Artist at the Classical Brit Awards with Terry Kenny looking on, 6 May 2000.

Recording one of the songs for *Dream a Dream*, my third album.

Me and Billy Gilman recording 'Dream a Dream'.

Jolie's having breakfast by the pool, so if Charlotte wants to meet her, she'd better come now.'

Richard was a real hard taskmaster and I knew he'd never let me go in a million years. Nothing was allowed to interrupt our lessons, except, as it turned out, Angelina Jolie. Usually if there was an interruption, he'd say, 'No, no, no. You've got to focus. You've got work to do.' But because he, like all men, fancied her, he said it was OK, I could go. So what did I do? I refused. 'I can't. I've got nothing to say.' What an idiot!

Dad was going nuts at me. 'What do you mean you won't go? You must. You go and meet everyone. You can't say no to the one person *I* really want to meet.'

I stood my ground, though. I was such a big fan of hers that I was too embarrassed and tongue-tied, so I chose geography over Angelina Jolie!

I loved LA and everyone I worked with there. I never had to work as hard as I had to in New York, where most of the American TV and media are based. Apart from appearing at the Hollywood Bowl, I'd mostly only go there because I was asked to appear on TV programmes such as Jay Leno's who, out of all the TV hosts, was the most fabulous man and always gave me presents. He said I reminded him of his mother when she was young. Odd, but I took the gift regardless.

The sun always seems to shine in LA and the sky is always blue. Everyone's so laid-back that it was my kind of town. The only thing that pissed me off was that I never got to see enough of it. Every day, I'd have to take my three hours of tuition while my family went out shopping and sightseeing, then once they got back, I'd usually have to go and work. It's bad enough having to go to school in your hometown, never mind when you're in LA where there's so much going on.

Now that Dad was travelling with us, our routine changed a bit. Mum did all the front-room stuff, talking to my manager, the lawyers and the Sony people and generally making sure that I was being treated right. She has a real business brain and knew instinctively how to deal with people. Wherever we went in the world, Sony provided us with a schedule of everything they wanted me to do and then Mum went into battle whenever there was too much. Due to the child employment laws that state minors can only work eighty days a year, Sony were usually on fairly rocky ground, so Mum often got her way.

Meanwhile, Dad did all the back-room stuff, from ironing my clothes and carrying the bags to sorting out the rows that used to blow up between Mum and me. We are both really quick-tempered and ready to say what we think. People used to think we were falling out big time, but once we have our say, any disagreement blows over as quickly as it began. Dad was always understanding and very careful not to get in my space, whereas Mum would constantly get on my nerves. There's no one else in the world who can push my buttons like she can. She can do my head in. I so often wanted to knock her out! At the same time, though, we love each other to bits. I've never been able to let an argument last for longer than five minutes. Life's too short. If there's something on my mind, I say it and try to sort things out.

Having them there made all the difference to me. As we toured, I went through every emotion in the book, resentful at having to do things I didn't want to, yet thankful I was being asked to do them. Whatever I was feeling, my parents insisted that I do everything we'd agreed on politely and with a smile. One moment I'd hate them, but during a performance, they'd always be there with glasses of water, throat pastilles and costume changes, and I'd love them all over again. When I didn't know what to say in between songs, I'd always ask Mum.

'Just talk about what you've done in their city.'

'But I haven't done anything except have my tuition.'

'Then talk about what you did in the last city. No one will know.'

I always tried to big up wherever I was because the audiences seemed to like that. She was right. Sometimes I felt grateful to her and at others I'd feel bitter as I sat down for my lessons while she and Dad went out to explore. Visiting new places and meeting new people was always great, but with that came the stress, boredom and exhaustion of work. I was having a wonderful, privileged existence, doing something I loved, but I experienced a confusing rollercoaster of feelings along with it.

I was asked to present the award for Best Newcomer at the MTV Awards in New York at the Metropolitan Opera House in September. How cool was that? Every single famous person in the charts was there: Madonna, Mary J. Blige, Kid Rock, Lauryn Hill, Will Smith, Jay-Z, Ricky Martin, P. Diddy, to name but a few. And I'm there with my fucking mother! If I'd been there with a friend, we could have rushed around collecting autographs, pretending we were cool, but I felt so self-conscious being with Mum, who was *so* old – she was only thirty-three, but you know what I mean! My feeling so out of place and embarrassed wasn't helped by her constantly asking in a too-loud whisper, 'Who's that? Who's that?'

Inside I'd be dying. 'That's so and so.' Shut up!

Although I sang classical, I listened avidly to all the pop

music and I loved Faith Evans, P. Diddy, Lil' Kim and Christina Aguilera at that time. We were sitting right behind Jay-Z, who turned round and said, 'Charlotte Church? Nice to meet you. I'm a really big fan.' What a sweetheart. That meant the world to me. Whenever I've met him since, he always makes an effort. I think he saw that Mum and I were well out of our comfort zone, sitting in the middle of all these hip fashionistas. Nobody really knew what this little girl was doing there, but he made the effort to say something and I was so chuffed.

I had rehearsed presenting the award with Wyclef Jean, but when the moment came, our presentation didn't go quite as I'd expected. He'd been nice to me all day and we started off all right, with him asking me whether he could give me an A or a C. I started singing, but then he started rapping over me. I was well pissed off. You cheeky bastard, I thought. You didn't do that in rehearsal. I was so determined to get the last bit in that I just sang it anyway and got a huge round of applause. My biggest worry was pronouncing the winner's name right. Germaine kept telling me to think of M&Ms, so that I'd get it right. 'And the winner is . . . Eminem.'

What a brilliant night. The show went on for hours and I met everybody. Backstage was like a circus or a freak show, with the wild costumes and all the women so heavily made up. Pamela Anderson was walking around in a corset and massive stupid hat; Richard Branson picked me up for a photo; to my mum's excitement, David Bowie was there, although I wasn't too interested in a man who looked so skeletal, though his wife, Iman, reminded me of Nefertiti she was so beautiful. Most exciting of all was meeting the Stereophonics. Naturally, we united because we were all

Welsh together, stranded in a completely weird and different environment.

The whole of 1999 was schizophrenic. One minute we'd be in the States, the next back in Cardiff, with me snatching some time at school, and the very next we'd be somewhere in Europe. A highlight was singing for John Major in Geneva, where we stayed in a hotel overlooking the lake. One night my parents had said goodnight, and had gone with Richard, Rhodri and Catherine down the road for a meal. I was watching TV in my room, knowing that Jonathan's PA, Cerys, who was travelling with us, was in hers. Suddenly my TV turned itself off. As soon as I turned it back on, it turned itself off again. Outside was pitch black, so when a tapping started on the windows, I completely freaked out. I swear to this day that there was a ghost in the room. I don't believe in ghosts, but there was definitely something there.

That day we'd gone round Château de Chillon, a medieval castle on the banks of the lake, and had seen the dungeons. They were pretty creepy, so maybe that had given me ideas. Whatever the reason, I knew I had to get out of that room, because whatever it was didn't want me there. I left the room, nearly crying with fear, and went downstairs to ask the receptionist if she knew where my parents were. She sent me down to the bar, but the bar was in darkness with all the chairs piled on to the tables. CRASH! One of the chairs tipped on to the floor. I fucking legged it out of there as fast as my legs would take me, tears of terror streaming down my face.

My last resort was to call Cerys. I was incredibly calm as I asked her if she knew where Mum and Dad were. She didn't know the restaurant, but offered to come and keep me company. By this time, though, I had come to feel about her in the much the same way as Jonathan and would rather be on my own scared shitless than be with either of them.

Eventually Mum and Dad appeared and I flung myself at them, crying my eyes out. 'I can't believe you left me.' Poor Mum felt terrible and burst into tears while Dad tried to calm us both down. That was the one and only time I've met a ghost.

The Ford ad was finally released on 1 November in ninety-eight countries at 9 p.m., reaching millions of people all over the world. At the same time 'Just Wave Hello' was released as a single, quickly followed by the release of *Charlotte Church*. The album went straight to number one in the classical charts and to number eight in the pop charts. The Sony PR machine cranked itself into gear with another huge schedule of appearances for me, so the whole circus began again, with TV and radio appearances, press interviews and gigs all over the country.

One of the biggest audiences I performed to that year was at the 1999 Rugby World Cup final in Cardiff. All my family love rugby, so it was a big deal to be asked to sing in the stadium before the match. There had been a brilliant semi-final that year between France and New Zealand. France turned on the French flair and beat New Zealand, who were considered pretty much the best team in the world, so the final was between France and Australia. But first of all I had to sing. Why would the crowd want to hear me?

I planned to wear the red coat I wore on the cover of my second album and a black top with 'FEVER' written on it, jeans studded with pink and clear rhinestones and pink Miu Miu flat shoes. Nice pieces individually, but together they made a fucking awful outfit. Nonetheless, I laid them all out in the guest bedroom at home, ready to put on after I'd done my hair and make-up. When I went back, they'd vanished.

'Mum, where are my clothes?' I yelled.

She'd only gone and thrown them in the laundry. Time for a massive row that went on as she retrieved them and began to iron them. I was just ready in time to drive through streets that were heaving with rugby fans. I warmed up in my dressing room below the stadium, practising scales and keeping myself calm. I could hear the roar of the crowd as the official stewards led me through the players' tunnel into the stadium, past the dancers, past the flags, past the orchestra and the drummers to a little white stage in the middle of the pitch.

I felt really silly. Mum had told me to say, 'Let's raise the roof.' So I did, before I noticed that the roof was already open! I sang 'Just Wave Hello', but no one was really interested. They must have been thinking, Fucking come on. Bring on the rugby. The game itself was shit. France always blow hot or cold, either turning it on or being a bit average. That day they were a bit average and lost 12–35.

Almost before we'd had time to turn round, we were on our way back to America to promote the new album and single, flying from one city to another, without time to think. Although much of the time we stayed in hotels and were taken to places we would never have otherwise been able to visit, Mum and Dad must have found it difficult always living out of suitcases and not being at home with their friends. I think my dad definitely missed his workmates and I learned later that Mum was more stressed than I'd realised. She seemed to thrive on every second. She's a strong woman and she learned quickly, getting the hang of how the industry worked, so she could be very awkward. A lot of the Sony people were scared of her but had a grudging respect for her. After all, she was only being awkward for my sake. She was like a lioness protecting her cub, making sure that no one took advantage of me by working me too long, too late or too early.

Macy's department store in New York holds a Thanksgiving Day Parade every year. Thousands of people line the street to see the bands, floats, cheerleaders, clowns and massive helium balloons representing loads of cartoon characters. I love Macy's, so I was chuffed to be asked on to one of the floats. I had no real idea what the parade involved and hadn't bargained for standing on a float for four hours, stuck between a giant Snoopy and a huge clown, waving and miming to 'Just Wave Hello' over and over again in the pouring rain.

I'm hopeless at doing my own hair, but I'm usually good at my make up. By the time I was thirteen, I'd picked up enough tips from the make-up artists I'd worked with. But that day was so cold that what I did all went to shit. With the sun well hidden behind the clouds, the harsh light made my face look ashen, accentuating my enormous kohl-rimmed eyes so I looked a bit like a panda. Despite all that, the crowds were fantastic, shouting my name, waving at me and yelling at me to sing. I was amazed that they recognised me at all. I hadn't really realised that I was becoming more of a star there than I was back home.

Finally, having been all around Manhattan, we ended up in front of Macy's, where I had to perform, singing 'Just Wave Hello'. Right in my eyeline were Mum and Michael Lalla, another Sony PR person, who jumped to his feet and started shouting, 'You are the vessel of this little one, darling. You are the vessel.' Mum was just as bad. 'I am the vessel.' Oh, God. I just wanted to knock her out. Shut up. You're showing me up again. I don't want to make out that my family were always drinking, but one or two might have gone down that day to ward off the cold!

Michael was very camp and hysterically funny. He often took us out when we were in Manhattan. After the parade, he and John Vernile took us to a Russian restaurant that was my favourite. They served massive chunks of meat – pigs, cows, deer, everything – and would slice huge chunks off on the spot for you. Nothing else, no veg, just meat. I could never get enough of it. At least it made up for what had otherwise been a bloody horrible day and put a smile back on my face.

We had done so much travelling that year that all I could think about was being at home with my family and seeing in the Millennium with them. I was invited to sing for the Pope at the Vatican with Plácido Domingo and at London's Millennium Dome celebrations in front of the Queen, but all I wanted was to *cwtch* at home. I'd been performing throughout the year and we all desperately wanted some time to ourselves.

I had already performed at the Dome, just four days before Christmas, to celebrate the opening of the Ford-sponsored Journey Zone. I took Kim and Jo, two of my friends from school, with me so we could have a look round what was being billed as a cultural extravaganza and lasting monument to the glory of the millennium. Lots of the zones hadn't been completed, but we were excited to see as much as we could. The fact that it turned out to be the biggest white elephant in the world and a massive waste of money was a real shame, but there you go. Afterwards we all flew to Holland for a meeting with the record company and some sightseeing. Once I got home for Christmas, I just wanted to stay there.

Somewhere along the line, I'd had to name my best and worst films *ever* in a newspaper interview and had named *Notting Hill* as my worst because of all its sloppy romantic lines. Not long after, I received a letter from the film's screen-writer Richard Curtis, which said something like:

I know you're not a big fan of mine. I promise my next film will be a hard-hitting sci-fi action adventure. But please would you appear with Lenny Henry at Cardiff City Hall on Millennium Eve to raise money for Comic Relief?

I badly wanted the evening off, but the letter was so funny that I couldn't resist saying yes. A big stage had been set up out-side City Hall with a live link-up to America and I just had to sing quite early in the evening, then I could leave them to it. All my family, including my cousins Linda and Nadine, came down, and afterwards they came backstage where we had our photo taken. I hadn't seen them for ages so that was brilliant. Outside there were thousands of people milling about the streets and we joined them on our way to the Millennium Stadium to watch the Manic Street Preachers. I pushed Elliot's buggy into the stadium. Because I was so young and because I was Charlotte Church, no one from security both-ered to check the buggy, which was just as well. Mum, Dad and Caroline had hidden a few bottles of wine for everyone under the blankets. We clinked all the way to our box, past the bar that was at least twelve deep, and settled in for a bril-liant, brilliant night. The stadium was packed, the atmosphere was amazing and the Manics couldn't have been better. The countdown to New Year was deafening and at the last stroke of midnight the sky exploded with fireworks.

We were invited to the after-show party at the Marriott Hotel, not far away, but we lost Bampy. We spent a good hour searching the stadium but couldn't find him anywhere. In the end we decided to go to the party without him. Of course, the first person we saw there was Bampy, chilling out. Nana had been so worried that she went absolutely nuts when she saw him. It's always best to start the new year on a high note!

Mum, Dad and I knew that our start to the new year was not going to be pleasant. We had already put the wheels in motion and we were heading towards trouble, although I don't think any of us realised quite how much. After touring with us for three or four months, Dad came back to the UK to confirm to all that Mum and I hadn't exaggerated about Jonathan. At last, in December 1999, we decided to take action.

CHAPTER 9

Trial by Media

TIP:

*No matter who you are, nothing will
prepare you for the moment when the
British press turn on you. They are world
masters at building up celebs and then
knocking them down. Weirdly, if you
can survive that and come out the other
end unscathed, you will have earned
their respect.*

Counsel took one look at the documents, taking into account my age when they were signed, and immediately said we could drive a coach and horses through them. He told us he thought the contracts were unfair, we had been pressurised into signing them and that he thought Jonathan's case was weak. We had made an appointment with a barrister in December to find out whether we had 'just cause' for sacking Jonathan, and what he said was exactly what we wanted to hear. The fact that a leading barrister was so positive about my situation freed us to go ahead, confident that there wouldn't be any negative repercussions. If only we had known then that Jonathan's lawyers were probably telling him the exact opposite and that it would be for a judge to decide who was right.

Finally, in the first week of 2000, a letter was sent by my lawyers to Jonathan, telling him of our decision. The letter went out by first-class post on Friday, but to our complete astonishment, Jonathan phoned Mum on Monday as if it was business as usual. She quickly realised that he was either ignoring the letter or he hadn't received it. Yes! The great British postal system had let us down! She immediately called Mark, who hurriedly faxed Jonathan a copy of the letter and then . . . SILENCE.

A week later, Jonathan did try to call Mark, but because Mark was probably going to end up as a witness in court on my side, a different law firm now had to represent me in the dispute and Mark was unable to talk to him. Things went quiet for a while before there was an incredible press blitz. In the stories it seemed that Jonathan had been extremely badly treated and had been fired for no reason: the papers said we hadn't even had the guts to phone him personally, but had hidden behind a lawyer's letter. What they failed to mention was that our contract with him was quite explicit – notice had to be served in writing – and we had simply abided by those terms. My mum was painted as a money-grabbing stage mother from hell and Jonathan was the injured innocent.

When this sort of situation had arisen in the past, the courts and the press usually supported the artist. Managers were often seen as cigar-chomping, greedy, manipulative people and the artists as innocent victims. But not this time. Fortunately for Jonathan, the Spice Girls had recently fired their manager, Simon Fuller, who had received a great deal of public sympathy. I know that Mark and my parents feel that Jonathan benefited as a result of this new mood in the press, which swung opinion in his favour.

To make matters worse, my biological father was threatening to sell stories to the press about my family. I think we could probably have just about put up with all the unfavourable coverage we were getting, but this was the last straw. Poor old Terry Kenny was wired up as if he was in the Secret Service and went with Mark to meet him, where they successfully caught him on tape trying to extort money from me. My mother freaked out, and because she told me everything that was happening, I was terrified but angry too. The press were dying to publish my biological father's stories, but we took out an injunction to stop him talking to them. As we all know, truth counts for nothing in this business. Meanwhile, Paul Burger agreed to hide the whole family from the media in a fabulous Tuscan villa until the furore died down.

With all this added pressure, when Jonathan's lawyers proposed a meeting to discuss some sort of settlement, we were damned if we were going to negotiate anything with him. As far as we were concerned, he wasn't going to get a penny. One of the best barristers in London had told us that the contracts were unenforceable, so we were going to stick to our guns.

In hindsight, I can see that behind the scenes, Sony weren't helping matters. All the way through the Sony people advised us to keep a dignified silence. 'Don't say anything. Don't feed the fire,' they said, which was unbelievably frustrating when the press made us appear more and more deranged and demanding. By keeping quiet, we effectively lost the PR war.

Having the press turn against me, and particularly against

my mum, was horrendous. She took the brunt of it and we were shocked and upset by how vitriolic and unpleasant the journalists who had once supported us were. They painted a picture of a deprived childhood with greedy parents who begrudged giving away even a cent of my earnings. Not being able to answer back and explain our side of the story was unbelievably stressful. This was my first lesson in how the media can set out to destroy someone by running reports without checking the truth behind them and by exploiting people even only halfway connected to celebrity. Suddenly the rosy glow that had bathed my career so far was losing its blush. I was seeing another side to the world of showbiz, and I didn't like what I saw.

Despite all this, the show had to go on. I spent a relatively quiet January at home, going to school and catching up with my close friends. But at the end of the month we set off on a massive eight-week world tour. Sony wanted me to crack other world markets, so they'd fixed up a tour that included Japan, Singapore, Australia, Hawaii, Brazil, Canada, New York, Los Angeles and Sweden. This latest hectic round of promotion started with showcases in New York, Toronto and Los Angeles, followed by all the usual TV appearances and press interviews. I even did my very first signing in the KCET store in LA, marked for me by the fact that I was wearing tiny glasses for the first time. I'd decided that wearing glasses looked good, so I pretended to be long-sighted so I could have some. That wasn't a phase that lasted long.

I was so worried that no one would come, but the signing was massive. About 3,000 turned up, so people were being turned away at the door. I was there for hours, signing every photo and album cover put in front of me. I was exhausted by the end of it, but overawed and humbled by the fact that so many people had taken the trouble to turn up. It really gave me a sense of how big I was becoming in America. It was a relief to leave all the nastiness at home and be somewhere I was appreciated.

We left America for the countries around the Pacific Rim. In all these places, we'd follow roughly the same routine. Soon after we arrived there would be a meeting with the Sony people to find out exactly what I was expected to do during our time there. Sometimes I'd be way too tired, so Mum would go to the meeting alone to cut down my workload or negotiate a compromise. I've never been able to sleep during the day – once I'm up, I'm up – so I'd never sleep on the flights and Dad would make me go to bed when we arrived somewhere. As soon as I got up, I'd do my tuition and then go to work.

I found myself very drawn to the Far East. I loved how different it is from the West: its colour, vibrancy and spirituality. I've always been quite a spiritual person, and am interested in exploring different philosophies and religions. I don't have any particularly strong beliefs myself, but I like to try to understand other people's faiths. I've read a lot of the Bible and want to go back to the Koran too, though I found reading it long and very hard. Buddhism interests me as well. At the time I was in Singapore, someone had given me the *Tao Te Ching*, a tiny book with a couple of phrases or guidelines to life on each page. They made such perfect sense to me. Nothing else I've read has grabbed me quite as much as that book. If I ever feel any turmoil in my life, I still go back to it.

I was particularly fascinated by the Eastern system of astronomy as it's quite different to ours. I was told that astronomically I was a fire tiger, so I found a book that told me all about Chinese astronomy, which seems much more specific to individuals than Western astrology, where the same character traits can apply to so many different people. In general, though, fire tigers are meant to be magnetic personalities, full of enthusiasm for life, optimistic, honest and fair. Quite so!

Wherever we went in the Far East, and not just in Japan, I was showered with amazing presents – an MP3 player, a stuffed toy, dresses, GameBoy games. Perhaps it wasn't such a spiritual affinity I was feeling after all!

In Singapore, we stayed at the Raffles Hotel, a fabulous throwback to colonial days. The Sony people made our stay good fun, as they did whenever we visited again. This time they took us to see the Chinese New Year celebrations. China Town was packed with people meandering through loads of stalls selling biscuits, oranges, waxed duck and meats. The smells of cooking wafted everywhere. We saw a massive and spectacular street parade filled with music, decorated floats, stilt-walkers and brightly coloured, twisting and twirling dragon dancers. Thousands of people lined the street to watch. We were taken to the night safari in Singapore Zoo, where we rode in a tram through different landscapes, watching out for clouded leopards, flying squirrels, bats, rhinos, giraffes and every animal you can think of. My other abiding memory of Singapore is the muggy heat and driving monsoon rain. One day it rained for hours, so the water was inches deep outside the TV studio we were visiting. We couldn't go anywhere so, to my delight, we had some time off.

The workload was intense. A hard day in any of these countries meant getting up at about 5 a.m. to be at rehearsals for one of the early-morning TV shows at 5.45. Live sound check. Wait around. Make-up. Get dressed. Interview. Sing surrounded by a thousand candles because no one ever came up with anything different for a 'singing angel'. Sign autographs. Then it was back to the hotel for my tuition from nine to twelve. However tired I felt, Richard would make me concentrate solidly as I listened to him and asked questions. After lunch, I'd probably do a couple of press interviews, a photoshoot and then maybe a concert, a showcase or a Sony dinner in the evening. Finally, at about nine or ten in the evening, we'd get back to the hotel, where I'd fall into bed, ready to be up and start my tuition at nine the next morning. No wonder I'm so averse to hard work as an adult. Nowadays, as soon as I start feeling a bit busy or flustered, it's Fucking get me out of here – I'm going home.

My fourteenth birthday was overshadowed by the news from the UK that Jonathan had formally filed a lawsuit against us for breach of contract. We were on our first trip to Australia and were celebrating in Taronga Zoo, Sydney. I was really pissed off that a camera crew came with us to record every moment, including me kissing a kangaroo and stroking a koala, but nothing could really spoil our trip to Australia because it had turned into a massive family occasion. We were met at Sydney Airport by Bampy's three sisters, who had moved to Australia with their families years ago. There must have been about forty of them! Mum, Dad and I had never met them before, so it was all very emotional but brilliant.

I was really happy because Jo, one of my good school friends, had come too, so she and I could chill together when the adults went out. The only hitch during the week-long trip was when she and I went to Bondi Beach on my day off. We dutifully did the old 'Slip (on a T-shirt), Slop (on a hat), Slap (on the sunscreen)', but I forgot to put any sunscreen on my forehead or the tops of my feet, so when it came to doing my showcases at the Sydney Museum of Contemporary Art and in Melbourne I had a shining bright-red face and feet. I looked a bit silly, but there you go. It didn't seem to stop the audience enjoying the performances.

From Australia we went to Hawaii, where Ford invited me to sing at a conference that included a few days R&R – well, someone had to do it. They even paid for us to go on a helicopter ride over Hawaii's Big Island. We swooped down into the lush green valleys and were shown where the opening scene of *Jurassic Park* was shot. Then we flew down to cross the mouth of the Kilauea volcano, where fiery red lava flowed into the sea and steam hissed up from the water. The land was constantly growing as the lava cooled. That half of the island is completely barren, just cooled and hardened lava that looks like I imagine Mars does. Seeing something of what Richard had taught me in action was amazing. As we swung away and up into thick cloud, the helicopter was thrown around in the thermals. Mum and I were hanging on to each other for dear life. Neither of us had been happy about flying since we were in a plane to Dublin that got struck by lightning and this trip didn't help our phobia. That was the low point of a fantastic few days, though.

The real high point came when we got to swim with dolphins in a tidal lagoon at our resort. Six people were taken at a time while the others watched, queuing for their ten-minute turn. We stood at the edge of the lagoon as the dolphins swam towards us, weighing us up with a beady eye before flipping away in a neat turn. We stepped into the cold-water lagoon as the trainer encouraged them to perform tricks that we rewarded with a bit of herring. Their final trick was to 'kiss' each of us for a souvenir photo. The whole thing was a little bit commercial, but that didn't take away from the amazing experience, during which they communicated an intelligence I've never experienced with any other animal.

The countries we visited on tour often threw each other into sharp relief. Sweden was cool, elegant and sophisticated, but in Brazil I got to see the terrible conditions in which some people live. The extreme contrast between rich and poor is right in your face. There we were in our beautiful five-star hotel in Rio, while out of the window we could see one of the vast *favelas* (shanty towns) crowded on to a nearby hill. We were told that 160,000 people lived there in 50,000 shacks built of anything people can lay their hands on. There's scant electricity and only basic sewage. We could see tiny kids at the bottom of the thousands of steps that led to the top of the hill. Apparently they were scouting for drug dealers and would run up to warn them if the police turned up. I was fascinated and horrified. Our man from Sony told me that he had been mugged near a *favela* in São Paolo. They took his wallet, his jewellery and then shot him five times in the legs. I was like a sponge in those days, soaking up information. Wherever we went, I wanted to learn, and I did.

The weather was heavenly in Brazil, the hotel had a fabulous pool and the people were beautiful. In one of the breaks between work, we were taken to a water park that was opened especially for us. Scaffolding covered everything, making it all look really unsafe – British health and safety would have had a field day – so it was a wonder we didn't break our necks. Lifeguards watched Mum, Dad, Richard, Catherine and me as we whizzed screaming down the slides. We'd never been anywhere like that before.

In one of my appearances in Brazil, I sang 'Tormento d'Amore' with Agnaldo Rayol, a love song that's used as the theme tune of a Brazilian soap. I felt incredibly awkward because Agnaldo was much older than me. He looked as if he must be nearly ninety, and as he sang, he had to stare adoringly into my eyes. I squirmed with embarrassment, thinking, Just get me out of here.

Just as weird was my appearance with him on the Brazilian equivalent of *Top of the Pops*. After we'd sung 'Tormento' again, I was interviewed by the presenter, a beautiful, tall woman with short blonde hair. She spoke in Portuguese and I had a translator telling me what she was saying through my earpiece. The trouble was that the audience around us was going nuts, so I couldn't hear a thing. Then the music started up again. I was confused but joined in with Agnaldo, who had started the song again. It was just as well I did, because it turned out that the ratings for the channel went up while we were singing. If you've got viewers, you want to keep them, so you do the same thing again! We sang it three times and I couldn't stop laughing.

Despite experiencing so many different cultures and meeting so many fascinating people, the tour was gruelling and seemed never-ending. We were all dying to get home after being away for so long and agreed that we would never stay away for longer than three weeks in the future. I was so glad to get back to school again and catch up with what had been happening, but no sooner had the spring term ended than I was off to America to appear at the *Heroes for the Planet* Concert, a TV special sponsored by Ford Motors and filmed in San Francisco. One of my favourite moments came during the morning of the concert. I'd been driven in a new Ford

Think electric car to Nob Hill, one of the smartest residential districts, where I was to present a cheque to the mayor, whose name was Willie Brown. I was creasing up at those two names.

That evening, I was due to sing several songs to break up the programme as sixty-five people were honoured for the amazing things they had done for the planet. The show was presented by Haley Joel Osment, the boy who starred with Bruce Willis in *The Sixth Sense*. We bonded straight away. He's kind, sweet and clever and he has the wisest eyes. He was much shorter than me then, and dressed in a suit with his hair slicked back in a funny old-fashioned style, he looked much older than his age. He gave me a beautiful topaz and silver bracelet that I really cherished and have kept to this day. Afterwards we stayed in email contact for a while, but we eventually lost touch. I did see him a couple of years later in the film *Pay It Forward* and cried buckets – very unusual for me.

Finally we met up again last year, this time at Ant and Dec's All*Star Cup at Celtic Manor outside Cardiff. Gav and I were there and – this is really bad – we got Haley drunk. I was so happy to see him again. Even though he must have been about eighteen, he looked exactly the same, though his voice had broken. Once his parents had disappeared to their room, he joined us in the bar and Gav started buying him sambucca shots as we chatted. He talked about getting into his high-school band, but I was very worldly wise and advised him, 'Stick to what you do best. You're a brilliant actor. I know we all want to swap and try another career, but it always goes wrong. Just don't do it.' Just as well I didn't take my own advice! Perhaps he won't either.

As the evening went on, Gav and I had a stupid argument

and stormed upstairs together, leaving Haley drunk as a skunk and all on his own. I still feel terrible about that, especially as we found out he had to go to LA the next day so we couldn't even say goodbye. Not surprisingly, I haven't heard from him since, but it was lovely seeing him.

Whenever I was on the West Coast, I was invited on to *The Tonight Show with Jay Leno*. I was extra excited when I heard that Tom Cruise was coming into the studio to sign a motorbike for charity while we were there. We'd been warned not to bother him or stare at him. He wasn't coming in to be part of the show, just to sign the bike, so we should leave him be. That was all fine by us: we were so busy at that point, we didn't have time to meet people. We just wanted to get on, do the job and get out of there. We were in my dressing room, a shabby little room with smudged white walls, navy carpet and sofa, wires running across the ceiling and a TV hanging up on the wall – touring is not all glamour. Richard was sitting with his laptop in a corner, sorting out my lessons for the next day; Dad was ironing my dress for the show, while Mum had popped out for a cigarette. I was getting ready for the show, using a beauty mirror to put on my make-up, and looked like something out of *Clockwork Orange* with only one eye made up, thick with mascara, when there was a knock at the door.

Dad answered it and there was Tom Cruise with his two kids, one on his hip and one standing, holding his hand. We were completely open-mouthed.

'Hi,' he said. 'I'm sorry to interrupt, but I just wanted to come and say hi. The kids are really big fans of yours. Where are you guys from? Ireland?'

'No,' said Dad, coming to. Then, to my disbelief, he told some shitty Irish joke. I know he was nervous, but he couldn't stop.

I was sitting there, like a one-eyed panda, thinking, Just shut up, Dad. Shut up. Tom didn't seem to mind, though, and laughed and asked us a bit more about what we were doing this trip. We relaxed and started chatting. Then, to my horror, I saw Mum behind him. She'd somehow missed him coming down the corridor and had only just cottoned on to what was happening. She madly gestured at me to introduce her, pointing and waving so that I'd notice. As if I couldn't!

'Sorry,' I said. 'Behind you is my mother.'

There she was flashing her best smile at him as he said what a pleasure it was to meet her. He didn't stay long, but what a lovely unassuming guy. He didn't have to visit, but doing so meant the world to us.

Although thousands of people enjoyed listening to me sing, there were plenty of others who liked to take a pop at me. I had received some criticism from music purists for pushing my voice too hard too soon. My detractors seemed to think that I stepped on to a stage and just screamed out the songs. In fact, Lulu was always very careful with my training and never made me reach beyond my natural capabilities. They also implied that I did nothing but give concerts, when in fact I did very few. I usually had plenty of breaks between them, and when I did perform, I only sang five or six songs. What did they know?

Made anxious by the criticism, my producer, Jeremy, had even taken me to a voice expert, who reassured us all that I was doing everything perfectly. I was influenced by one critic, mind, but not in the way she might have hoped. When I met her, she shook my hand so feebly that from then on I took everyone's hands with a vice-like grip, just to show that I was made of stronger stuff. Although I didn't take any of this too seriously, I was thrilled to be nominated for two of the new Classical Brit Awards, which were held for the first time in 2000. Perhaps this would help silence my critics.

The awards were held at the Albert Hall and my parents came along to give me moral support. The set was an amazing gothic-looking affair that must have cost shitloads of money. Vanessa-Mae opened the show with an electrifying performance. Both of us were nominated for Young British Classical Performer, but lost out to the conductor Daniel Harding. I thought I looked the bees knees that night in a red and gold outfit as I stepped on to the stage to sing 'La Pastorella' and 'Guide Me O Thou Great Redeemer'. By this point in my career, I was much more aware of my appearance. My hair was layered and, although Mum wouldn't let me have it highlighted, I had blonde extensions put in. The long list of awards came and went without my winning anything, until suddenly I heard my name: I had been awarded Best British Artist! I was so chuffed but completely unprepared. I went up to accept the award from Chris Smith and blurted out something unmemorable, thanking everyone I could think of. Then I returned to the table, clutching the trophy as if I was never going to let it go.

The awards themselves were criticised in some quarters for being too populist, but I believe that anything that widens the appeal of classical music, bringing it to the attention of a new audience, is a good thing. It shouldn't be viewed as the preserve of the traditionalists, who can be so stuffy. People like Vanessa-Mae, Nigel Kennedy and Bryn Terfel do great things in making people understand that classical music is enjoyable and not just for the élite few.

*

At last I could spend the summer term settled mostly at school, revising for the end-of-year exams. Mum still insisted that education came first. My ambition was to go to university, where I thought I might study philosophy or English before auditioning to train as a classical singer with the WNO. I was booked to go to Boston on 14 June for a private concert, so I had to take the last of my exams with me. The concert was difficult because I had to sing as soon as we arrived there and my voice had completely gone, but in the end a slug of brandy was enough to get rid of the croak. The exam, on the other hand, was much easier than I'd expected. I had to take it in my hotel room with Richard invigilating, which felt a bit odd. Thanks to Catherine and Richard's brilliant tuition, I came through with pretty high marks all round, even getting 95 per cent in geography.

While all my mates were having their summer holidays, I was back in Air Studios working, recording my third album, *Dream a Dream*, for release the following November. By now the whole recording business was becoming a habit and the magic was wearing a bit thin. I think it was for some of my UK fans, too. This would be the third Christmas in a row that I'd have an album out and the press we'd been getting, largely thanks to the impending court case, hardly encouraged people to support me. However, in America, quite the opposite was true. There I could do no wrong.

Dream a Dream was a Christmas album, made up of twenty Christmas songs, from one of my favourites 'Ave Maria' to 'Joy to the World' and 'Silent Night'. The sleeve was going to be a painting of me done by Amanda Dunbar, an amazingly talented Canadian artist only four years older than me, who I'd met on *The Oprah Winfrey Show* earlier that year. The original is hanging on my mum's hall wall. For the recording, Sony had laid their hands on a Christmas tree, which I decorated with tinsel and baubles and every time I finished a song, I was allowed to open a present. Lulu and Sian Edwards, my conductor, were with me in the studio while Grace and James were in the control booth as usual, along with Mum and Dad. To be honest, compared to the first two albums, recording this one was a piece of piss, and after five days, we had it in the bag, except for the title song, 'Dream a Dream'. This was going to be a duet – the first I'd ever recorded – with Billy Gilman, a twelve-year-old country and western singer from Rhode Island who was the latest thing in the States. Some bright spark at Sony thought we'd be cute together.

The first half of the year had taken its toll emotionally and physically as the amount of travelling we'd done had been phenomenal. God knows how many planes we must have taken, how many hotels we'd stayed in or how many interviews I'd given as we jetted round the world. The knowledge that the court case with Jonathan was looming was putting a lot of pressure on us, too. During the course of the year, there was endless correspondence between lawyers and the long process of preparing witness statements. After all this, we were ready for a holiday. Mum had booked two weeks in August in St Lucia and Grenada, and we were taking Terry and my best friend, Kim, with us.

Although we were totally exhausted and ready to wind down, we weren't allowed to stop quite yet. Paul had arranged for me to record another film for PBS in Jerusalem. Mum went nuts, ranting and raving that we were going too soon after the album, that I was exhausted from recording and that my voice was cracking, but nobody listened. When you're dealing with the big boys . . . what they say goes. They'd sit her down and explain that they'd spent this much money, that this was the only slot, that they'd booked a top director from PBS and on and on. She had no option but to cave in – and she did.

CHAPTER 10

Losing the Magic

TIP:

*When you're so tired you can't think
straight, try to keep things in perspective.
It's only a job. Remember all the good
things it brings, not just the bad.*

The sun beat down as we walked along the Way of the Cross, unable to believe that we were really walking through Jerusalem in Jesus's footsteps, following the fourteen stations of the cross. The queue outside the Church of the Holy Sepulchre was enormous. I felt bad because we were allowed in before everyone else when they had obviously been queuing for hours. Unsurprisingly, someone objected and a scuffle broke out. We were elbowed inside quickly by our minders. Mum and I both found being inside the church profoundly emotional and cried as we walked round, especially when we saw Christ's tomb. We stood there saying our prayers beside a group of chanting, crying nuns, and I saw one man crawling on his belly, imitating the exhaustion of Christ. Being there was an unforgettable experience, perhaps only bettered by our visit to the holy crypt in Bethlehem's Church of the Nativity, where Jesus is thought to have been born. Steps lead down into a dark cave where you can touch the actual spot – that's pretty special.

When I wasn't rehearsing, we wandered through the bazaars, which teemed with people, head-scarfed women and Orthodox Jews in black coats and hats, despite the heat. Being in the crowded Old City, making our way through its narrow cobbled streets, transported us into the past. The smells of cooking and spices were carried on the air, and as the day drew to a close, the white-washed buildings turned orange under the setting sun and people rushed to prayers.

The whole trip was made more demanding by the fact that I was filmed wherever we went. Mum says that I whined and moaned all the time about how exhausted I was, even on our one precious day off.

The concert took place in the courtyard of the Tower of David. I was excited about singing there because it was such a beautiful location, especially when it was lit up at night, although I didn't understand where the audience was going to sit. In the end, they managed to squash them in front of the orchestra. It was a balmy night and I wore a sparkling sleeveless red top and skirt that I loved, but once again, looking back, I looked more like a frigging gypsy! Another fashion disaster.

After the concert, I had to sing again at Dormition Abbey, just outside the Zion Gate. We were in a freezing-cold church without an audience at one in the morning with me singing carols alone with an orchestra. Mum was like an absolute banshee, trying to get the director to hurry up or stop filming, while I got moodier and moodier. The fact that I'd stayed up the night before reading *Harry Potter and the Prisoner of Azkaban* till three o'clock in the morning didn't help! I'd been lying in bed thinking, Shit, I'm really tired and I've got the concert tomorrow, but I couldn't stop reading.

At last we finished, only to be told that we were expected to be up three hours later at five in the morning so we could get to the desert and film before it got too hot. Mum went nuts. She needn't have bothered, though, because it didn't make any difference to the production team: they were adamant. I dragged myself out of bed the next day, then had my hair and make-up done yet again, ready for action.

Don't ask me where they got a fucking camel from, but they did. They wanted me to ride it along a ledge that was about two metres wide with a massive drop on one side. I was like, 'You're joking! I can't do that. We'll fall off.'

They were so persuasive, convincing me that camels are unbelievably sure-footed, and soon I ended up on its back, absolutely shitting myself. I have to say, the shot does look great in the documentary, but the drop beside us couldn't be seen. What really made me mad was that they also dressed me up as Mary. I know I was only fourteen, but I did have a *bit* of fashion sense by then. In my book, there's back-dated and there's back-dated. And I felt a bit back-dated! I had to talk to an archaeologist to find out how Mary would have lived. That was fine, interesting even, but the clothes!

Despite our exhaustion, being in Israel was amazing. I was in awe of its history, the places we visited and things we saw there. Occasionally we were aware of tension in the air and could even hear explosions in the distance, but the serious troubles began only a few months later. We were incredibly privileged to have been able to visit when we did. My only regret was that, yet again, Nana wasn't with us. Although she had visited Israel when Bampy went there with the band, I wished she had been with us to see all these places that would have held so much significance for her.

Another big American tour was lined up for the end of the year, when we were going to visit Minnesota, Tennessee, Atlanta and Milwaukee, side-stepping to Hong Kong and Singapore for two private concerts, then finishing up in Los Angeles, Baltimore and Toronto. But before that kicked off, I had time to squeeze in one of my favourite events, Wiltshire Festival's Classical Extravaganza at Lydiard Country Park, where I'd also performed the year before. The conductor, Joe Alexander, is fabulous and the audience isn't anything like your normal classical audience. They were much rowdier, wildly shouting and applauding. Mind you, that year the concert was memorable not for my singing or the audience, but for being the night when I got a little bit inebriated for the first time.

After the gig, we went back to the hotel, where the conductor and my dad's ex-boss were buying drinks for me, Abi and Kim, who had come with us. Although we were underage, I can be quite persuasive when the mood takes me and I knew how to get what I wanted. We were ordering Hooch, which looks conveniently like Fanta. My dad didn't trust me as far as he could throw me and immediately suspected we were up to something, but Mum was so trusting that she hadn't a clue. Dad insisted on having a sip, then went completely nuts and sent us straight upstairs. I knew I'd let him down and cried my eyes out. I gave him some sob story about how hard my life was and how I wanted to be like my friends, and he bought it hook, line and sinker and ended up apologising for shouting at me. Kids, eh! Bless him. Abi and Kim were gobsmacked at my success. I was well pleased with myself, even though we were back on the Fanta for the rest of the night.

Every album I brought out in America did better than the one before. *Dream a Dream* went straight to number seven on the Billboard album chart and quickly went platinum. It was the most successful Christmas album by a British artist in the American album charts ever! Almost everywhere I went to perform, I received standing ovations and great treatment from the media. I was beginning to see the difference between the American and British media. In America the privacy laws are much more draconian than those in the UK, and they were more interested in news than gossip.

The big event of that American tour was the annual Carousel of Hope Ball at the Beverly Hilton in Hollywood, a do that pulls in all the movers and shakers to benefit Diabetes Research. Everyone who was anyone was there: Sydney Poitier, Kevin Costner, Dustin Hoffman, Goldie Hawn and Kurt Russell, Bo Derek, Joan Collins and Jennifer Love-Hewitt; there was even a surprise appearance from Michael Jackson and Elizabeth Taylor. I walked past a neon-white Michael Jackson, who was so pale he seemed to be glowing.

Mum and I were looking fabulous in dresses made by Canto Castillo. Mine was deep burgundy, corseted, satin and sleeveless with a full skirt and train and lots of petticoats. I'd graduated at last from those hoops that I'd refused to wear under my very first long dress! Once again I had been lent jewellery that was absolutely lush – a million pounds' worth of diamonds and rubies from Harry Winston this time. With my hair a little bit up and a little bit down, I felt like a princess. Mum's dress was just as beautiful, black and fitted with an off-the-shoulder plunging neckline, but she'd had a real hair disaster. Having it chemically straightened and dyed two months earlier had made it start to fall out, so she'd had to have it cut really short and was dying with embarrassment. However good we thought we looked, though, Dad looked sensational. No designer outfit for him. Mum had bought him a tuxedo for £100 from somewhere shitty in Cardiff, but it had all the gay men swarming round him likes bees round a honey pot: 'Oh my God, James. You look amazing.'

Before the show, there was a drinks party where everyone was dressed up to the nines, including Morgan Fairchild and another woman, who were standing back to back, both wearing the same blue dress. I didn't see their faces when they turned round, but that must be death in Hollywood.

We were introduced to Sidney Poitier, one of the nicest men we met and a real gentleman. We were chatting and he turned to talk to my mum: 'You must be Mrs Church. I'm looking forward to your daughter's performance.' To my horror, she completely ignored him, turning away in mid-conversation to say, 'Oh my God. There's Sam Neill. He's my favourite.' I nearly battered her! As soon as I could, I went nuts at her for being so rude. But not before she'd pointed at Dustin Hoffman, who was sitting on his own. 'Stop pointing, Mother.' Her eyes were out on stalks the entire time but, funnily enough, the only time I was completely starstruck was when Michael Clarke Duncan came over to us. He shook my hand as he said, 'I'm a big fan of your voice, Charlotte.' All I could say was, 'Oh my God. I loved you in *The Green Mile*.' Pretty impressive, eh! There were loads of celebrities I didn't recognise, including a distinguished old man with a walking stick who was applauded by everyone when he walked in. Mum and Dad were overawed to be in the same room as the actor Gregory Peck, but his name meant nothing to me.

During the show, I sang 'Bali Hai' from *South Pacific* as part of the cabaret. Toni Braxton and Ricky Martin were also on the bill. There was an odd moment when Michael Jackson took to the stage with Ricky Martin but didn't sing, he just hugged him and waved at the audience. Get off the stage. We're watching Ricky. Later, when they saw the photo of me with Ricky, it was one of the rare times when my schoolfriends got a bit envious.

The following day, Marvin and Barbara Davis, who established the Children's Diabetes Foundation, held a reception at their home for all supporters of the charity and the artists from the previous night. It was one of the largest residential compounds in Beverly Hills, with miles of drive leading up the hill to a massive thirteen-bedroomed – at least – mansion with separate guest houses. Two donkeys with their names branded on their backs grazed in the back garden. In the huge marble hall, a grand staircase descended from the upper floor – only in Hollywood. Everything was old-fashioned and ostentatious. Wherever you turned, you would trip over one invaluable antique after another and there were more books in the library than I had ever seen. Jackie Collins befriended us and was nattering away. She introduced us to her sister, who I thought looked down her nose at me and offered her hand like royalty. I gave her one of my very firm handshakes. Going somewhere as showy as that and hearing people slagging off Clinton for not turning up brought home how many worlds away we were from Nana and Bampy's house in Cardiff. I know which one I'd prefer any day.

Behind the scenes, our impending court case with Jonathan was rumbling on. Not a day went by without a phone call from our lawyers or someone in the press, making it a very difficult time. A date had been set for a hearing in November when everything would come to a head. All of us were feeling horribly stressed out at the prospect, especially my mother. She had already taken so much flak from the press and we knew that any court appearance would just fan the flames. None of us wanted that for her. Finally we accepted the fact that even though a leading counsel had said we could get out of the contract, it didn't mean that Jonathan was just going to roll over and walk away. He was obviously going to fight for the last penny.

The issues at the heart of the case had always been whether or not I had realised exactly what I was signing at the age of twelve, even if my mother had received legal advice, and the question of whether any contract is enforceable against a minor. His lawyers argued that even if I was too young to understand it all, the amount of money I had earned meant that the contracts must have been to my benefit, and in any event, my mother, who had countersigned everything, certainly did understand what she was letting me in for.

About a fortnight before the hearing, we did try to settle out of court at the last moment, making Jonathan what we considered a reasonable offer. But he refused – he seemed keen to take it to trial. I was ready for that. I was sick of the way the press had portrayed me as a poor, vulnerable thing and wanted to appear in court with my mother so that people would see us united together. I knew that I was strong enough to take the stand and look straight at Jonathan with my iciest stare.

Once we'd offered to settle he must have suspected that there was every chance we wouldn't proceed to trial. However, on the first day of the case, he got his chance to put his side of the story, as the plaintiff always does, and then on the next day, he agreed to settle. All that anyone heard was how badly we were supposed to have behaved while we never had the chance to make public our side.

After the court case, something shifted in Mum. I think it coincided with, or perhaps even prompted, her becoming ill with what has recently been diagnosed as manic depression. Although she's told me that she self-harmed in her twenties, I'm pretty sure that's when she started again. I never saw her do it, thank God, and I only learned about it later. That's something I've never been able to understand. I know that everyone deals with their problems differently, but I can't see how cutting into your own flesh can make you feel momentarily better. Mum was always worried and on edge, either very hyper or very down, and her attitude changed. Dad coined the phrase 'power happy' to describe her because she sometimes acted as if she thought she was indispensable, and she began to talk to people in a different way, being very dismissive and curt. I remember how bothered Dad and I would get about it. 'Just chill out, Maria,' he'd say. 'Let things go as they are and they'll be fine.'

She really was a powerhouse, though, unafraid to say what she thought and doing her best for me, every time. Once we arrived at a hotel somewhere in Japan completely exhausted after an overnight flight and were greeted by loads of people and taken straight to breakfast. All I wanted to do was go to bed, but all they wanted to do was go through the schedule. I was looking at it, thinking, There's no way I can do all this. Then I looked at Mum, willing her to sort it out. And she did. 'She's fourteen, she has three hours of tuition to fit in every day and there's no way she's working these hours. Not only is it against British law, I won't let her.' Thank God for that. Thanks, Mum.

Even though we were on the same side, she and I argued all the time about everything and anything. I love her to bits but, like most mothers and teenage daughters, we were always at loggerheads. I never agreed with what she had to say, whether it was to do with me, my career or anything else. Whatever she thought, I thought the opposite and said so. We didn't care where we were or who was there. We didn't have an ounce of pride or need for privacy, whereas Dad was always trying to keep the peace, saying, 'Shut up, people are looking,' or, 'Walls have ears. Be quiet.'

Being a referee must have been hard for him, partly because my mum can be a bit nuts, partly because I was a stroppy teenager and partly because so much other stuff was going on around us. My relationship with Mum was a bit confused at this point. I hadn't had a proper manager for almost a year, so Terry had effectively taken on the role, with Mark and Mum helping him until the business with Jonathan was sorted out and we could appoint someone new. So was she my mum or was she my PA? That was weird.

If I had a big problem, I went to Mum, but I took all my day-to-day complaints to Dad. Right from the very beginning, he was the one who dealt with the little everyday things. He was the calm one who'd get up for me if I was sick, who'd bring me a glass of water and rub my back. He was the one who could cook, too. Mum admits herself that she's hopeless in the kitchen, not helped by me being a finicky eater as a kid. Back then, fruit and vegetables were swear words to me. I lived off toast, chicken chargrills, chicken dinosaur nuggets, bacon and microchips. That was my standard diet, largely because Mum couldn't work the oven and they could all be cooked in the microwave. I loved it when Nana cooked them properly. Now I look back, I can't think why I loved them so much, they're so greasy and disgusting. When I was nine I was taken to hospital with suspected appendicitis, only for the X-ray to reveal that I was severely constipated. Bring on the broccoli, Mum! That's when Dad took over the cooking. When he went away on a Lions tour, he stocked the kitchen with food for us, but Mum had to call him in Australia to find out how to work the oven! We lived on asparagus and steak for three weeks until he came back.

Now, released from the kitchen completely, Mum was having to make some crucial decisions, and she was probably petrified of making a mistake. She would check the small print of every contract, occasionally spotting a small but critical point that even the lawyers had missed, thereby saving me thousands of pounds. She wasn't scared of going direct to whoever the deal was with and haggling face to face until they gave in, then she'd tell the lawyers to rewrite the appropriate clause. It takes a lot of balls for a businessman, never mind for an inexperienced mother from Wales, to do that. No doubt she worried away about these details to Dad when they were alone, so he got it from both sides. He's like me, in that we both have the ability to see a situation from all angles. He could see how my mother was struggling and how hard it was for me. Although there were massive highs, there were also massive lows. Living in each other's pockets like that wasn't easy, and looking back, I think they did an amazing job.

One of the real problems was that I'd had enough. I didn't want to go on touring any more. The novelty had worn off and it had become really hard work. I understood how the business worked by now and that I had to meet the PR people, journalists and the Sony representatives to excite them about the product. I could switch on my enthusiasm as if I was answering the same old questions for the first time, but I was finding it boring doing it over and over again. I didn't want to have to be nice to everyone I met any more and I hated not being at home. Nonetheless, I kept Bampy's catchphrase in my mind: keep smiling. And I did. I was gaily giving interviews all over the world, saying, 'If I ever don't want to go on, I'll just give up.' That was bollocks! I had to present a positive front to the world because that was the professional thing to do, but also because I wanted people to think that I was in control of things. I was going through a stage where I didn't want to do anything. I had my allowance and a job to do – that was it.

Mum knew just how I felt and it upset her. She was a mother who wanted her child to be happy and hated it when I wasn't. But although she was stressed, she had also found a job that she was really good at and she enjoyed having control over what we did. Her usual reaction to my moaning was to shout. One of our most memorable fights happened over my GameBoy. I was so addicted to playing it that I started being rude to people, ignoring them when they asked me questions or trying to cut interviews short so I could get back to my game. I played it all the time and it drove Mum mad. One night, we were in a hotel room somewhere in Germany when she woke at 2 a.m. to find me playing *Pokémon*. She was furious because I was always moaning about how I tired I was and there I was wide awake in the middle of the night.

'Stop it, Charlotte. Turn it off,' she ordered.

'I can't. I'm on a really good bit. I can't pause it.'

Suddenly she grabbed it out of my hands and chucked it out of the window. Dad and I couldn't believe what she'd just done. I ran two floors downstairs to find my GameBoy in bits all over the pavement. I was distraught. I'd been on about level 52 and she'd destroyed it for ever.

'I can't believe you did that,' I screamed. 'I hate you.'

But Mum stood her ground and laughed. 'It serves you right. All you've done is play that damn thing and be rude to people.'

It took me some time to forgive her!

Dad was quite different. He was always the more logical of the two, and if I ever complained about what I had to do, he'd say, 'You're just having an off day. If you give up now, you'll regret it for the rest of your life. Every job in the world has its bad side. If you worked in an office or a factory, you'd hate that too. This is just work. Work's getting up in the morning, being somewhere all day that you don't want to be, with people you don't particularly want to be with. That's all this is, but you mustn't forget all the good things that come with it.'

He was right. I had to remember the fantastic places I'd been and the people I'd met. I loved singing. And I was rich! In the end I decided to stick with it, giving it one or two more years to see what happened. Although the court case was over, there was still a bit of the year left and more appearances booked: appearances that for once I was looking forward to because my favourite time of year had come round again.

Having switched on the Oxford Street Christmas lights, I flew to Washington for the National Tree Lighting Ceremony at the White House, the last Christmas the Clintons would be there. Washington looked magical, with fabulous, really classy Christmas decorations everywhere, ten times better than anything in the UK. The ceremony traditionally takes place on a stage at the Ellipse, just in front of the White House, where the national Christmas tree is planted. A model train runs around it and on the 'Pathway of Peace', another fifty-six smaller trees are planted, one for each state, each territory and the district of Columbia. I was wearing a pink cashmere jumper, but it was freezing cold so I grabbed Richard's red-and-white Welsh scarf that said 'Wales' on one side and '*Cymru*' on the other. Not a great look, but it was warm and it made me feel patriotic.

After Billy Gilman, Kathy Mattea and the cast of *Fosse* had performed, Santa introduced me. I sang 'Winter Wonderland', 'Silent Night' and 'O Come All Ye Faithful' before we were joined by Bill, Hillary and Chelsea Clinton, who stood behind bullet-proof glass as the President spoke, then lit the tree and we all sang 'The First Noel'.

Every year, the Plácido Domingo Society hold a Christmas concert in Vienna, so ten days after celebrating Christmas in Washington, I sang with my favourite of the Three Tenors, Plácido Domingo. It was so great to discover that as well as having an unbelievable voice, he's a lovely, lovely man. 'I love your voice,' he said to me. 'It's very rich. You're much more a mezzo than a soprano.' That's a real compliment, particularly given my critics, who had no idea how hard I trained with Lulu, how I used my voice or how I controlled it.

As I still dreamed of becoming an opera singer, I was dead chuffed to be singing in a beautiful theatre with Plácido Domingo, Vanessa Williams – who I will always remember for wearing too much blusher under her cheekbones. I agree with wearing it there, but there is definitely a mark and she stepped right over it – and Tony Bennett. He's a nice old man but I can't help feeling he should retire now. Wouldn't he have a nicer life? I think of him in the same way as I do Tom Jones – both lovely men and huge musical icons, but their voices are going now, their vibrato slowing with age, and I think they should go and live a little, spend their money and enjoy their kids and grandkids. It's time to give up. Come on, guys.

That evening, I wore a beautiful dress by Vera Wang which was worth about $18,000. It was covered in tiny gold beads and weighed a ton, but it looked fabulous, despite being a pain in the arse to wear. The concert was going well until Plácido Domingo and I sang 'O Holy Night' together. As I hit the top note – B flat – my jaw locked. Nothing like that had ever happened before. I was just starting to panic when it snapped back into place just as quickly as it had locked, and we finished the concert with no one being any the wiser.

Mum, Nana, Auntie Margaret and Jo came with me to Vienna, so we had a fabulous time wandering around the Christmas markets in the snow. Fairy lights were twisted up in the trees and around stalls selling fabulous Christmas food like sugar-coated peanuts, toffee-apples, gingerbread and mulled wine, as well as traditional crafts. Everywhere there were elaborate Christmas decorations with beautiful old wooden Santa Clauses and nativity scenes, and outside the town hall was an open-air skating rink surrounded by stalls selling all kinds of ethnic food. What a lush place and so Christmassy.

At last we got home to have our own Christmas in our new home in Whitchurch. Despite all the touring and the court case, we had managed to move house. Number 4 Gerddi Ty Celyn was much bigger than our previous homes and we loved it, despite the electric gates that were always broken. We'd been looking around for a while and bought a new house so we could specify some of the things we wanted: a lovely indoor swimming pool, a jacuzzi and a sauna. Mind you, we never really used the pool. Once when we were away, it sprang a leak but kept filling up automatically, costing a fortune in water bills. The house was beautifully done out because Mum hadn't got her own way all the time. If she had, it would have looked like a flock-wallpapered Indian takeaway. Her taste is *so* not the same as mine.

My new attic bedroom was lush. It was about forty feet long and ten feet wide; it reminded me of a bowling alley. Originally I'd wanted to decorate it using an ancient Egyptian theme, but that was way too difficult, so I ended up going Oriental instead. My huge, wrought-iron bed had wicker chests of drawers on either side and a big Oriental chest at its foot. All the soft toys I'd collected from around the world competed for space on the pillows. A long, narrow coffee table was laid with chopsticks and surrounded by four Chinese pillows. Elsewhere I had a Chinese lantern, a parasol and various beautiful Oriental pots and ornaments that I'd been given when I went to Japan and China. On show on the window ledge were all the pages I'd torn out of my autograph book – Rowan Atkinson, Robbie Williams, Stephen Fry, Jackie Collins. Every time the door opened, they'd all blow off in the draft and I'd spend ages meticulously putting them all back up. At the other end of the room were two sofabeds from Argos, so I could have sleep-overs. I loved having somewhere I could have my friends round, with room to chill out, gossip, watch TV and listen to Robbie Williams, Santana, Eminem, Destiny's Child and All Saints – our favourites at the time.

None of this took the nasty taste of the court case out of our mouths, though. I was tired and I was sick of all the shit that seemed to come with my career. I loved to sing, but not the rest of it. My mother had to put up with so much. The whole experience meant I lost a lot of my innocence. For the first time, I was learning something about the true nature of fame. I didn't feel guilty for being the cause of all this trouble, but I did feel sorry for my mother. I wanted the world to know that she wasn't the person portrayed by the media, but a brilliant mum who had done everything to encourage, support and protect me. My blood boiled at the injustice of it all. I'm all for fairness in life and I wanted to put across our side of things, but I couldn't because all the PR advice we were getting said, don't get into a war of words. Not that it would have made a blind bit of difference if I'd tried. I'd had my first taste of what the British press were capable of and I hated it. I felt jaded, cynical and quite bitter about them. Having seen the way things could be twisted made me very wary of doing interviews. If only I'd known how much worse it was going to get, I might have given up there and then.

CHAPTER 11

Hell's Angel – Not!

On 20 January 2001, the Bushman was inaugurated as president of the United States. It was a chilly, grey day, steadily drizzling with rain. I was to be part of the two-hour line-up of celebratory entertainment that included Andrew Lloyd Webber and Ricky Martin. The streets of Washington were closed off for the inauguration parades, so everyone involved took a special bus from the hotel to the Lincoln Memorial. My mum and dad had to go in the car with John Vernile, so I went alone on the bus, sitting next to Kelsey Grammer, aka Frasier. He told me that we shared a birthday and that his girlfriend couldn't be there because she had diar-rhoea – too much information! Although I wanted to sing at the event, I was completely oblivious to the political nature of the situation and the significance of which stars were there and which weren't. Anti-Bush protesters shouted at us as we went past and Secret Service men surrounded the stage that was set up on the steps of the Lincoln Memorial. When my turn came I sang 'Take Care of This House' – a bit Julie Andrews, but there you go.

After the show, all the performers went into a marquee set up by the stage. There were flowers everywhere and drinks for the celebrities and senators. President Bush came round to thank us all, and when he got to me he asked where I was from.

'I'm from Wales,' I replied.

'What state is Wales in?' he asked.

'Um. It's not in America, it's in the UK.' I felt really embarrassed for him.

The next day I flew to New York to appear in a concert with Wyclef Jean in the Carnegie Hall to benefit the Wyclef Jean Foundation, which is dedicated to music education for kids. Eric Clapton, Whitney Houston, Mary J. Blige and Destiny's Child were lined up for a wicked concert. Stevie Wonder was the evening's surprise guest, and he sang an amazing version of 'Gone Till November' with Wyclef. I duetted with Wyclef, too, singing 'Summertime' from *Porgy and Bess.*

The after-show party was in a downtown club somewhere in SoHo. All the VIPs were in a cordoned-off section upstairs but we watched all the rappers go downstairs. There were a lot of heavy-looking, pistol-packing dudes hanging around, so it was a weird old atmosphere. As I came out of the toilet, a big black guy bent towards me. 'D'you want some of this?' He nodded at a small pack of white powder in his hand.

'Errr . . . no, thanks. *Daaaad!* Where are you?' This was way out of my comfort zone. Although I'd heard about drugs, I'd never been exposed to them before, so it was a bit of a shock and I wanted out of there. Fast!

Now Jonathan was safely off the scene, it was time to appoint a new manager. Because I was spending so much time in the US, it seemed logical to take on an American management company. Peter Grosslight introduced us to a number of potential managers, including Irving Azoff, a legend in the music business. He has handled all the big stars, among them the Eagles, Steely Dan, Seal and Christina Aguilera. Irving was a little powerhouse, about five feet one with a high-pitched west-coast drawl, the most accomplished schmoozer around and a man with a fearsome temper. I'd heard a rumour that once, when he wasn't invited to a party, he sent the host a boa constrictor with a note, saying, 'Now you've got two. This one and your wife.' But if he's on your side, you couldn't ask for more. Mum and I decided that he was the man for us. By this time, Mark Melton had left P. Russell & Co. to set up his own company, so he remained my lawyer and trustee in the UK, helping Mum out when she needed him, as did Terry. Together they effectively acted as my manager at home, while Irving handled everything else, with the help of Sarah Ferguson-Jones in his London office. At last I had a team of people I felt completely comfortable with. I'd already learned that when you find good people in this business, you stick with them.

Irving and his gorgeous, diamond-studded wife, Shelly, invited Mum and me to the Grammy Awards ceremony that was taking place in LA on my fifteenth birthday. The night before, I celebrated with Mum, Julie, Germaine, Catherine and Sophie, a friend from Cardiff. The Stereophonics were live at the El Rey Theatre and we had special clearance for Sophie and me because we were underage. Sophie and I wanted to look the part for the Welsh boys, so I spent ages curling my hair into tight ringlets, while the gorgeous, almond-eyed Sophie wore something fabulously provocative. We all left the hotel in a long stretch limo with blacked-out windows. Boy, did we think we were the business. Just before we got to the venue, the adults stopped the car and got out for a cigarette. While they were outside, Sophie spotted decanters filled with clear and amber liquids that I recognised as vodka and Jack Daniels. We agreed that it was a good idea to down as much as possible before the others came back. She took the Jack Daniels and I took the vodka. Vodka is like my mother's milk and, knowing her, it probably was!

We managed to hold it together for the first fifteen minutes at the El Rey, but all I remember is hearing, 'Ladies and gentlemen, the Stereophonics . . .' After that, it's just random flashbacks of arguments with bouncers, sliding down walls and trying to hide Sophie while she peed in an alley. All the women were pissed off that we'd betrayed them and, because they'd had to bring us back to the hotel, cut their evening short.

When we got back to our room, my mother plied us with water, coffee and dry toast. I felt so sick and my head was spinning. Someone ran a cold bath for Sophie and she got in fully clothed. The only thing I can remember after that is waking up the next morning fresh as a daisy – still drunk, probably. Sophie had to tell me what had gone on the night before. Apparently we'd thrown up in the car and back at the hotel, while Mum went totally nuts. I couldn't remember anything about it.

We apologised to Mum, who was fuming but had hidden the sick-covered sheets from Dad. She wouldn't tell him, if I promised never to do it again. Luckily he had been out and missed the whole thing, otherwise he'd have gone mental. For some reason she did tell him about it when I was nineteen and he did go mental, which I thought was slightly pointless, but there you go.

The next evening we went to Clive Davis's pre-Grammy party, which was held in a massive hotel ballroom where millions of dollars had been spent transforming it into somewhere beautiful. Clive is another top music mogul who in those days was running Arista. Alicia Keys played a Beethoven piano sonata brilliantly before giving her first performance of 'Falling'. We were completely mesmerised by her because she looked so different. Her voice had a real earthiness with its gravelly texture and amazing range. She didn't sound like anyone else. Luther Vandross and Dido sang, too. Luther was silky smooth, the consummate professional, but beside him Dido seemed breathy and unimpressive.

Then it was on to the Grammys themselves. Irving thought that it would be a good networking opportunity for me, and he was right. Everyone was there: Madonna, Destiny's Child, Britney Spears, Justin Timberlake. I sat next to Jill Scott, an amazing R&B singer from Philadelphia, whose voice is so smooth it's like honey. It took me ages to work up the courage to ask for her autograph, which she happily gave me. The highpoint of the evening for me was when everyone sang 'Happy Birthday' to me when I got up to present an award. I felt very honoured and self-conscious. It was a long night as the ceremony went on for hours and hours, although it was pretty cool seeing the most famous artists in the world performing in sets that must have cost thousands of dollars to put together.

The after-Grammy party was in a massive marquee full of Sony chiefs, including the Welsh-born head of the Sony Corporation of America, Sir Howard Stringer; Tommy Mottola, head of Sony Music Entertainment; and Peter Gelb, head of Sony Classical. Tommy had an incredibly expensive bottle of wine that he wouldn't let anyone touch, although I seem to remember Howard helping himself when Tommy wasn't looking. Tommy sat at his table, cigar in mouth, with his wife and a guest as if he was someone very special. We loved Howard Stringer that night because he got a bit inebriated and cut through all the bullshit, taking the piss out of everyone's pretensions. We felt a bond with him because he's a Welshman through and through, born in the old St David's Hospital, just like me. He always made sure I had all the latest Sony gadgets and, better still, he always took our phone calls. In this business, it's rare to get straight through to the man at the top, but he always picked up his own phone.

Howard was the exception in a room full of men with huge egos. He was funny and straight as a die. As a fifteen-year-old, I could never understand what the others did that qualified as hard work. As far as I could see, they had meetings, listened to music, signed people and decided where the money went, while all of us artists worked our bollocks off. While they travelled first class or in chauffeur-driven limos, we made do with business class and taxis. Not that we had such a hard time of it, I admit, but I really resented their lavish lifestyles. It seemed to me that they and the people who surround the stars – PAs, bodyguards, managers and the like – were the divas, not the stars themselves. While the stars were slogging their guts out, trying to survive their promotion schedules, everyone around them was living the high life.

I was dying to go over to Destiny's Child, but their bodyguards were eyeballing me as if to say, 'Don't you dare.' I went over anyway, but one of the guards said, 'You shouldn't come over while the girls are eating.'

'But I only want an autograph,' I protested. Fortunately the girls heard and were happy to sign for me. They weren't swamped with people and knew I'd disappear straightaway, but their guards took themselves way too seriously.

As my career had been steadily building in the States, Sony decided to concentrate their promotional effort there. Somehow I had cracked the American market – something that's notoriously hard for a British singer. I'm not sure how I managed it, but I guess it was a combination of luck and hard work. It's obviously harder to get round America than the UK to promote an album simply because of the size of the country. Some people aren't willing or are unable to put in the time and energy you need for that. During the first half of 2001 we had a two-month tour that covered the whole of North America, travelling from North Carolina to Florida, Texas, Quebec, Ontario, Connecticut, Michigan, New York, Boston, Minnesota, Virginia and more. So much for our vow that we'd never be away for more than three weeks at a time!

For once we travelled in a private jet, like the top brass, except that the top brass never had to endure in-flight geography and maths lessons. When you're travelling as much as that, one concert or book signing seems much the same as another. You don't have time to explore the different cities and you're busy meeting so many different people and staying in so many different hotels that it all becomes a bit of a blur, however fabulous they are individually.

Wherever we went, crowds of people turned up to see me. Most of them were lovely, but we did get some wild, weird and wonderful fans too. I used to get a bit freaked by the ones who thought I was an angel sent from heaven or that I'd been touched by God. Some of them would cry and reach out to touch me. 'I've touched the angel,' they'd sob. I didn't really know what to say to them, but I knew I had to be polite, keep smiling and say thank you, while inside I was thinking, It's only me.

Walking past a fence at an open-air concert, all I could see were the arms and hands of people who hadn't got tickets reaching under the fence, holding slips of paper and autograph books. I ended up crouched on the ground, signing autographs for people whose faces I couldn't even see.

Once, a guy with blue hair was waiting for me at the stage door.

'I've dyed my hair blue for you,' he said. 'I heard it was your favourite colour.'

'Great,' I replied. 'Thank you.'

'I had brain cancer,' he explained. 'But every time I listened to you singing, the tumour grew smaller and smaller, so dying my hair is in honour of you.'

There were many more strange stories. A nun wrote us an eight-page letter explaining that I had been touched by God, who had sent me to restore the faith of young women. One lovely old lady who used to come to a lot of the American concerts still writes to me and sends me pictures. Mr Swan must have been in his sixties when I first met him in Cardiff. He was shaking when we met and was quite in awe of me. Afterwards he sent me a beautiful piece of jewellery every birthday and Christmas. One woman sent my nana a Christmas card every year, asking how I was; then her family phoned and told Nana she was dying. When Nana told me, I sent a letter saying how sorry I was and that our family was praying for her. Her son wrote back to say that receiving it meant the world to her, describing how her face lit up. Another woman's grandmother was suffering from Alzheimer's and she claimed that the only time her grandmother smiled was when she heard my records.

To have touched so many people's lives is incredibly humbling, but sometimes it led to some quite nasty stuff. I've had a lot of scary-arse letters and we even had a bomb threat at school once. I know there's also been a lot of shit I haven't been told about, such as kidnap threats and stalkers. Knowing the details would do my head in, so I don't ask. The one I did hear about happened while we were in America. Apparently a man staying in a Cardiff B&B had been into the locker room in Howell's. The police tracked him down and found pictures of me all over the walls of his room, as well as a shrine set up surrounded by candles. He was a real nutcase and was extradited home to Europe.

Despite all this, I still worried that no one would come to see me. I needn't have, because wherever we went, thousands of people turned up. Security was always laid on, but I was also always accompanied by John Vernile, a couple of Sony representatives and Mum, Dad, Richard and Catherine. Fans who buy an album and want an autograph are one thing, but I try not to think of the more obsessive ones because it weirds me out. Although I'm quite strong, I am terrified of staying alone in a house at night because of them.

Once the tour was over, I could settle back home again, although various concerts or appearances always cropped up.

My family have always been staunch Labour supporters, so they were delighted when I was invited to sing at a pre-election Labour Party rally in Bristol. I took the warm-up spot and sang 'Summertime' and 'Dream a Dream' before Tony Blair took to the stage, sleeves rolled up, to deliver his speech. Afterwards, he complimented me on my singing, but I took the opportunity to tell him exactly what I thought of having to pay 40 per cent tax on my earnings when I still wasn't old enough to vote. I was really pissed off about it then and still think it's unfair now. He looked embarrassed and laughed it off before going on to talk to someone else.

When we all left the rally, I was weighed down with bags while Mum hauled my suitcase full of outfits and carried the flowers I'd been given. As she followed us up the stairs, Tony Blair turned round and noticed her. 'Oh my God, Charlotte. Look at your mother. No one's bothered to help her.' He ran back down to her. 'I'm so sorry. You look as if you're about to keel over. Let me help.' At that moment, the security guys stepped in and took the case, but Tony Blair was definitely Mr Charming.

Having sung with Plácido Domingo at Christmas, I was looking forward to singing with Pavarotti at a summer concert in Hyde Park. Russell Watson and I were to sing the 'Drinking Song' from *La Traviata* with him. I had learned and rehearsed the soprano part especially. Russell and I went to see Pavarotti before the show. He was in make-up, sitting there like a big Father Christmas with just a towel round his waist having his eyebrows and beard pencilled in. He seemed friendly enough and shook our hands before we discussed our performance. Then he barked at me, 'When I point at you, you sing.'

'I only know the soprano bits, Maestro,' I replied. 'But as long as you point to me when it's a soprano bit, I can sing that.'

His people had warned us that we had to call him 'Maestro'. Monstro, more like.

'No. You should know the whole song,' he insisted, too aggressively for my liking.

'Well, I don't.' I was trying to be as polite and reasonable as possible. 'I'm a soprano, so I'm afraid I've only learned the soprano part.'

He obviously wasn't impressed.

We left him to finish getting ready, but five minutes before we were due on stage, Russell and I received a message saying Pavarotti would be singing with his own soprano! We weren't needed after all. We were well pissed off.

The summer holidays had become synonymous with my recording a new album, and this year was no exception. However, when it came to the fourth album, *Enchantment*, Sony's control over the content lessened as Irving took over. He recognised that I was growing up and needed to develop my career, so he decided I should be positioned as more of a crossover artist than a child soprano. He also introduced me to a new producer, Keith Thomas, who had worked with stars such as Vanessa Williams, Faith Hill, Michael Bolton and Luther Vandross. Luckily for me, Keith couldn't come to the UK, so I had to go to LA to record, stay in the Sunset Marquis and, when we weren't working, enjoy the sunshine. The big studio had sofas to lie around on, while outside there were tables and chairs where we were served beautiful food or I played snooker with Dad.

Enchantment did include a couple of operatic songs, but several were from shows such as *West Side Story* ('Somewhere'), *South Pacific* ('Bali Ha'i') and *Carousel* ('If I Loved You'). Some were old favourites that I'd been singing for a while, and others I had to work hard with Lulu to perfect, such as 'The Flower Duet' from *Lakmé*, 'The Laughing Song' from *Die Fledermaus* and 'A Bit of Earth' from *The Secret Garden*. My voice had matured and become richer, but now I was older my repertoire could expand to include songs about love without seeming too stupid.

What also made this album special was working with the brilliant flamenco guitarist and arranger Jesse Cook, whose CD I had listened to on tour when I was younger. His music was so lively and passionate and he put his own distinctive stamp on some of the tracks. My top song was his version of 'Habañera', from the opera *Carmen*, using big Brazilian drums and flamenco guitar, which really captures the spirit of the opera. I thought it was ten times better than the original, although I know my critics felt that we took the song too far from its purist form.

We also reworked the traditional lullaby, 'The Little Horses', to include drums and guitar. During my travels, I had heard the French composer Erik Satie's 'Gymnopédie 1'. As well as the melody, I loved its simplicity and elegance, so I asked whether Jesse and Keith thought we could do something with it. They did. At the time I had a real thing about gypsy violin, so Jesse found someone who could play it as well as the flamenco guitar, and so 'From My First Moment' was born, probably my other favourite song on the album.

After the success of my duet with Billy Gilman, everyone was thrilled when the producer David Foster approached Sony to suggest that I might want to sing with his new protégé, Josh Groban, a wicked up-and-coming crossover artist with a flawless tenor voice. As a result, Josh and I recorded 'The Prayer' together, a beautiful song written by Carole Bayer Sager and David and originally recorded by Céline Dion. Our voices complemented each other's perfectly. David Foster is a legend in the music business; he's passionate about his work and has worked with all the major names, including Michael Jackson, Paul McCartney, Lionel Richie, Neil Diamond, Dionne Warwick, Céline Dion and Barbra Streisand. The list goes on and on. We were to discover that David was also a warm, generous guy who, with his then wife and co-writer, Linda Thompson, invited Mum, Dad, Josh and me to dinner while we were in LA.

I'd spent most of that day recording *Hollywood Squares*, a popular US celebrity quiz show, where I'd been made up to meet Whoopi Goldberg, a really cool lady who bothered to come to the green room and give Smarties to all the kids. Afterwards, we'd gone back to the hotel to get ready for the evening. Josh was due to pick us up at 7.30, and Mum and I were in the two separate baths in our LA hotel suite when the whole building began to shake. Out of our fifteenth-floor window, we could see skyscrapers swaying like trees in a gale. We leaped out of the baths, which looked as if they might come off the walls at any minute, and ran to the doorway where we stood, half-wrapped in towels with shampoo in our hair, screaming our heads off. The earthquake was over in minutes, but they were the longest and most terrifying of my entire life. We both thought we were going to die, buried in the rubble of the hotel. We found out later that this was the largest earthquake felt in the LA basin since 1994. Fortunately, no significant damage was reported and life quickly went back to normal, so we just hopped back into our baths!

Josh picked us up as planned and we were driven to David's estate in Malibu. We'd thought the Davises' Beverly Hills house was glamorous, but this was ten times grander and another glimpse into how the other half lives. Again, there was a long drive leading up to the Hollywood-style mansion that was completely cut off from the rest of the world, surrounded by trees and acres of land. Inside the house, fairy lights twinkled up the stairs, and everywhere we looked, ornaments of angels looked back at us. Before dinner, David took me over to meet Barbra Streisand. She looked pretty scruffy to me in pink cords, a pink jumper and almost no make-up, but there was a definite aura around her. What I remember about her most of all were her hands. They were like a hand model's, with long fingers and a perfect French manicure. She was very charming and interested in me, what I sang and what we were doing with David.

At dinner we were on Barry Manilow's table. He and his manager had us in stitches, regaling us with Hollywood gossip. I couldn't help noticing that Mum and Dad were the only people drinking wine, though – everyone else was on water, drinking a little bottle each. Afterwards, we all moved into another beautiful room, where David sat at the grand piano and started to play. Josh and I were asked to sing first, then Paul Anka took over, followed by lots of the other guests. The only two who didn't join in were Barry Manilow, who said he refused to unless Barbra would, and Barbra Streisand. Instead, she made Mum's night by plonking her arse next to her on one of the settees and talking to her about me. This was all too much for Mum, who was gasping for a cigarette, so she snuck outside, not through the door that led to a patio of tables, chairs and ashtrays, but through another. When she'd had her smoke, she knew she couldn't stamp the stub out on the terrace, so she tried to bury it in a flower pot. The earth was so dry she had to scrabble like a mad thing, and came in, mission completed, her hands covered in dirt. When she told me afterwards, I nearly died, but we had a good laugh about it.

We were the last there, along with Josh, Barbra and her husband, sitting round a table with David and Linda. David turned to Barbra and said, 'One of Charlotte's favourite songs, one of the ones she sang when she was eight or nine, is "Don't Rain on My Parade".'

'How could she have sung that?' Barbra didn't believe him. 'She's a soprano. Besides, it's a big song.'

'It's true,' chipped in Mum.

'Sing it for me,' Barbra said. 'Please.'

I felt a sharp kick under the table and Mum's voice in my ear. 'Go on, Charlotte. Sing for Barbra.' I was so embarrassed. Yet again my mum had put herself next in line for the execution squad. Even she admits that, at that moment, she was behaving like the pushy mother in *Gypsy Rose Lee.*

I hadn't sung the song for ages, but nobody would listen to my refusals. After I'd stood up and given it my best shot, David turned to Barbra and said, 'Meet the new you, Barbra.' She didn't say a word, just smiled. Grimacing inside, more like.

Recording *Enchantment* took about two weeks. Sometimes Germaine and Julie would come and visit us at the studio, or, if we finished early, we'd go down to Venice Beach. I stayed there a couple of nights with Julie, walking her dog and waking up to the sound of the waves. In the evenings we'd eat out at the best restaurants: Crustacean, Ivy at the Shore, Le Dôme and Mr Chow's. Nana and Bampy came over to see me sing at the Hollywood Bowl again, and we even managed to fit in the launch party to N Sync's new album and the prèmiere of Jackie Chan's new movie *Rush Hour 2*.

What I was beginning to find hard was the way the press were starting to comment on how I was growing up. I didn't mind them noticing what I was wearing, but journalists were getting more personal. I had boobs now and wanted to start dressing differently, but the press had a bit of a problem with that. Everyone seemed to want me to remain the innocent twelve-year-old angel, but that wasn't going to happen.

At the *Rush Hour 2* première I was wearing a blue top that was perfectly decent, quite tight-fitting but no low neckline. The next day's headline was CHARLOTTE'S LOOKING CHEST SWELL. I was so uncomfortable after that that I wanted to wear a big baggy hoody for the rest of the year. I couldn't, of course, but it did make me more self-conscious for a while. My mum was OK with most of what I wanted to wear, but my dad was much fussier. I remember having some beautiful sexy tops: one of them was a completely backless woollen polo neck, and the others were a little bit low-cut. My dad only went and left them all in a hotel room in LA. He maintained it was an accident, but I'm pretty sure he did it on purpose.

I have never been seriously influenced by what people write about me. In an odd way, what they said made me even more determined to live my life the way I wanted without being dictated to by anyone. I wanted to find my own style and stick with it, but whatever I wore seemed to provoke comment. Nothing more so than the leather bustier, trousers and jacket I wore with a sparkling belt and choker at the *Showtime* concert at the Millennium Stadium in November. The next day, the papers went mad – HELL'S ANGEL: CHARLOTTE GOES HELL FOR LEATHER. I had ditched my little girl image at last and was getting ready to move on. Yes, folks, I was growing up!

CHAPTER 12

Stitched Up!

Like most people's, my relationship with my parents as I was growing up was mixed. I loved them to bits and knew I didn't want anyone else travelling with me, but at the same time I didn't want them there either. They were my parents, for God's sake. What self-respecting fifteen-year-old wants to spend all that time with their parents? I would have hated not being with them, but at times they did my head in.

The older I got, the more I missed my friends back home. It wasn't that I felt lonely when we were on the road, but I was isolated. Nobody, not even Mum, understood what it felt like being me. When I wanted sympathy for the amount of work I was doing, no one would give it to me. Although Mum and Dad were always there for me, they couldn't understand what it felt like to be so famous so young. I had gone through a unique experience. In the same way, I couldn't understand what it was like for them having a famous daughter, though I can see how weird it must have been for them when I was recognised almost everywhere we went. We were stuck in our separate bubbles. We had brought one or two of my friends on the road with us during the school holidays, and that helped me a lot. I felt much better when I had a friend there to share all the amazing things that were happening to me, but even so, there was nothing like being back home with them.

By now I had a small group of close friends: Naomi, Kyla, Jo, Kim, Charlie and Abi. Naomi and Kyla were friends from outside school, who had neatly slotted in with the rest of us. Naomi is feisty and hysterically funny. She always knew the latest dances and the words to all the latest songs, so we thought she was very cutting edge. With her high cheekbones, full lips and elongated green cat's eyes, she looks Maori and makes the most of it with cool hair and make-up, plus the latest stylish outfits. She's the sort of person people naturally flock to, and although she doesn't try to control things, she became a bit of a gang leader.

Kyla has beautiful milky coffee-coloured skin with exaggerated Egyptian eyes, and when she doesn't kill her hair by straightening it, she has stunning tight curls. Curly or straight, every hair has to be in place. She's quite softly spoken, but most importantly she has a heart of gold. We all hung out together whenever we could when I was at home, often having sleepovers or going to the cinema.

On Saturdays, we'd go to Savoy's Sandwich Bar, where a couple of my friends worked. There were about fourteen of us crammed in the tiny shop, unintentionally intimidating potential customers. We'd hang out there, looking nice, but if any of the boys came near us, we'd get all embarrassed and

One wrong step and we'd
have been over the edge...

At the Carousel of Hope
Ball in Hollywood in 2000
— everyone who was anyone
was there.

With Placido Domingo, Tony Bennett and
Vanessa Williams in Vienna.

Singing at the Christmas Concert in Vienna
wearing a fabulous Vera Wang dress decorated with gold beads that weighed a ton.

Explaining geography to the new US President, George W Bush.

Going Greek at the Grammy Awards on my 15th birthday.

Duetting with the man himself at the Wyclef Jean Foundation Concert at Carnegie Hall, New York, January 2001.

Finally ditching my little girl image at the Red Dragon FM Welsh Awards, Cardiff, October 2001.

On the road and loving it — not! More inflight tuition with Catherine.

Cutting the cake on my 16th birthday.

Singing with Josh Groban at the closing ceremony of the Winter Olympics in Utah, 2002.

A definite style by-pass on my part! Walking into Cardiff City Centre with Catherine Zeta Jones and Ian Botham in aid of the Noah's Ark Appeal, Cardiff Basin, 27 April 2002.

Richard Kendal/BBC Photo Library.

My heart was pounding when I guest-presented Have I Got News For You.

On the red carpet, meeting some fans at the premiere of I'll Be There in 2003.

Dave Hogan/Getty Images

Being introduced at the Oxford University Union in November 2003, by President of the Union, Marcus Walker.

Living it large in Ibiza. Me and Naomi after a legendary night at Pacha nightclub.

hide. I felt quite safe there with all the girls. The only thing I couldn't do with them was hang out in the street, where I'd be recognised, so we'd go to someone's house instead. I'm sure they were more adventurous when I wasn't there, but that didn't matter. A few were allowed to go to Zeus, the under-18s nightclub, but I know my mother would never have let me go. She would have been among the parents who thought we were too young, and she was right. Anyway, we'd have got bored with it soon enough. I did try to go clubbing a few times, but because everyone in Cardiff knew exactly how old I was, I could never get in. False ID was pointless for me because I was almost always recognised. I tried all sorts of disguises: glasses, putting my hair in different styles, ridiculous heavy make-up or none at all, and hats. The only thing I wouldn't play down was my clothes, because I had to look cool.

Once Jo, Kim and I asked Dad for a lift to the cinema. When we got there, there was nothing on that we fancied, so we went to Reflex, a cheesy Eighties bar. It wasn't our style, but we had to go to pretty shitty places if I was going to get in at all. When they let us through the door, we sat there for an hour, too scared to even have a drink, then met my dad and lied about how good the film had been. Pathetic, I know.

Sometimes we'd get past the door of a club, but then some-one would recognise me and say, 'It's Charlotte Church.' Then the whole club would be whispering and the next thing, it was the bouncers, 'Charlotte Church? Get out!' The only club that would let me in was RSVP, a proper R&B club that was always packed out on Saturdays. It was really rough with fights kick-ing off all the time, but we had a great time there, drinking and dancing. I know my parents worried that we were hanging out with the wrong sorts of boys and blamed that on our having been to an all-girls school, but I was enjoying myself and I didn't care what they thought.

I loved that gang of girls and did almost everything with them. Being with them helped keep me grounded. They weren't really interested in what I'd been doing, unless I'd met someone they were keen on, so when I came back it was never a question of what I'd been doing that they'd missed out on, it was all about what *they'd* done and *I'd* missed out on. In fact, I don't think I missed too much. I'd get home after three weeks away, imagining how much I'd missed, but the local radio station Red Dragon would still be playing the same old songs. The same people were going to the same places, getting drunk, dancing to the same music. I soon realised that nothing was that different, whereas for me, things were always on the move.

At the end of the year, I was off to the States again on a six-week tour to promote *Enchantment*, which was released at the beginning of October. Jesse Cook came with us, but at least he was spared the chaos of our tour bus. I took the double bed intended for the artist, while Rhodri, Mum, Dad, Richard, Catherine, the tour manager Tom Consolo, who was one of Irving's management team, and Arnie Roth, the conductor, all bunked up in the 'coffins'. The most I can remember about the tour was being completely knackered, although Mum insists that it was nothing to do with hard work and more to do with the fact that I played my PlayStation until three or four every morning.

By this time I thought I'd learned how to be careful with the press, how to watch out for saying things that can be taken out of context and twisted. Perhaps the worst lesson came after 9/11. I was flying back home from Chicago when the Twin

Towers were hit, and two weeks later, I went with Mum and Dad to Ground Zero. I wanted to go there to try to understand this massive landmark in American history and to pay tribute to the people who had lost their lives. I didn't want to take one of the VIP tours, surrounded by photographers, but preferred to visit anonymously. I had spent so much time working in New York that I felt like an honorary New Yorker and consequently felt as close to what had happened as all my American friends did.

I had expected the area to be silent, with people going down there to pay their respects. We weren't at all prepared for people climbing over cars to get the best picture and taking away debris as souvenirs. Apart from that, being there was an extremely emotional experience and one of the most humbling, moving experiences of my life. People were standing in huddles crying for those they'd lost, and burning candles in their memory. There were thousands of 'missing' posters pinned up and it was heartbreaking to see. Afterwards, I felt that perhaps I shouldn't have gone, because it was a gravesite and very personal to all those who had lost their friends and family there.

The day we flew back to London, I was booked to do an interview with Jasper Gerard, a *Sunday Times* journalist. My PR person was tied up and had asked Mum if she would sit in on the interview, but Mum had to go to a meeting. This was one of the rare occasions, if not the only one, when I was on my own. We talked for two hours, and I came away having enjoyed our time together, feeling that we'd had a proper conversation instead of my having to answer the usual questions. During it, we talked about 9/11 and I told him about having been to Ground Zero. I also said that I'd been at the UK

National TV Awards where two of the New York firefighters had been flown to London to present the Award for Most Popular Soap. I felt that these two men represented a group of incredibly brave men whose courage and sacrifice had been like nothing else. They weren't TV stars, they were heroes. Having them present this particular award seemed to me to demean their heroism and showed the producers in a bad light.

When the interview appeared in print, I felt what I'd said had been taken out of context and twisted to sound as if I thought what the New York firefighters did on 9/11 was all in a day's work. As for my visiting Ground Zero, the impression was given that I had been expecting a red carpet to roll out. Nothing could be further from the truth.

My mum believed me when I said I hadn't been fairly represented, although my dad was less sure. Everyone else went mad. The people at Sony were apoplectic. To begin with, the public reaction to the piece was muted, until about ten days later, when the piece was quoted in the *New York Post*. Thanks, Mr Murdoch! After all that singing at your wedding! The rest of the US press swooped on it before the whole thing bounced back across the Atlantic. A typical headline of the time read, VOICE OF AN ANGEL SPEWS VENOM. I received sacks of hate mail, mostly from America. In some ways I couldn't blame the senders because I would have been as upset as they obviously were if I thought someone had the views being attributed to me. Among them were death threats, so wherever I went in the States after that, I had to be accompanied by an armed bodyguard. I was devastated and scared by what was happening. I hated the thought that people would believe that I was really cold and mean.

Soon afterwards, I was appearing at Disneyland when someone shouted, 'What about the firemen, Charlotte?' I felt terrible but the only thing I could do was ignore him. What else could I do? If I'd tried to explain, I knew we'd get into a wrangle, and I was scared that more remarks would be taken out of context by the press, who were just waiting for me to slip up. I had released a formal statement that made my true feelings clear, but I didn't know how to put things right until someone working in my PR's office in New York told me he had a cousin working in the first unit of firefighters to arrive on the scene. I arranged to visit the station so that I could at least tell some of the men what had really happened. They accepted my explanation, and I hope that I managed to make up a little for the misunderstanding.

I couldn't grasp what I had done that made someone dislike me that much. Why would anyone twist an interview to make me look so unsympathetic? I was beginning to understand the idea of 'spin' and the lengths the press will go to for a headline, no matter what the cost to the subject. I knew I should try to put it to the back of my mind, but I worried about it for weeks. Mum once found me crying my eyes out before going on *Parkinson*. She tried to pull me from the show, but I knew that would make people think even worse of me, so I insisted on appearing. I was being kept busy as usual, doing various TV appearances and concerts, such as *GMTV*, *Open House with Gloria Hunniford*, the *Showtime* concert and the *Royal Variety Performance*, where I met the legendary Lennox Lewis. He was lovely but absolutely massive. When he shook my hand, he practically engulfed my whole forearm. So much for my firm handshake!

During that time, Frank Skinner was one of the people who

supported me. I was a guest on his show, and instead of patronising me, like so many others did by talking about how I'd grown up, he turned the conversation to talk about how nasty the media can be. I was relieved to find someone else who'd been on the receiving end. The whole episode made me grow a much tougher skin. In future, I would have to be more guarded over what I said and about who I trusted.

I've supported the Noah's Ark Appeal ever since it began in 2000, with the aim of raising the money needed to build, equip and support the first dedicated children's hospital for Wales. I think every child has the right to the best medical treatment, and until now Wales has been the only European country without such a hospital. The very first time I helped fundraise was when I was fourteen and appeared with Chris de Burgh. I hadn't a clue who he was and had never heard 'Lady in Red', so it never occurred to me that wearing a red dress might not be such a bright idea. When he called me up on to the stage to sit on the piano stool next to him, I nearly died. You're joking! I hate you for this, Mum, I thought. You knew who he was and that he'd sing this song and you still let me wear red. As we were in front of an audience, I had no choice but to go up and sit there with him, but all I wanted was to go home.

A year later I was fundraising for them again, this time with my first ever solo concert in Wales. I had performed my first solo concert at the Avery Fisher Hall in New York earlier in the year, which had been a big deal for me. People always expect that because of all the trickery involved with making CDs, I won't be as good in concert, but I always felt that my voice came into its own when I performed live. The New York concert had gone well, especially with Jesse Cooke as my support act, but in Cardiff, there were so many of my friends and family in the audience that I was completely petrified. My usual pre-concert calm had flown out of the window as I prepared, and because the whole thing was being filmed for PBS, the show perhaps didn't have the spontaneity it should have had. After a slightly shaky start, I gave it as good as I'd got. By this time I hated 'Pie Jesu' with a passion, and if I could avoid singing it, I did, so most of the songs I sang came from the new album, *Enchantment*, which I'd recorded earlier in the summer.

One of the upsides of being famous is that you can help make a difference to other people's lives by lending your name to charity appeals. I've always loved making fundraising appearances. Apart from the Wyclef Jean benefit concert and the Noah's Ark Appeal that year, I was asked to appear at the MGM Grand Garden Arena in Las Vegas for the Andre Agassi Foundation, which is designed to benefit at-risk children. Headlining were the singers Tim McGraw, Faith Hill, Nita Whitaker and Stevie Wonder, along with Robin Williams, Elton John and Don Henley from the Eagles. I'd spotted my black dress with a plunging neckline in one of the Vegas hotel shops and I loved it – yes, again! – and was feeling good.

At the pre-show press conference, someone asked Robin Williams a question that sent him jumping over the press tables, running round going nuts. We were all like, What the fuck is he doing? After the show, we had a photocall back stage, so I said something like, 'It's been nice to meet you. I think you're amazing.' What else could I say? It's so hard to think of something to say to someone who you know isn't really interested in talking to you. I told him I came from Wales.

'Wales,' he said. 'Shakespeare.' And then he went nuts again, going on about Shakespeare, Wales and whales. I was totally confused. It was intriguing to meet him, but in the end I managed to pull myself away so that Mum and I could leave, but not before Elton John had apologised for ignoring me when he'd been having a tantrums and tiaras day at the Grammys. Elton apologised to *me*! How nice of him was that? He chatted to me, commenting on how my voice had matured and asking how I liked being in America. Andre Agassi was a real sweetheart, too, and one of the most humble men I've ever met. He was so over the top with his thank yous. That, on top of the standing ovation I'd received, meant I went away more than happy. The whole event raised $4.2 million, so it was an amazing and worthwhile thing to be part of, even if it was a bit mad.

By Christmas, I think we must have visited every state in the US that year. Sony had wanted saturation and they got it. When *Enchantment* came out in October, it went straight in at number fifteen on the national Billboard chart, while in the UK it only reached number twenty-four. As far as I was concerned, though, my own enchantment with the business was flagging.

I was looking forward to a quieter new year, when I was going to be allowed to be at home, concentrating on my GCSEs, once I'd had my sixteenth birthday.

CHAPTER 13

In the Spotlight

TIP:

When it's time to leave home, try to do it
without falling out with your parents,
however annoying they might be.
Arguing with them makes the whole
thing a million times more stressful.

Until my sixteenth birthday, the press had pretty much left my private life alone, but I knew the gloves would be off when the clock struck midnight on 20 February 2002. Someone had even set up a website counting down the days until it was legal for me to have sex! How sick was that? The idea really disturbed me. The press picked up on it, and by reporting the site and criticising it, they seemed to plant the subject in the minds of the whole nation. It would have been better to say nothing and leave the sick website in the dark. Fortunately, I was really comfortable with myself or I guess I could have got quite screwed up about it. I never felt that I was lagging behind my friends in anything and was looking forward to celebrating my birthday in style.

I'd been given some bottles of sake, so the evening kicked off in my bedroom, away from the prying eyes of my parents, who would never let me drink. My closest friends came over and we got pretty drunk as we got ready for the party. Everyone was dressed up and I thought I looked lush in a fucking awful outfit of thigh-high black boots, a pleated denim skirt and a black long-sleeved top with a massive bling-bling diamanté belt. Then we hit the town. About seventy or eighty of my friends were invited to a club we'd hired, and God knows how many others tried to gatecrash. The only people I wouldn't allow in were my parents. They weren't happy about being banned, but I wanted to have a good time without them watching. When the DJ booth broke down I went nuts. 'You're taking the piss. We can't have a party without music.' So we had to move the whole thing to the upstairs bar. Although we were under strict instructions to be non-alcoholic, of course we managed to smuggle in some alcohol and had a wicked night. I danced the whole time and loved every minute, although I didn't feel so great when I turned up at a *Hello!* photoshoot the next morning.

Naomi and Charlie dragged themselves out with me, then the three of us flew out to LA with Mum and Dad for a couple of days before we went on to Utah, where I was performing at the closing ceremony of the Winter Olympics. As usual, we stayed at the Sunset Marquis, where the girls were overwhelmed by the lush surroundings and celebrity-studded company. We were due to go to Club Moomba, a hot nightclub in West Hollywood to celebrate my birthday again, and that afternoon, the three of us were secretly smoking out of the toilet window, when Mum called, 'Charlotte! There's someone on the phone for you.'

I picked it up to hear a stranger's voice speaking in a nasal West Coast drawl. 'Hi there. Is that Charlotte Church?'

'Yes. Who is it?'

'This is Dave from Rays, a club in downtown LA. We're doing a Charlotte Church transvestite night, and they're all going to get dressed up as you and sing some of your best hits, like "Pie Jesu". We'd love to have you there, if you'd like to come down. It'll be a blast.'

A transvestite club? I'm only sixteen. But I was so well trained I knew just what to say. 'I'm so sorry,' I said in my poshest voice. 'I'm studying for my GCSEs and I've got to revise. I'd love to have come otherwise. Tell them all, good luck.'

'Shut up, you silly cow. It's Robbie!' Dave's accent had completely changed!

Silence. Robbie? Do I know a Robbie?

'Robbie Williams.'

Ha bloody ha. Dietrich, our favourite waiter, and Robbie had set me up and I'd fallen for it, hook, line and sinker.

I'd met Robbie a couple of times and once he'd even written me a poem – of sorts: 'Don't start smoking, When you hear my live vocal, You'll know I'm not joking.' His live vocal sounded more than fine to me, so I'd ignored his advice. I think he must have been a bit lonely because he said he'd come up to our villa and was there within minutes, giving us no time to get ready. He and I chatted for about half an hour, but for once Naomi and Charlie were dumbstruck. 'What's the matter, Charlie? Cat got your tongue?' he asked. She was so embarrassed. We were made up that he was there, though. He didn't have to come and see us, but it was an amazing thing that he did and he even sang me 'Happy Birthday'.

The following night we were in Utah. The reflection of the

lights twinkled off the snow and ice in the huge Winter Olympics stadium, where there was a great air of expectation and excitement. Because Irving Azoff also managed Christina Aguilera, he took the three of us to meet her, but she just didn't seem to want to know. We were stunned by how she behaved: she barely looked at, never mind spoke to us. I do know how hard it is when you've got people in your face all the time. I won't say that it takes nothing to be nice, because if you're on show all the time, it takes a lot. I'm more chilled about all that now, but when I was a moody, hormonal teenager, I didn't want to be nice to anyone, so I knew how she felt, but there was still no need to be that off-hand.

More exciting was going to meet Jon Bon Jovi, who was also appearing. John Baruck, one of Irving's management team, took me into his trailer and I said, 'Hi. Nice to meet you, Mr Bon Jovi.' I might as well have been invisible. I was wondering how much make-up he wore on the TV because he looked much older than I'd imagined, but he couldn't hear my thoughts, so that's no excuse. He started talking shop with John, who interrupted him by saying, 'Charlotte's a singer.'

'Yeah. Do you remember the time when . . . ?'

'She's singing "The Prayer" with Josh Groban this evening.'

'That was fucking awesome, man . . .'

And so it went on.

The concert that night was incredible and featured Kiss, N Sync, Moby, Gloria Estefan and Earth, Wind and Fire. Josh and I sang just before the Olympic flame was extinguished, standing alone on a big circular stage, Josh in a cool leather jacket and me in a lush white sheepskin coat. I tried not to remind myself that I was performing to my biggest TV audience ever – close on 1.6 billion people were thought to be tuning in – and instead concentrated on the song, which I always found very emotive and uplifting.

We left the States to go back to Cardiff and school. GCSEs were looming, so my work schedule was deliberately limited that year. I was determined to do well so I could go on to A levels. The only other concert I did in the first six months of 2002 was at the Megaron Mousikis in Athens, where a fundraiser was held for the construction of the American-Hellenic Arts Center of Halandri. I was invited to take part in a series of cultural events that included performances from the New York Ballet and José Carreras. The concert was on a Friday night, so we had some time the next day to explore Athens. We took the funicular up Lycabettos Hill, then explored the narrow streets of the Plaka before climbing the Acropolis and wandering around the Parthenon. I loved seeing the remains of ancient Greece and imagining what life must have been like back then.

Apart from that, I pretty much kept my head down and concentrated on my revision, with the odd TV appearance here and there until my GCSEs were over. Nick Fiveash, a lovely cuddly bear of a man, had taken over from Nicky Chapman as my TV plugger. He thought that the odd guest appearance would keep my profile up and give me a chance to do something different, so I guested on *The Kumars at No. 42* and as a panellist on the terrifying but funny *Have I Got News for You*.

The other first was recording James Horner's music for the film *A Beautiful Mind*. Two weeks were set aside for my first recording with a live orchestra, and we finished in two days. Recording with a live orchestra was a new experience for me and I loved every minute of it. The score that James had written was beautiful and I felt privileged to be part of it. Mr Horner himself was a bit of an odd bod, very focused on his music, though mostly off with the fairies. I found this combination mesmerising and he instantly became a bit of a hero of mine. With Will Jennings, he wrote 'All Love Can Be', one of the most haunting and ethereal songs I've sung, which appears at the end of the film. Mum really believed that it would be as big as Céline Dion's 'My Heart Will Go On', but unfortunately it didn't happen.

The one thing I did want to be part of was Ian 'Beefy' Botham's amazing 229-mile walk to raise money for the Noah's Ark Appeal. Catherine Zeta Jones, the other appeal patron, flew in specially from America, so we met in Cardiff Basin, where we were surrounded by hundreds of well-wishers. I was in an incredibly unflattering pink tracksuit, with my hair scraped back, hoop earrings and specs on the end of my nose. I don't think you can learn style – you've either got it or you haven't – so I was still putting together the same old shitty combinations. I was so glad to see Catherine looking in a right state too, with her navy tracksuit bottoms and white top with some Hi-Tec trainers. I remember thinking, At least have some Nikes on your feet, love! After about three-quarters of an hour, Beefy appeared and we joined him for the last two miles, which took us through the packed streets of Cardiff. I had to run all the way to keep up with them, so thanked God I was only 'walking' the last two miles.

I arrived at Cardiff Castle completely knackered, with my face the colour of a tomato, but I was glad to have been part of such a good cause. While I recovered, Catherine and my mum were sneaking a sly cigarette, tossing the butts into a 2,000-year-old grate so no one would see! Catherine is a really lovely woman, so natural and friendly. There was a big do that evening, at which she looked absolutely stunning, but she still kept disappearing for a cigarette with my mum and my auntie. I so wanted to join them, but I'd managed to keep my smoking secret. I knew they'd all go mad if they found out.

Up until then I had always been incredibly self-righteous about smoking. If any of my friends smoked, I'd go on about how it made them smell and how it would kill them, but I changed my tune after I went with one of them to her mother's house, where we were allowed to drink Malibu and Coke. Her mum even let her smoke. After a couple of drinks, she said, 'Go on, have a cigarette.'

'OK,' I said, taking one. 'I'll try it.'

Most people claim that they had to work really hard to start smoking, that they hated it to start with and had to keep trying until they got used to it. Not me. As far as I was concerned, the taste of the alcohol was so minging that the taste of a cigarette, especially a menthol one, was quite welcome. I didn't mind it at all. I already knew my vocal chords were as strong as old rope. I hadn't taken much notice of advice like don't eat mince, curry or dairy foods and avoid air-conditioning. I was young and didn't give a fuck. If I wanted a curry, a bar of chocolate, chewing gum or a cigarette, I had one. Nothing had happened to me so far, so I wasn't really worried about my voice. I was enjoying doing something that I knew my parents would kill me for if they ever found out. But there was no way that they were going to.

I wasn't recording a new album that year, so I had the summer to myself. I felt that I'd come to the end of a road and that I wanted to develop my singing in other directions, although I wasn't quite sure where yet. Obviously I couldn't remain an angelic twelve-year-old with a unique voice for ever, and there were enough people of my age who could belt out a chart contender to give me some stiff competition if I crossed over to pop. I'd always liked many different types of music – rock, R&B, Motown, classical, you name it – and knew I was capable of singing most of them, so it was just a question of finding what I was most happy with.

In the meantime, Sony was going to release *Prelude*, a compilation of my favourite and most popular songs, for Christmas. I agreed with Sony that after the *Prelude* tour I would have a break for a couple of years. Although I wasn't going back to school, I still imagined that I might go to university with my friends in two years' time. But right now I had a film to make.

I'd been for a number of film castings when I'd been in LA, but had never got anywhere. I wasn't used to failing at anything, but I'd failed at these. I decided that if I'd done that many without being offered a part, then I obviously wasn't any good. Don't flog a dead horse, girl, I said to myself. Stick to what you're good at. Once I'd come to that conclusion, I wasn't really that interested when other film projects were suggested. However, Peter Grosslight hadn't given up. He introduced me to Morgan Creek, a production company that decided to base a whole project round me. It was incredibly flattering, so I decided to give it one last go. I reckon that if I put my mind to anything, as long as I focus I'll probably be OK. A little natural talent and lot of dedication go a long way.

I met Craig Ferguson, who would be the writer, director and star, to talk about my life. He went away and came up with a script that was very loosely based on Liv Tyler's discovery that her dad was Steve Tyler from Aerosmith. Originally called *The Family Business*, the film was eventually called *I'll Be There*. I was daringly cast as Olivia, a talented singer growing up in a small Welsh town. She discovers that her dad (Craig) is a rock star and tries to reunite him with her mother (Jemma Redgrave). The film appealed to me because it was small and British. I was aware of the flak Britney had taken when she made her Hollywood debut in *Crossroads*, but this was on a much smaller scale. I thought I'd give it a go and if no one liked it, so be it.

The cast and crew were brilliant to me. Craig could always make me laugh, and Jemma was fabulously understanding whenever I couldn't get something right. They made the whole thing as enjoyable as they could, but I hadn't expected the long hours of waiting around in trailers while the cameras were reset. Sometimes we'd be called at six in the morning, but then wouldn't be needed until two in the afternoon. I'd read my book, talk to my friends on the phone, chat to the make-up girls or spend time with Jemma. Because Craig was directing, he was usually busy. Serious acting didn't come easily to me. Craig was always telling me to 'make it smaller', trying to tone down my whole performance, but I'm not really a quiet person, so that felt a bit unnatural to me. I struggled to give him what he wanted, but when I eventually watched an early cast and crew showing, I could see that I was shit.

I felt so pissed off because I'd gone straight into this after my GCSEs. Everyone else was on their summer holidays and here I was working, staying with my parents in a shitty rented house in Slough and secretly smoking my brains out. I had all the tricks up my sleeve to stop them finding out – open windows, mints, blaming other people! Things between us were as complicated as they'd ever been. One minute we'd be getting on fine, the next we'd be screaming our heads off. Not that our relationship seemed much worse in many ways than those between my friends and their parents – all of us were flexing our muscles and straining for independence. It was our situation that made us different, but none of us realised that we were heading towards crisis point.

I had my own room in Slough, but it was the pits and really impersonal. One of my friends, Dilly, came over to visit from Cardiff during filming. She was pretty cool and a bit of a rapper. We'd surreptitiously smoke out of the window, then think we were really clever, drowning all the butts in a half-full Oasis bottle that I 'hid' in a corner.

Not long after her stay, I was given a week's break from filming. I was so excited when it was time to go home, so I jumped into the back seat, ready to go. Dad was on the phone, but as he put it down, he turned round.

'D'you want a drink?' he shouted, chucking the Oasis bottle at me, all the cigarette ends bobbing about in the orange liquid.

'They're not mine, Dad,' I protested. 'They're Dilly's. Honest.'

'I don't believe you.' He was furious. 'You're telling me that Dilly smoked more than twenty cigarettes in the two days she was here. You're a liar.'

'Shut up, James,' Mum chipped in. 'We can deal with this better.' Usually she was the one who screamed and shouted while Dad was the quiet, reasonable voice of calm. Not this time. 'James! Stop shouting. Just be quiet for a minute.'

But he was so angry. It was as if a dam had burst. He yelled about how I'd damage my voice and how I'd lied to them. Of course I had; that's what most teenage kids do, isn't it? I wasn't a particularly bad teenager. I wasn't rude or disrespectful, I was just normal. But he went on and on about my attitude, dragging up every petty example that he could think of. Apparently I was lazy, untidy, didn't wash up, didn't want to do anything for anyone, was always on the phone. Sounds like a teenager to me!

'James, don't,' Mum kept interrupting.

But it was too late. I was a typical headstrong sixteen-year-old who thought I knew it all. 'Forget it,' I yelled. 'I'm leaving home and there's nothing you can do to stop me.'

My mother desperately tried to calm things down, but there was nothing she could do. Something had finally snapped and my mind was made up. We had been cooped up together for too long. However much we loved one another, there's not a teenager on earth who would be able to live with their parents as closely as I had. Touring together was incredibly stressful, like living in a pressure cooker. I'd grown to hate the way my mother seemed to enjoy the control she had over everything and the dismissive way she sometimes treated people. My dad and I had always got on well, but recently even he was beginning to seem like a pain in the arse. He had to deal with my mum and, for a quiet life, he often sided with her against me.

I also got fed up because sometimes, when people came directly to her instead of going through my London manager, Sarah Ferguson-Jones, she would agree to my doing things I'd prefer not to. If she agreed to something, it was then awkward to say no, and anyway, she'd guilt-trip me into doing it. For instance, she was the one who got me on to *The Brian Conley Show*. To be fair, she was getting phone calls morning, noon and night from the insatiable PR machine at Sony, who wanted me to compromise my classical roots by singing with him.

Brian's a lovely man, mind, but he's not a singer. I had to sing 'Dancing in the Moonlight' with him – one of the most over-played songs at the time – and it was all so wrong. I was still a classical singer and I felt, no offence to Brian, that I shouldn't have been on his show. I was sixteen and dancing around a forty-year-old man as if we were at a family wedding. I got in a right strop with my mother over that.

Everything came to a head in this stupid row, when things that should probably have remained unsaid were screamed at each other! My response was to think, Fuck you. I'm moving out because I can. I've got money and I can. At that time the trust gave me an allowance of around £250 a week, and any major bills went to Terry, so all I had to do was ask.

As soon as we got home, I packed what I needed in black bin liners and moved out to stay with friends until I could find something permanent, going back to Slough to finish filming on my own. Sarah stayed with me in the same shitty rented house and my friends came up to visit. If I hadn't been so upset, it would have been a teenager's dream. I had phoned Terry and Mark, my two trustees, and asked them to help me. I didn't even have a bank card of my own, so Mark came down once a week to take me to the cashpoint and get out what money I needed. Dad worked with them to make sure that when I got back to Cardiff I moved somewhere safe. When I rented a really small terraced house in Pontcanna, he made sure that almost every security system known to man was in place to protect me. I took the coffee table from my bedroom to keep me company, but the house was partly furnished already with cheap wood-block floors and greyish-white paint on the walls. If anything, it was like a hospital ward, but at least it was mine.

Back home, my mum was having a nervous breakdown. She and I are as stubborn as one another and neither of us was going to give way first. She thought I was behaving immaturely, but more worrying still for her was that I was a very rich sixteen-year-old who would make a great target for kidnappers. After all the stalkers and weird fans we'd experienced, nothing seemed impossible. She and my dad were worried sick that something awful would happen to me now that they had no control over me.

Of course the press went to town over our fall-out, saying I had 'sacked her as my manager'; but she had never been my manager, ever. If anything, she acted more like a PA. And although she didn't like agreeing, we did mutually agree that, now that I was sixteen, I could manage on my own. I didn't need my parents to travel with me everywhere I went. Show me another teenager who has left school and takes her parents to work with her! As Mum has always said, it was a natural progression. We just didn't handle it very well.

Now I understand better the reasons why Mum was so devastated. Then I was just another teenager who didn't bother to imagine how hard it must be when your only child leaves home. Nor did I give a thought to the fact that we had made Mum redundant at the same time. My dad was OK with the decision not to travel with me any more. Even if they weren't there, he knew how well I'd be looked after by my management and Sony. My mum couldn't be reassured though. I didn't realise that I'd taken away her life force. She had been really good at minding me and thrived on the way of life we had and her involvement in my career. By the same token, she gave a structure to it, and without her I would have lost a lot of my money on the way. Now those days were suddenly over and she had no control over anything any more. When I left home, many of the people we'd met through work who Mum trusted as friends stopped dealing with her and started contacting me direct. Professionally, of course, they had to, but it was incredibly hurtful for her and made her feel as though she didn't exist. Most of them, bar John Vernile, didn't even bother to phone and find out how she was. I think that stinks, but right then I didn't care.

Our relationship broke down completely, and as a result, for about six months my family and I didn't speak to one another. I couldn't see what I'd done wrong and felt the situation was all their fault. OK, I was young, and perhaps I shouldn't have left home, but shit happens.

What made the situation worse was the small detail of my going out with Steve Johnson. I started seeing him after my birthday, while Naomi hooked up with his best friend, Joshua. I knew right from the very beginning that this wasn't going to be a great relationship, but I was too busy rebelling against my mum to admit it. She didn't make a secret of the fact that she was unhappy about me being with him, but that only fuelled my determination to stick with him. Every time I was asked about Steve in public, I was incredibly positive, but if I look at one of the documentaries made about me at the time and listen to what I was saying, I just think, You silly cow, you weren't thinking that. Even though I went out with him for more than a year, I knew it would never last. I knew there would be an end and I was just waiting for it to come. Everyone makes mistakes, and he was one of mine. Ultimately, my family were absolutely right about what they said, but it took time for me to see that.

Bampy, my grandfather, was the only person who kept the

lines of communication open. It was hard for him, mind. His whole family had been ripped apart and all of us were upset. He phoned me every week to try to organise a get-together. Bampy knew that I was the key to making it right, and I could easily have helped him, but I didn't want to. I didn't want to go back to my old life. I liked my new one. I'd be really short with him, giving out my standard line: 'Mum and Dad are the adults. Why does she have to be so stupid? Why is it my fault? Why does it have to be me who has to go and see them?' I put it off for as long as I could, although I was missing everyone badly, but Bampy never gave up and eventually I caved in. He made us all go for Sunday lunch down the Romily pub, and God, it was awkward. The only one I really talked to was my bampy. Realising how upset he and Nana were made me put things right as best I could. I started speaking to Mum and Dad again and went round to see them occasionally, although I drew the line at moving back home or giving up Steven.

My GCSE results were in – I'd got three A*s and four As! I had already made the decision not to continue with A levels immediately, but to take some time off to take stock before I made a decision about where to go next. The results came hot on the heels of the other award I won that year: Rear of the Year! I didn't know whether to be pleased or embarrassed, but decided that it was a bit of harmless fun, dressed up in my best jeans and went to accept it. I swear there were more photographers at the photocall than at any other I've ever done. What was this public obsession with my body?

Since I had left home, the press had stepped up their invasion of my private life, and it seemed as if I could do nothing without it being reported. It's hard enough being a teenager, trying to find out who you are, without having a camera stuck in your face every time you make a fool of yourself or having journalists try to worm stories out of your friends. Fame gives you a lot of good things, but it also makes you very vulnerable. Everyone seems to want a little piece of you. The press had a field day with the fact that I had fallen out with my family, and even worse was their obsession with me and Steven. He was repeatedly painted as a lad from the wrong side of the tracks. Perhaps the worst thing that happened was when a couple of reporters set Steven up while I was in Los Angeles, singing with Paul Anka at the Dinner of Champions, an event that benefited the National Multiple Sclerosis Society. I especially wanted to be there because that year it was also honouring Howard Stringer and Sony for their support. Meanwhile, the story spread in the UK that Steven had agreed to sell a story about us for £100,000. I obviously have no idea what really happened between him, his friends and the reporters who invited them to a hotel room at the St David's Hotel in Cardiff Bay, but at the time I chose to believe he was innocent.

From then on, the press wouldn't let go. According to them, I was on the road to hell. What bollocks! I was just a teenager, trying to sort out myself, my life and my career. Everything I did was reported: where I went, what I did, who my friends were. I absolutely hated it, but my nana advised me to ignore the paparazzi and keep on smiling. That way, they wouldn't get the pictures they wanted. The first time I was caught having a cigarette, I was with a friend who assured me nobody was outside the house, but as I walked out: click, click, click. The next day's headline was CHARLOTTE THE SCRUFF HAS A PUFF. I did look pretty scruffy, to be fair, but I've never cared about that. Some days I wake up and feel like making a real effort, while other days I can't be bothered, but the paparazzi are always there to record it.

In the end, I went on the offensive. When my greatest hits album, *Prelude*, was released in the UK, interviews were lined up on *Today with Des and Mel* and *Parkinson*. Among the general chit-chat, Parky asked me about all the rumours flying around about me. Although I felt awkward about being so comprehensively grilled, I answered everything. I made it very clear that my mum was still involved in my career, but to a lesser extent than before. Yes, drugs were available on the entertainment scene, but I wasn't curious about them at all. As for Steven? I believed he wouldn't sell a story about me. No, my mother didn't approve of him, but mothers often don't approve of their daughter's first boyfriend. The press had blown everything right out of proportion.

'Are you in love with him?' asked Parky.

'I think so,' I said, embarrassed to be asked something so personal.

'You'll get over it,' came the reply.

How right Parky was!

CHAPTER 14

Growing Pains

I was only sixteen and I had a 'best of' compilation out. How mad is that? Although I hadn't recorded anything new for *Prelude*, Sony had scheduled me to join Julie Andrews and Christopher Plummer on a massive fifteen-city tour of North America that ran for almost the whole of December. When the day came to leave, I cried all the way to Gatwick. Naomi was meant to be coming with me, but she was sick, and I had a splitting earache that was making me feel terrible. At the airport, I phoned Mum. 'I'm not going. I feel awful.'

'Come home then,' she said. 'We'll sort something out.'

I saw a doctor who advised me not to fly for three days as he thought I'd risk bursting an eardrum, and that gave us enough time to arrange for Mum to come with me. I was nervous about being on tour with her again after everything we'd been through, but there was no need – she was fabulous and so supportive, and we were soon getting on as well as we ever had.

A Royal Christmas was a spectacular extravaganza compèred by Julie Andrews and Christopher Plummer and featuring London's Royal Philharmonic Concert Orchestra, conducted by George Daugherty, the Westminster Choir, the Westminster Concert Bell Choir, principal and solo dancers from London's Royal Ballet, Winnipeg's Royal Ballet, Russia's Bolshoi Ballet, Ukraine's Kyiv Ballet, the Shumka Dancers – and me.

The first stop was Cincinnati, then Grand Rapids, Pittsburgh and Detroit. Almost immediately, word reached us that the British press was full of reports portraying me as a tempestuous diva having an emotional breakdown. We spoke to the family every day and it was awful to hear my nan so upset, firstly by the accusations and then because she couldn't understand who would make up such things. 'Why did you behave so badly, Charlotte? There's no call for that.' For what? The headline read, I DIDN'T AGREE TO NO MEET AND GREET. HELLO! and went on to explain how I'd marched off, refusing to see a group of disabled children after the Cincinnati show. Bollocks! It was true that I hadn't been told of the arrangements and was taken by surprise. I always prefer to know what's expected of me in advance, so that I can get my head round it before I go on stage. But of course I did the meet and greet – I would never let down the fans who put me where I am. The damage was done, though, and it opened the way for a horde of journalists to pick me to pieces on the basis of something that hadn't happened.

Next came the rumour that I'd made all sorts of ridiculous A-list demands for stuff like chocolate cake, Italian ham, sweets and so on to be in my dressing room. Cue stories about me not watching my weight. It's true that I had a rider in my contract specifying that I got some Strawberry Ribena (my favourite), fruit, water and towels, but that was it. On top of all that came the reports that the tour was a disaster. Yes, the early concerts weren't sell-outs, but the arenas the organisers had chosen were huge. Six thousand tickets were sold in Cincinnati, and that was the smallest venue we did. Given that my usual concerts were in front of about two thousand people, I was fine with that. As the tour went on and we got closer to Christmas, the venues sold out every time.

The ticket sales may have improved, but unfortunately the press reports back home didn't. I tried to let them go over my head, but it's difficult when other people are upset and angry on your behalf. I had no idea where the stories were coming from. I'm really not a diva, I don't throw tantrums and I did everything that was asked of me. I love singing and was grateful for the many amazing things that had happened to me, but I seemed to be caught in a vicious circle. As I tried to develop my personality and self-confidence, the press kept pushing me down. The one thing that kept me strong was my family, who were always there, pushing me back up again. Our rift had been completely mended. I understand that if you make yourself available as a celebrity, you have to accept that your private life will be scrutinised. I can see that if you're thirty, you've probably developed the inner resources to deal with the attention by then, but I was only sixteen.

Being in the public spotlight when you're young is like living in a goldfish bowl: everything I did was multiplied into a big extravaganza of a story that I hardly recognised. The press tried to pay people I knew for quotes to use so that, apart from my closest friends, who, together with my family, were a real source of strength, I didn't know who to trust. The press were still so hostile to Mum as well, and she didn't deserve that. As far as I was concerned, I was a singer doing my job, and nothing else needed to be mentioned. Sadly Fleet Street didn't agree. Being in another country, unable to speak for myself but knowing about all the negative press at home was shit. I felt completely powerless. The media were vilifying me and didn't let up. It was as if there was a giant game of Chinese whispers going on in which every story got more and more exaggerated as it did the rounds. In the end, the situation got so bad that I was given a spot on ITV's *News at Ten* to put across my point of view from America.

The concert schedule was hard work, day after day, city after city, with very few days off. Apart from being physically demanding, it was emotionally draining too. As always, whenever I performed, I gave it everything. Every night I sang two of my favourite songs, 'Imagine' and 'Bridge Over Troubled Water', perhaps the two most emotional songs in my repertoire. I've always believed in my voice, so whatever was said in the press at home wasn't an issue when I was performing. It was just the other twenty-three and a half hours of the day that were difficult.

Julie Andrews was the most gracious, elegant lady I've ever met, but Christopher Plummer kept himself pretty much to himself. I tend to keep people at arm's length when I'm working with them, too, just so I can focus on my work, so I completely understood. Besides, we didn't have much time to be together. We travelled everywhere in separate tour buses which had everything on board: a proper kitchen, a big double bed and bunks, a DVD player, a massive TV and a fridge. After we'd finished work, I'd come down from that post-performance adrenalin high by playing my XBox on the bus for a couple of hours before going to bed.

Although I was hating the tour, largely thanks to what was going on at home, I was cheered up when Noel from Hear'Say, an old family friend, visited me in Boston, and then my friend Beck came over for the end of the trip. She seems quite quiet and unassuming, but she's a bit of a dark horse, and inside there's a party girl who lives to have fun. At the same time, she's quite easy-going and never imposes herself on anyone. She's just happy to go with the flow, so was a great, relaxing person to have around.

By the time I got home, I was just relieved it was all over. I felt very bitter about what had happened and I wanted to curl up under my duvet and for the world to go away.

I didn't have much time to lick my wounds, though, because my single 'The Opera Song (Brave New World)' was coming out in January. In the autumn, Jurgen Vries (real name Darren Tate), a DJ, had sent me a demo. I'd never been into dance music, but this was a song that really grew on me. The whole thing worked very well, with a cool operatic burst in the middle. It was a bit Eurovision, but sometimes I like cheesy music like that. Recording it would be a huge departure from anything I'd done before, so I thought I'd give it a go. We recorded it in a room on an industrial estate somewhere in London and my voice sounded as perfect as I could get it: as clear as a bell, with that ethereal quality Sony liked. They decided to release the single. Mark and I were worried about the credit saying, 'Featuring Charlotte Church,' because we felt I might be putting my head on the block – if the press didn't like it, the guillotine would fall – so instead we agreed to 'Featuring CMC'.

The music had been knocking around the clubs for some time, but our version went crazy. Mark called me to say that all the DJs were playing it, there were remixes being made and phone-ins were being held to guess the identity of CMC. When the single went to number three in the charts, it was even more exciting. At first people thought the voice might be Kylie's or Christina Aguilera's. Weren't the initials a clue? They were shocked to find out it was me. Once the secret was out, I appeared on *Top of the Pops* with a whole dance routine – brilliant. Needless to say, although some people loved it, there were those who didn't. Once again, the friendly press stepped in to quote an opera singer and a music critic who both said my voice was shot and that I was throwing my talent away. I'm always sorry when someone doesn't like what I sing, but the answer is, If you don't like it, don't listen to it. Plenty of other people liked it.

Although my management say 'The Opera Song' signalled to them the direction my career might take, I certainly wasn't thinking that way at the time. I was fed up of talking career, career, career and was just living every day as it came, chilling out, having fun with the girls, being normal, going up to London for various big dos, such as the UKC Hero Awards or Julien MacDonald's show during London Fashion Week.

IBM asked me to Hawaii in April to perform three concerts. All they involved was a little rehearsal in the afternoon and a forty-five-minute performance in the evening. One concert was for American guests, one for those from the Far East and the last was for the Europeans, who, after a few drinks, were the rowdiest of the lot. The only spoiler was when Mum called me, absolutely furious, because I was all over the UK press again. I had changed my T-shirt when we transferred planes in Miami and put on a pink one with 'My Barbie is a Crack Whore' splashed across the front. I thought the T-shirt was funny and hadn't given it a thought when I'd changed, but Mum thought I should have known better. Obviously not. Now it was all over the papers. When was all this going to end?

When I wasn't performing in Hawaii, the time was mine to wander along the white-sand beaches, swim in the sea or pool and watch out for turtles lumbering down the sand into the sea. What will always stick in my mind is going whale watching with Sarah from my management office, a fabulous, classy rock chick who became a good friend. We were taken by a tanned, lean, grey-haired Hawaiian guy who had built his beautiful boat in traditional style, binding the wood together with rope. He had been watching whales all his life and knew their behaviour patterns better than any marine biologist. We motored out to sea, where the ocean was so clear and deep it looked like the night sky, bottomless. Huge humpback whales circled the boat, so close we could see the barnacles on their backs. Our guide told us that every year, all the whales in the world change their song simultaneously. He held a hydrophone into the water so we could hear them, just a few series of notes as they communicated with one another. I climbed into the water and pushed myself under the boat so I could hear them without the mic. It was one of the most magical experiences of my life, right up there with swimming with dolphins when I'd visited Hawaii before. When I was back on board, I couldn't resist phoning Mum to tell her what she was missing. The only thing she didn't miss was being stung by a tiny, almost invisible jellyfish that must have brushed by me, but the sting was soon eased by our man rubbing meat tenderiser on my leg.

My love affair with Roberto Cavalli's designs began on our way home from Hawaii. We stopped off in Vegas, where I was giving a one-off solo concert at the Aladdin Casino Resort. Walking around the designer shops in the hotel, I spotted the most beautiful dress I have ever seen in my life: a white corseted Cavalli number with a $7,500 price tag. If my mum had been there, she would have slapped me silly, but she wasn't, so I persuaded Sarah to charge it to the business. That evening I felt a million dollars and the concert went brilliantly, apart from the moment when I missed my opening for 'Bali Hai'. The orchestra stopped and I turned around. 'Did I just miss something here? Oh my God, everybody. I made a huge mistake and forgot to come in when I was supposed to come in. I'm so sorry.' The audience were lovely and didn't seem to mind. The only thing that annoyed me afterwards was that I wasn't allowed into the hotel's club because I was underage.

I was always up for a challenge, but being a TV presenter turned out to be one of the hardest things I've ever had to do. Nick Fiveash was thrilled to get me a spot presenting *Have I Got News For You*. I agreed to go on without having a clue what I was letting myself in for. When I'd been on the show as a panellist the year before, I always knew that if I cocked things up, the host panellists Paul Merton or Ian Hislop would come to my rescue. Being a presenter, though, was something else. The script came with four jokes for every question, so I could pick the one I felt most comfortable saying.

At least that made me feel like I'd put my stamp on things. Then I had to get used to reading the autocue, scared that the words would roll away without me, while someone talked to me through an earpiece, telling me I had to move things on more quickly. I also had cards to read, as well as being surrounded by amazingly clever, quick-witted people. The whole experience was pretty intimidating to say the least. I had a mic attached to the front of my dress and I thought that all anyone would hear was my heart pounding – it felt as if it was about to jump out of my chest. Ten minutes into the show I began to calm down, and once I got into the swing of things, I even began to enjoy myself.

Afterwards, everyone seemed to like the recording, and I've had more people mention it to me than anything else. I suppose they thought I was some stupid child star who was fast turning into a has-been, thanks to all the reporting in the press. Suddenly they had this new respect. That was pretty cool.

The rest of the year may have been relatively quiet on the career front, but it was all change in the housing department. Mum and Dad sold the big house and bought the first of what would be their two hotels, publicly announcing that they were stepping down from their involvement in my career. I took the opportunity to move house again, too, this time to a brand-new flat down in Cardiff Bay by St David's Hotel. One side of the living room was all windows that led on to a big balcony overlooking the bay, and there was a huge bathroom. I did the whole place up myself, so it looked lush – cream carpet, white walls, red leather sofa, a rug and my trusty little table that had been with me for years. Everything else came from Ikea or

BoConcept and looked quite modern or, dare I say, manly. I must have been going through a masculine phase.

On the nights we went out, five or six of my friends would come over, some of them straight from work, and we'd have a couple of drinks and something to eat. If I hadn't started cooking then, I'd have lived on Pot Noodles for the rest of my life, so we'd usually have chicken Caesar salad or chicken stir-fry. In the summer we'd sit on the deck and have barbecues. For afterwards, I had a revolving cupboard full of sweets and chocolates. Then we'd get ready for the night ahead. I'd do everyone's make-up because I'd learned so much from all the make-up artists I'd met, and we'd dress up and do our hair. All of the girls used to save their earnings to buy clothes and make-up, so we'd dress really well.

We'd either head off to RSVP or to Emporium, another shit-hole where everyone was buzzing on Es. We were quite good girls and alcohol was enough for us. None of us ever did drugs. I'd seen too much in the music business to ever want to touch them. Besides, I got crazy enough on alcohol not to need anything else, and it only takes one rogue pill and you're dead. We were all spurred on by each other, drinking and taking to the dance floor to rival Beyoncé. That was enough for a brilliant time. I remember once, when I was throwing up outside RSVP, Abi came out, looked at it and suddenly projectile vomited. Astonished, we looked at each other and burst out laughing before going back in and carrying on dancing. We were nuts and I loved every second of it.

Sometimes we did get into trouble, but we were having so much fun we didn't try to hide it. We thought we were wicked. Other girls didn't like that and they certainly didn't like me. They used to square up for a fight: 'Charlotte Church? What the fuck do you think you're doing round here? You stupid bitch. Come here and I'll fucking knock you out.' The first time it happened I was shitting myself, but then, after a couple of drinks, I reckoned I was just as hard as they were. 'Come on then,' I shouted. I always felt safe knowing that I had all the girls behind me, although I reckon I could pack a good punch if I had to – I think. I've never tried, mind. I've never had a fight in my life and I wasn't going to start then. My mouth got me out of all these situations. 'Why do you want to fight me? You think I'm something I'm not. So get away from me because I'll knock you out.' Problem solved!

I reckon that if I'd cowered back, whispering, 'Look, I'm not looking for trouble,' they would have glimpsed a bit of weakness and picked on me some more. If I gave as good as I got, they'd just reply, 'You're a bitch, right. Just watch out next time,' and leave us alone. But there never was a next time.

The boys never gave me any trouble. They seemed quite intimidated, but if any of them did come up with a cheesy line, I'd run a mile or use my standard line, 'Get the fuck out of my face.' Nice! My interaction with boys had been fairly limited until then, so that side of things seemed slightly unnatural. Besides, I had Steven, my boyfriend.

At last life was good. It was normal. I was having a break from my family and my career. I enjoyed not working, doing my own thing, just lazing around in my house always listening to music, thinking about what direction to take my next album, flirting with different ideas. I had come such a long way since I was an eleven-year-old kid, starting out in the music business with no real ambitions, desire for fame or idea what she was getting herself into.

CHAPTER 15

Tissues and Issues

Walking down the red carpet between my mum and dad
towards London's Leicester Square Odeon for the première of
I'll Be There, months after filming it, was pretty nerve-racking.
The press and fans hung over the barriers, shouting out, asking questions and wanting autographs. I chatted to as many
people as I could before heading into the cinema. There were
more people than there had been two days earlier when the
film had its first British première in Cardiff's UCI, but
strangely I felt less nervous. All my friends had been at the
UCI showing, and I'd felt so self-conscious about my performance that I spent the entire time cringing in my seat. That
had been a very dressed-down affair, but London was all glitz
and glamour. Afterwards, there was more time to meet the
fans before we were swept off in two silver Mercedes to the

after-show party. It was a brilliant occasion, so I felt bad for Craig when, over the next few days, the reviews were negative. He, Jemma and I had given various TV and press interviews, but it wasn't enough to put bums on seats. I knew I couldn't act, but no one wants to be told that by the papers, especially when you've done your best. I made a resolution not to rush into another film. My best obviously wasn't good enough.

For the first time in four years I wasn't bringing out an album at Christmas, which meant I could focus on doing a few things that were a little bit different. I have been asked if the interviews I'd done for *Q* and *The Face* marked the start of my 'rebranding', but if they did, it wasn't deliberate. I'd been approached by a documentary-maker, Chris Terrill, and agreed that he could film me for nine months to make a film for BBC TV. Sony, Mark and I thought that this would be a good way to get both sides of my life across to the public. I wanted people to see that the press reports weren't true and that when I was out of the spotlight, I was an ordinary teenager trying to find out which direction the rest of her life should take, just as my friends were.

Having said publicly how difficult I found learning to live with the press intrusion into my personal life, it felt very odd going to the *Daily Mirror* offices to meet the editor, Piers Morgan, one of the men responsible for hounding me. Normally I wouldn't have set foot in his office, but I had been asked to speak at the Oxford University Union. Following in the steps of such inspirational speakers as Nelson Mandela, the Dalai Lama and Winston Churchill was pretty daunting, although I felt better about it when I heard that Kermit the Frog had done it, too! I was the youngest person ever to address the Union, so I wanted to make sure I spoke about something close to my heart and said something provocative. I also wanted to show that there was more to me than the drunken rebel portrayed in the newspapers. The obvious subject seemed to be press intrusion and celebrity, giving me the ideal opportunity to fight back, so I went to see Piers to try to get the picture from the other side. When I asked him, 'Didn't it matter to you that I was only thirteen or fourteen at the time?' all he could say was that I should stop whinging and moaning. He couldn't explain why a young teenager should be just as fair game as an adult. Everything I said, he managed to twist, not ludicrously, but so that I could see his point of view, even though I absolutely didn't agree with it. I thought he was a pig, but a clever one.

When it came to addressing the students, I was absolutely shitting myself, sure that only about four students would bother to turn up. Give me a song and I can sing in front of an audience all day long, but public speaking isn't my thing. Why ever would they want to listen to what I had to say? They'd probably heckle me or ask impossible-to-answer questions. To my astonishment, the hall was full. I was sure they were all looking at me as if to say, 'Come on then, you seventeen-year-old. Let's fucking hear it.' At least Mum and Bampy were sitting right at the front where I could see them: the two non-intimidating members. I talked for about half an hour about celebrity and what a two-faced monster it is, as well as calling for a privacy law to protect minors in the public eye from press intrusion. I illustrated the talk with Chris Terrill's film of my interview with Piers Morgan, so the students could see both sides of the argument, as well as the worst of the newspaper headlines about me. The students made a brilliant audience and laughed at my jokes and seemed to appreciate what I had to say. It also turned out that I had worried about their questions for the wrong reasons as the first was, 'Do you prefer singing or sex?' Not easy to answer with Mum and Bampy's steely gazes fixed on me, so I said I liked them the same!

Without an album to promote, I was having a relatively quiet year in terms of public appearances. The only solo concert I gave during the last six months of 2003 was in Hong Kong, where I was invited to take part in the Hong Kong Harbour Festival. The city was wicked. I loved being able to walk through the busy markets and shopping malls or take a boat round the harbour with no one taking any notice of me. I was just some European girl being followed by a man with a camera (Chris) and no one cared. We went through the bird and flower markets, me shrieking when a grasshopper (local delicacy) leaped from its cage on to my shoulder! I burrowed through the stalls, thrilled to find a lush knock-off Vuitton bag for £20. The first concert we saw was an amazing open-air gig against the Hong Kong skyline. Prince was headlining in a top performance, where he played every instrument, danced and sang all of his hits. I was heartbroken when no one would come with me to the secret after-show gig he was doing in the Dragon Club because they were too jet-lagged. Another night, we saw a really good Craig David concert, and then it was my turn.

This was going to be the last time I would sing as the 'Voice of an Angel'. It hadn't sunk in until Mark Melton, who was acting as my UK manager, pointed out that from now on, my repertoire would be completely different, which pulled at the heartstrings a bit. I had begun to experiment and was co-writing songs with various composers and lyricists, and through that I was starting to find a new direction quite organically. Preparing for the last time was weird. The older I'd got, the more nervous I was before a show and this was no exception. I suppose I was more aware of all the things that could go wrong. As I warmed up in a tent behind the open-air stage, I felt as though my stomach was going to leap out of my mouth. I was wearing the lush Roberto Cavalli dress I'd bought in Vegas, so at least I knew I looked good. The audience was fabulous and all of them wanted to enjoy themselves, so I came out to thunderous applause as I began singing 'Tonight'.

Sometimes during a performance, I went on to automatic. I'd be singing but wondering at the same time whether or not I'd left the iron on or locked the front door. At other times – and this was one of them – I'd be completely focused on the songs, eyes shut, concentrating. The time vanished, and before I knew where I was I was singing the last number, 'Over the Rainbow'. Suddenly it was all over. I should have been euphoric, but instead I felt flat inside as I said goodbye to a big chunk of my life.

The 'Voice of an Angel' wasn't the only thing I said goodbye to at the end of 2003. Shortly afterwards, and not really to my surprise, my relationship with Steven ended. We had gone to a nightclub together, but I left early. Subsequently, a friend of my driver's reported having seen Steven kissing someone. I'd heard similar rumours before, so I wasn't completely surprised. When our relationship began, I'd felt completely adored by him, but that feeling had disappeared a long time ago. When I confronted him with the story, he immediately swore his innocence, but his expression and failure to fight back gave him away. This time he didn't try to make up with me. As far as I was concerned, we were finished there and then. That was it. After he'd left, I put all his stuff in black bin bags, and the next day I dumped them outside his mother's door. I never spoke to him again. For the first few weeks I felt as if I'd lost the second chunk of my life. Whenever you split with someone, it's hard to get used to being on your own again. I couldn't eat and felt miserable, but it wasn't long before I started looking at the positives. I lost loads of weight so for once I was skinny, happy and going out with my friends all the time, and of course my family closed ranks around me.

I moved out of my flat in the bay because I didn't want to stay in that area any longer. My dad found me a coach house to rent, which was round the corner from theirs: he wanted me close by so they could keep an eye on me. I didn't mind that because as far as I was concerned it was far enough away from them to maintain my privacy. My new home was a shitty little house with one tiny living room, a downstairs toilet and a little kitchen. Upstairs there were two tiny bedrooms and a bathroom. It wasn't the greatest place on earth, but I still moved there with my trusty coffee table.

My mother came furniture shopping with me and advised me not to buy a white sofa I fell in love with. I bought it anyway, but she was right: after nine months of friends, drink, food and make-up that sofa was hanging by the time I moved out into a flat in the converted St David's Hospital, where I'd been born. To be fair, I was more than happy having my friends round there. It wasn't a time when I wanted to be on my own. My mum always worried that they were using me, but whether or not they were, I liked having them around. I had money and they didn't, and I wanted them on my level, so it wasn't that they were taking: I was giving because it was easier. Hanging with them kept me sane.

For a laugh, I went with Naomi and Sarah to the launch party for Justin Timberlake's new album at the Rex Cinema in London. Sarah was a bit of a lightweight when it came to drinking – she was meant to stay sober so she could organise me. Of course, me and the girls never wanted her to, so we used to try to get her merry if we could.

The party was packed, and at one point, I was on my way to the toilet when I slipped on a sausage roll. I didn't fall, as was reported, nor was I crossing the room to see Steven and his new girlfriend, although they were there. His being there was reported as being an embarrassment for me, but I wasn't embarrassed at all. I was completely indifferent to his presence and just carried on having a fabulous night. I'd met Justin a few times since we did *Touched by an Angel* and thought he was a sweetheart. He asked me what I was doing and when my new album was due. I introduced him to Sarah and Naomi, but as we chatted I dropped my lighter. Justin and I bent down at exactly the same moment to pick it up and, as we did, we crashed heads. I was mortified and probably as stunned as he was. I rushed off with Naomi following me, pissing herself because I'd looked such an idiot. Later I had to go over and apologise for not apologising.

The biggest night out in early 2004 must have been my eighteenth birthday. I started celebrating a couple of nights before, when a small group of friends and I drove to London in the coolest stretch limo. We spent the rest of the day at the Westbury Hotel getting ready. We all made an extra special effort, so that when we left for the evening, we looked the business. I'd just come back from a holiday in St Lucia with Kayleigh, so we were tanned and looking good. I'd dyed my hair darker and wore a beautiful Dolce & Gabbana black dress, diamond earrings from David Morris and tottering high heels, while the other girls were all cool and sophisticated in black too. We'd lined up several clubs for after we'd eaten at the Collection, a fabulous restaurant and bar in a converted warehouse. We didn't mean to drink much, but everyone at the restaurant was so generous, wishing me happy birthday, that we ended up being given eight bottles of champagne! I was being extra careful not to drink too much because there were photographers following us everywhere we went, and once those flashbulbs start popping, it's impossible to see where you're walking. I knew they'd be gagging for a photo of me on my knees or throwing up, and I was determined not to oblige. As we came out of Boujis, the first club of the night, we were immediately surrounded by cameras. I had a horrible panicky sensation as I tried to make my way through the paparazzi to the car, and then I swear someone pushed me. I just went down like a tree.

As soon as I got in the limo, I called my mum, who knew from my voice that I was telling the truth. I was gutted that they'd got the shot, although when I saw it I think it must have been a still taken from a video camera because I was caught in that split second when I had my 'falling face' on. The girls were all in tears, upset that I might think one of them had shoved me by accident, and they all wanted to go home. I wasn't having any of that, though. I knew that none of my mates would have done it, so we went to a couple of other places and had a great night. By the end of it, I was hammered. I just thought, Fuck it. They've got the photo now. I might as well. Sure enough, the next morning my face was all over the papers under the headline FALLEN ANGEL. I really had been as sober as a judge at the point the photo was taken, but I was made out to be completely hammered.

The following night I was back in Cardiff for my proper party with all my friends and my extended family at the Beverley, a really nice traditional pub with a lovely long wooden bar and one of those dodgy carpets that make your eyes go funny if you look at it for too long. Somehow the paparazzi got wind of where we were going, and there were about forty of them lined up outside, taking photos of all my family. Some of my old aunties felt like superstars for the night: 'Oh, I wasn't pulling my best face,' 'I hope they don't print that shot of me.' They were funny. Auntie Caroline set up all her gear so everyone could have a song and we made a real night of it.

The one thing the press wouldn't let go of was that once I was eighteen, my trust was dissolved and I could get my hands on my millions. Not so! I had never planned to overturn the trust. I always agreed with my mum that it was more sensible for me to have an allowance until I knew how to handle the money – I know that she was anxious that I would be targeted. She didn't tell me at the time, but a group of people in Bristol were reported to have hatched a plan to kidnap me. Thankfully that sort of story was kept away from me because it was too much for me to take on board. I didn't want to live my life anxious and always on the look-out. At about the same time, the police found a book belonging to a journalist, in which they found contact details for hundreds of celebrities: their families, friends, boyfriends, girlfriends, wives, kids. Inside were the addresses, postcodes, numbers and car registrations of my parents, Caroline, Nana and Bampy, Naomi and Abi. We were told that journalists would pay £50 to a mole at British Telecom for a private landline number, £100 for a mobile number and £500 for a police record. The police were trying to prosecute the journalist for invasion of privacy. Whether they succeeded or not, I don't know, but I hope they shredded him.

By this time, I was making real headway with a new album, working with a guy called Nick Raphael, a fast-talking, opinionated but in the end likeable A&R man at Sony. He had begun to talk to me about putting together an R&B album. He was sent loads of demos from different producers and songwriters and passed on the ones he thought I might like, or which he thought would be good for me. I was being hopeless, though. 'I can sing anything you want me to sing, Nick. I can sing opera, pop, rock, R&B, and I like pretty much everything, so I don't know,' I wailed.

'You need a theme, Charlotte,' he'd say. 'Something to hold the album together. You need to decide what musical style you want to follow.'

I knew he was right, but I was still no clearer.

Lulu was no longer on the scene to guide me now that I was changing the direction of my singing, so without her, I turned to my family, in particular my mum. She has a good ear and has always been the best judge of my voice, so I rely on her instinct to know what's right for it.

Some of the songs Nick sent had been written by Rick Nowels and Darren Hayes (Savage Garden). That September, I had gone over to LA with Sarah and Jo (Nick Raphael's assistant). I stayed with Julie Colbert for almost a month in her Venice Beach condo, putting in the time to work with Rick, but my heart wasn't in it. I hate being away from home and this was no exception. Rick was like an amiable schoolteacher, and he'd written with Mel C and Dido, amongst others, but I felt he didn't really get my voice.

We worked long days together as he made me record lines of songs over and over again until I felt like screaming. I remember puffing away on the old Marlboro Lights, thinking, I can't do this any better, but he wanted to do things his way, so that he could fiddle with my voice in post-production. I wasn't into that because the one thing I know I can do is sing, and I think you only need to fiddle with a voice if someone can't sing.

Eventually I came home, having recorded five or six songs that would go towards the final pick for an album. The song we chose in the end was 'Even God', which Rick co-wrote with Boy George. I was pleased to hear that usually Boy George hates other artists recording his songs, but apparently he loved our version, which brought tears to his eyes.

Songs were pouring in from all over the world – rock songs, ballads, country songs, pop – Nick filtered them through to me and I kept trying out the ones I liked, recording and working with different writers and producers, who were all helping me find my new voice.

I'd also started taking vocal lessons with Ian Shaw, an absolutely brilliant jazz vocalist and teacher who was helping me broaden my voice by teaching me a completely different kind of singing from the more classical style I had studied with Lulu. We worked on completely new breathing techniques and voice exercises. With him I learned to take short, sharp breaths, instead of breathing from my diaphragm. My lung capacity gave me surplus air that made me sound breathy when I was singing pop, so I needed to learn to control it. It takes different techniques to sing different styles of music, and I had to learn to adapt. Ian would come to Cardiff and we'd take a rehearsal room at the WNO, where he'd play piano and I'd practise all my new songs with him.

Everyone was saying I should try writing myself, but I felt the public already knew so much about me that I didn't want to put any of my personal thoughts and feelings into a song. I'd be giving away too much of myself. Besides, I didn't think I'd be any good at it. I'd written a couple of poems when I was about fourteen, my favourite being 'The Depth of Sorrow', and I knew I couldn't write happy things. It's much harder to write about good times because you're so busy experiencing them and holding on to the moment that you haven't time. Sad times, on the other hand, stick and there's so much more to say about them. Only now did I begin to realise that I could draw not only on my own experiences but also on those of my family and friends. The songs didn't have to be all about me.

The first song I co-wrote was with Fitzgerald Scott, who flew into London from Atlanta. He had two R&B backing tracks that I loved, so I sat down and wrote some lyrics. The words weren't bad, but my voice didn't suit the arrangement. I wanted to sing with my chest voice, but Fitz wanted me to sing with my head voice. They're two quite different sounds, not just because there's a difference in volume, but because there's a difference in tone. Lulu had taught me to sing properly with my chest voice to produce a sound that's deeper and more guttural than my head voice, which is much softer and sweeter. Fitz also co-produced 'Call My Name', one of the songs I collaborated on with Eg White and Wayne Hector.

I flew to Atlanta to work with Dallas Austin, a multi-platinum award-winning writer who, I discovered, didn't start work until nine in the evening. Short of something to do during the day, I was persuaded by Mark Melton and Fitz to go into the studio and record a couple of other songs Fitz had found. Mark and I disagreed about 'Crazy Chick'. He wanted me to record it, while I wanted to write some lyrics for the backing tracks of a half-written song. In the end, he cunningly suggested I record 'Crazy Chick' first, knowing that there wasn't time to do both. Just shows, the biggest hit of your career can be the song you like least. Weird.

My friend Beck came with me to New Orleans, where I was working on more songs for the album with the producer Dave Fortman. I loved the vibrant atmosphere of the city, especially at the weekend, when it erupted into one big street party, with Dixieland and jazz musicians jamming on almost every corner. As we didn't have ID to get us into a club, we found a restaurant where we thought we'd be fairly inconspicuous. Wrong! People were so all over us, trying to chat, that we got a bit scared and legged it back to the hotel after only two drinks. Not very adventurous of us, I know. Working with Mr Fortman was great, though. I love the big, lush sound he produced with Evanescence, but neither of the songs we recorded during that visit ended up on the album. A few weeks later, however, he came to London and we recorded 'Finding My Own Way' and 'Even God Can't Change the Past'.

Only days before I'd finished with Steven, Rob 'Can't Get You Out of My Head' Davis, Marcella Detroit and I came up with 'Easy to Forget'. It's strange, because the words suggest I had seen the end of our relationship coming. I love the hypnotic, lulling melody to that song, especially played on the acoustic guitar. I wrote several songs with Rob, including my only happy one, which is about my bampy – 'the way that you taught me and held me so dear has made me stronger inside' – but it never made its way on to the album.

Gary Barlow and Eliot Kennedy are two of the funniest men I've ever met. I met them because they had co-written a song that Sony wanted me to record. The song didn't suit my voice, but I went to Cheshire a couple of times, where Gary has a state-of-the-art studio in his house, to see what else we could do together.

I was a bit apprehensive at first, because when Gary was in Take That the first time round he looked like a miserable bastard. In fact, nothing could be further from the truth. He and Eliot are a ridiculously funny double act and I loved every second I was with them. Sometimes I'd arrive to find they'd already made backing tracks with a rough melody and might even have outline lyrics as well. On the times when they had nothing, we'd sit with a guitar and I'd tell them which songs or particular riffs I liked. They'd begin playing riffs using different chords and I'd pick the ones I liked or ask them to play something in a higher or lower register as we worked towards a verse and chorus structure. Then I'd begin la, la, la-ing along to get some sort of structure in my head that we could put down on tape. Only then came the lyrics. I would take my lead from the music, responding to whatever feeling it evoked in me. I prefer working in a minor key because it usually provokes sad thoughts. One time, they had a first chorus melody that they were playing on guitar but no backing track. When I heard the notes, I decided to write a song about Naomi, who was stuck in a difficult relationship, and that became 'Easy Way Out'. When I eventually played it to her, she got very emotional, but she did finish with her fella. Result.

My other favourite person to work with was Guy Chambers. Apart from helping Robbie Williams reinvent himself as a solo singer, Guy has worked with many other great singers. He's an interesting, eccentric man and an absolute genius who understands all the ins and outs of songwriting and can really think outside the box, so he comes up with fabulous melodies, great riffs and strong choruses. One day I told him that the following weekend my mum and I were getting hypnotised to stop smoking, and he jumped on this, saying, 'That's the first line of your song.'

Yeah, yeah. Whatever. That's really going to fit into a song! I thought.

Only Guy could take inspiration from something so ordinary. That was the starting point for 'Confessional Song'. Originally, there was a line saying, 'This is a confessional song,' but Guy suggested that we inserted a 'not'. I couldn't see the point of that at all, but he was right: the phrasing worked much better. He opened me up like a book, encouraging me to draw on my innermost feelings in a way no one else had managed. Of the people I worked with, he was the most experimental and tended to leave me to my own devices, so we made a good team, apart from the moment when he banned me from bringing Sasha (a Papillon puppy given to me for my birthday by my parents) into his studio because she'd shat in there. The carpet was a state anyway, so I was quite bitter about that! At least she found her way into 'Confessional Song'. Of the songs we wrote together, 'Casualty of Love', 'Confessional Song' and 'Let's Be Alone' were chosen for the album.

These were exciting times. I was meeting new people and discovering a new direction for myself. I didn't feel I was taking a risk by co-writing the songs. I'm not that ambitious and although I don't like failure I'm not scared of it, so I didn't worry about whether or not any of this would work. As a musician, I thoroughly enjoyed the process of co-writing and discovering that I could do it. In the end, I must have recorded about forty possible songs. Most of 2004 was spent going backwards and forwards, trying to get the songs as we wanted them. Sometimes, we didn't like what the songwriter had done on the production of a song, so we'd bring in another producer to take it further.

That's what happened when we brought Tore Johansson on board for 'Crazy Chick' and 'Moodswings'. I felt that the original production of 'Easy Way Out' lost some of the melody by being too hard rock, so we lost the heavy guitars and put on really nice strings. Sometimes we didn't like the sound of the vocals. I had a stinking cold when I recorded 'Show a Little Faith' with Steve Chrisanthou in a studio underneath a frame shop in Bradford. Everyone liked the vocal because my cold gave it a nice gravelly sound, but I thought I could do better. I recorded it again but this time it just didn't work, so we went back to the first version.

Once we were happy with a song, the tracks would be sent to the mix engineer, who makes sure everything sounds together and is tight. He might put some effects on my voice, maybe making it echoey for instance, although I think they can compress my voice too much, making it sound weak and thin. I know that can work for pop songs, but I think it can reduce the build-up and lose the passion in a song. After that we'd wrangle over the mixes. Months were spent working with loads of different people to get the best tracks possible.

The only person who wasn't too keen on what I was doing, or at least who came out and said so, was my manager, Irving Azoff. He really wanted me to work with American writers and producers to develop in the slick and polished style of American singers. But I liked the songs I was co-writing in the UK and I was enjoying learning so much and working with the songwriters and producers that Sony suggested. Besides, Wales was and always will be my home. I had too much going for me in Cardiff to want to spend so much time in America.

Irving and I agreed that there was no point in his managing me if we had such different ideas about my future, so we split perfectly amicably and Mark Melton, who had effectively been managing me in the UK, agreed to take over. I've known him for a long time and have huge respect for him. He's always constant and never flustered. If I don't want to do something, he goes all paternal on me as he tries to make me. If I dig my heels in, he sometimes goes behind my back to my mum and gets her to persuade me. I used to get pissed off because I thought this was quite underhand, but in hindsight, it's all turned out peachy, so he's forgiven now – and possibly even thanked!

CHAPTER 16

Crazy Chick

TIP:

Take your own path in life and enjoy it.
Don't let other people dictate the way.

The villa was conveniently between Ibiza Town and San Antonio: nothing too luxurious but with five bedrooms and a beautiful pool. The eight of us — me, Abi, Naomi, Becks, Lauren, Kayleigh, Kyla and Sarah — were sprawled fully clothed by the pool, our suitcases heating up beside us in the baking sun. The villa was locked and shuttered and there was no way in. After three-quarters of an hour, one of the holiday reps appeared, full of apologies. He opened the villa up and so began the craziest week of my life so far.

I'd already been to St Lucia with Kayleigh in 2004, when we stayed at Le Sport at the north end of the island. We had a brilliant time there, especially on New Year's Eve, when we joined loads of other people from the hotel to go to the Jump Up in the small town of Gros Islet. Walking down the main street, reggae and soca blasted out of every window, makeshift stalls sold beer, meat and fish, smells of cooking blending with the scent of wood and cannabis smoke. At the bottom of the street, there was a big space where everyone was dancing and it was brilliant.

That was the first time I'd been abroad on holiday without my parents, and only six months later I was away again, this time on a girls' week to Ibiza. On our first night we tanked up on the cheapest vodka from the little supermarket nearby, the stuff that makes your head bang as if you've been shot, before going to an MTV party at Eden. Not many people turned up, but we drank, danced and had a brilliant time, even though it was the shittiest party in history. I've never felt as ill in my life as I did the next morning. I was trying to compete with the other girls in the tanning stakes, but all I wanted to do was drown myself in the pool. There were only about four sun loungers and I insisted that one of them was mine because I'd paid for the villa. Some of the others were a bit pissed off, but most of them were fine with it. That was the start of our tanning competition. We all know how bad the sun is for your skin, but hey, lying in the sun is fabulous and a tan looks and feels good if you work on it carefully.

Sarah was like a mother hen, looking after us and trying to make us eat pasta and ham, even though none of us were interested in eating. Pasta 'n' ham is what we had pretty much night and day because there wasn't much else at the shop, although occasionally we'd have a bit of chocolate if we were struggling. We'd all get dolled up in the evening and take loads of photos with our disposable cameras. We had a wicked time. None of us argued or bitched, we all wore each other's clothes, did each other's make-up, compared tans, laughed about the night before and acted stupid because we were so hungover. We went out every night without fail and poor Sarah took us everywhere in a minibus. She remained steadfastly sober and, in the early hours of the morning, would hopelessly beg us to go home. We didn't discover until weeks later that she wasn't drinking because she was pregnant.

The best night we had was at Flower Power in Pacha. We went into Ibiza Town and wandered through the narrow old streets, where the bars sold four cocktails for the price of one. Once at Pacha, we dipped in and out of the different rooms – a Seventies room, an Eighties room, a hard-rock room and so on – until Abi cut her foot really badly. I poured neat vodka on it and she went nuts with the pain. I thought she'd kill me, but otherwise we had a brilliant time.

Boys were off limits. We'd never really been like that anyway, but I made it clear that if anyone was slutty enough to go home with someone, then they should go to the boy's hotel. I was expecting some arguments over that, but everyone agreed, which was very respectful of them. We were having such an amazing time that we didn't need anyone else's company. As Lauren said recently, 'That was the best holiday of my life and it will never happen again. We all got on so well, it was really cool.'

The paparazzi were having a field day, following us wherever we went. Stories about us appeared in the press back home every day, and there was no way of stopping them, though I did try. In Pacha, one of them stood right in front of me, blatantly pointing his camera. I was furious because we'd agreed with the photographers earlier that day that they could have one photo of us on the beach in exchange for leaving us alone. Understandably, some of the girls didn't want to be snapped in their bikinis or at all, but they agreed it was for the best if it got rid of them. So when I recognised this guy, I went mad. I thought I was She-Ra and He-Man combined as I chased him, screaming, round the club. Liam Gallagher, eat your heart out! I didn't catch him, though, and in the end I gave up.

Another morning we emerged from some club at 7.30 a.m., looking hanging in the bright sunshine but feeling very girl power. We got Sarah to take photos of us with each of our disposable cameras, but what we didn't realise was that behind the bushes were about ten paparazzi, taking photographs of us taking photographs of us!

Another time, they caught us eating the lush chicken bites at Café Mambo. That photo appeared in one of the papers with the girls' names and jobs all wrong. Of course, the girls were pissed off, especially the one who was reported as being unemployed when she wasn't. That's the trouble with the press: it wouldn't take much effort to do a bit of research, but half the time they're too lazy to bother.

The day we got back to Cardiff, Kayleigh and I were on our way out when we were stopped by a girl who shouted, 'Hey, Charlotte, you fat bitch.' Kayleigh went nuts, turned round and started pulling the girl's hair. I tried to pull her off, shouting at her to stop it.

'I'll fucking have you,' yelled the girl.

'Oh come on, Kayleigh. We've got much more drink to drink before we start fighting,' I said. I was used to people having a pop at me by now, and most of it was water off a duck's back, although it always upset my close friends. Finally she saw sense and tore herself away. I don't like fighting and have never got into a fight myself, but I was thankful for the way Kayleigh had stuck up for me. She was a good friend.

CHARLOTTE: VICES OF AN ANGEL – that was a typical headline from 2004. The press constantly made me out to be some kind of wild child, always drunk, clubbing, rebelling against my parents and going out with unsuitable boys. In fact, the truth was very different. I went out a couple of nights a week, went on two short holidays with my girlfriends and yes, I did get hammered, but nothing too excessive, and I did go out with two boys my mother didn't approve of. I wasn't brawling or throwing up in the streets (well, only that once!). Photos were taken that always caught me with one eye shut, looking much worse than I was. Once we were in a taxi at a garage when I wound down the window to call to Naomi, asking her to buy some gum. A paparazzo popped out with a camera right in front of my face, and in his photo I look as if I'm being sick. Another time I was photographed leaning out of my top window, a towel wrapped round me, throwing down the key so Kayleigh could let herself in. The picture printed was cropped so I looked as if I didn't have anything on at all.

However, a lot of stories were emerging that were close to the truth, and I began to suspect that one of the girls must be tipping off the press. At the time our little group had begun to drift apart. I think that often happens at that age as new boyfriends come on the scene and people take new jobs or move. I just let contact with four or five of them slip and none of us made the effort to keep in touch. I haven't spoken to them since, although I still miss them a little bit. Losing friendships is a hard price to pay for fame, but fewer stories have been leaked to the papers since.

It was hard to see how I was behaving any differently from thousands of other teenagers. The difference was that no one wanted me to grow up, even though it was inescapable. All I wanted was to be the same as my friends, going out, having a good time and going home. I wasn't working in a nine-to-five job like most of them, but having worked hard over the previous five years, I didn't need to. I lived off a strict allowance from my trust, so although I had more money than my friends,

I certainly wasn't loaded. I was working hard, putting together the new album, and if I'd been drunk as often as the papers made out, I wouldn't have been able to work at all!

In November 2004 I met Gavin Henson, dragging him off the street one night to join my family in Charlstons Brasserie. As we left, Mum really embarrassed me by asking him to give me his number. Because my phone battery was dead, Gavin gave it to Ian instead, before he disappeared into the night. I didn't forget him, but I tried to put him out of my mind. I knew I couldn't go out with him because I was involved with the second big mistake in my private life, who went by the name of Kyle Johnson. Although the relationship was running out of steam, I'm always a one-man woman. I would never two-time someone. More importantly, I still had some work to do on the album. Mark and I had hoped that Sony would release the new album at the end of 2004, but they were adamant that we needed a couple of songs that would be big hit singles.

The final decision as to which songs should go on the album was down to an amalgamation of people: me, Mark, Nick Raphael and the Sony boss at the time, Rob Stringer, the younger brother of Sir Howard. I squabbled with Nick all the time, but on the whole I trusted his opinion. Rob made it clear that Sony would be laying their necks on the line by putting up the money to produce and market the album, so I had to listen to them. We all wanted to use the strongest songs, but we fought over a lot of them. Even when we agreed on a song, we'd differ on which version we should use. Sony loved a keyboard version of 'Casualty of Love' that to me sounded like a demo. I hated it and wanted to use the version with the Brazilian drums. I fought for it and I won. I wasn't being difficult for the sake of it, but I like what I like. After all, Sony might be taking the risk, but I'm the one with my name on the album.

Finally we agreed on the twelve strongest songs, which included 'Crazy Chick', 'Moodswings' and 'Call My Name', the three that were recorded quite late in the day because Sony thought they were the hit singles the album needed. I felt their inclusion made the album more obviously commercial, but also more bland. I was a bit disappointed that it wasn't exactly what I'd wanted for my breakaway album, but of all my albums, it's the one I'm most proud of and contains the songs I like performing most.

All that remained was to think of the title. We'd been banging our heads together trying to think of something catchy and appropriate when a friend of my mum's came up with the answer. I was in the pub, ranting about my break-up with Kyle. After we split, he did what I consider the lowest of the low and, like Steven before him, sold a story about me to a newspaper. I found out about it the night before it appeared, which is when I ran into him at a local club. He came in with his friends and I couldn't help myself: 'You stupid little shit! You're no better than the shit on my shoe! I can't believe you did that.' He looked at me and said, 'You bitch.' So I punched him. I was like, 'You're a wanker! Please!' As I was relating all this, Mum's friend looked at me and said, 'Ah, tissues and issues, love.' That was it! We had our title.

I really wanted the album to do well, but as usual I had no expectations. I knew that there'd be a lot of people willing it to do badly because there's nothing the British press like more than the sight of someone falling from grace: the more spectacularly the better. I was going to do everything I could not to give them that satisfaction, but there was nothing I could do until the release of my first single in June and the album in July, so for the time being I was going to make the most of the calm before the storm, chilling out, watching the rugby and enjoying a new endeavour that had begun with a picture I saw in the paper.

A couple of weeks before the start of the Six Nations, a photo appeared of Gavin and Shane Williams in the new Ospreys kit. Gavin was lifting a weight with two girls in Ospreys strips beside him. The first time I'd seen him, he was wearing a suit, but this time you could see that he was buff. That beautiful photo ignited my lust! I just had to find out more about him. Round at Abi's, we Googled Gavin Henson and loads of photos came up of him playing rugby. 'God, Charlotte. He's minging.' She laughed, but he wasn't and she knew it.

I watched the Wales v England game down the Robin, the first of the Welsh games in the 2005 Six Nations. My mum and dad had bought the pub at the end of 2004, so now it was even more than our favourite local – you couldn't keep us out of it. There was a massive atmosphere as everyone was loving the game. I was on the cheeky Vimtos, wearing my Welsh jersey and feeling good. The game had been brilliant and Gavin had played really well. Near the end, he had to kick a vital penalty, and the whole pub fell absolutely silent. You could have heard a pin drop. Then, as Gavin lined up the ball, my mother said, 'If he kicks this now, you're going to be gutted.'

'Whatever, Mother. Shut up.'

The ball rose up and sailed between the two posts and everyone went nuts. I couldn't wait any longer. I'd been thinking about him a lot, but this put my feelings into overdrive. I realised that I really wanted him! I called Ian. 'Have you still got Gavin's number?'

'Oh, baby.' I could hear something bad coming. 'I lost my phone.'

You are fucking joking!

That night I went into town with my trusty friend Beck to find him. Beck was a sweetheart and followed me everywhere. I had never felt like this in my life before: finding Gavin was my obsession. We went to every bar and club that I could think of where he might be, and ended up in Charlstons again. Maybe he would know to find me there. I was so deflated. It was 3 a.m. and I'd drunk everything I could drink and looked everywhere I could look. I'd bumped into Rupert Moon, a retired Welsh player, in Sodabar and begged him for Gavin's number, but he insisted he didn't have it. I'd even asked random people in the street if they had Gavin Henson's number. I'd been so certain that I'd find him and that everything would be amazing. Beck kept consoling me, saying, 'Don't worry. He'll be in touch.' But she didn't understand my desperate need and feeling of failure. Besides, I wasn't so confident that he would call me.

Days later, I found someone who got hold of Gavin's phone number for me. I texted him: 'Hi, this is Charlotte Church here.' What I didn't know was that the boys on the team had already been teasing him because of all the suggestions in the press that I'd turned him down. One of them had texted him, pretending to be me, and he fell for it hook, line and sinker, so when he got my text, he was really wary. He texted back, asking me to call him. He had to make sure it really was me this time.

Even though it was such early days, my parents were so

excited for me: he was a Welsh hero and my mother thought he was gorgeous. I've never been so nervous about calling anyone. I was expecting him to have a Cardiff accent – why? I had spoken to him after all – and I assumed that he'd like quite rocky music and all the latest bands, but when I spoke to him he had a beautiful low, soothing voice with a nice Welsh lilt and not too strong an accent. He told me what had happened with the boys and why he was being so cautious, but he also said that he'd been looking for me the night of the match. We must have been in all the right places at the wrong times.

'What sort of music do you like?' I had to know.

'Phil Collins, Huey Lewis and the News, Lionel Richie. That sort of thing.'

Fuck! Turns out he's a cheesy Eighties child. I was so shocked. But I loved all the little touches. For instance, once when I texted him, asking what he was doing, he replied, 'I'm "out here on my own", in my house.' The only time I had ever sung 'Out Here On My Own' was when I performed at the Millennium Centre, the day after I met him in November. I knew then that he must have watched me on TV, so that was sweet.

The Six Nations was in full swing so Gav was training hard, which made it difficult to meet up. I was at Naomi's once when he texted: 'I'm going to Rome, but if you'd like to spend a nice Valentine's weekend out there with me . . .'

'Oh my God, Naomi. Read this.' I was almost in tears.

I texted back: 'That's the most amazing thing anyone's ever asked me, but I can't.'

'I was only asking to see what your response would be,' was his reply.

Oh God, don't go cold on me now.

For about one and a half weeks, we texted one another constantly. Gav was completely focused on his rugby, so we couldn't meet. He certainly couldn't be seen with me, and some people in his camp thought it was a bad idea for us to be together at all. They only knew the image of me portrayed by the press and, not surprisingly, they didn't much like it.

We finally had our first date on Valentine's Day. We couldn't go anywhere because he was such a superstar and the press would go mad if they caught us, so instead he invited me to his house. I made a huge effort, taking hours to curl my hair and do my make-up, and deciding what to wear with Abi and Naomi's advice. I plumped for my jeans with my *Scarface* T-shirt. Doesn't every man love that film? At least it would be something to fall back on if the conversation dried up! Naomi kept reassuring me, 'Don't worry, Charlotte. You're going to be fine. He's going to love you.'

Abi was the only one who could drive at the time, so she drove me to Pencoed, putting up with me chain-smoking in the front seat as we worked out a fall-back plan in case it all went wrong.

'If you let my mobile ring twice then hang up, I'll come and get you.'

'What if we get on?'

'Then don't ring. Whatever.'

I knew Gavin wouldn't smoke, so I put out my last cigarette, doused myself in perfume and ate practically a whole packet of mints before we arrived. He answered my knock and stood in the doorway looking fucking amazing. He was just in from training, so he had his kit on and his hair was all spiky; it made quite a statement, but it added to the whole appeal. He took me into the massive kitchen – black slate floor, oak units and

I'll never get over the buzz of seeing my name up on a billboard. This was taken in 2003.

Saying goodbye to the Voice of an Angel. My farewell concert in Hong Kong, 2003.

Me and Caroline never need an excuse to get up and sing.

I've supported the Noah's Ark Appeal since it began in 2000.
Here I am blowing out the candles on my 18th birthday cake in
the children's ward at Heath Hospital, Cardiff.

Sharing a joke with the Queen and Kate Moss, J. K. Rowling and Heather Mills at the reception for Woman Achievers at Buckingham Palace, March 2004.

Singing the Welsh National Anthem with Max Boyce and Katherine Jenkins at the Millennium Stadium before the Wales—Ireland game, 2005.

Filming Crazy Chick,
my first pop video.

Chris Lopez

The dancers on the
Call My Name video
gave me more support
than I expected!

Charlie Chapel. Take a reality check. Yes, it's me (on my TV show).

Holly Goodchild

Chris Lopez

With Catherine Tate on her 2005 Christmas show, with Chas and Dave.

Holly Goodchild

Chatting with John Barrowman on my show and below, singing with Jamelia.

PA Photos

Me and my man. A moment alone in the long lenses of the paparazzi. This was taken in Antigua, 2005 (without our consent, mind).

Dave M Benett/Getty Images

(below) Dressing up for the latest Walkers Crisps commercial.

Holly Goodchild

Finding out that I'd won the Glamour Solo Artist of the Year Award in June 2006. A fabulous moment.

Me and Gavin — I knew he was 'the one' as soon as we met.

granite worktops, central island. First impressions? For a bachelor's pad it was really nice and very clean. I was quite impressed. Everything was quite masculine, except for the single red rose in the sink. He picked it up and gave it to me, muttering, 'Happy Valentine's Day,' all embarrassed.

We walked through to his living room, where I sat awkwardly on the edge of the white sofa with my rose, wondering what the hell to say. In the modern fireplace, blue imitation coals burned with a sultry flame that suited the mood. Neither of us really knew what to do, we were so embarrassed and self-conscious after all the build-up. As the TV was on, we watched a bit of *Coronation Street* to bridge the gap as we got chatting. We soon forgot *Corrie* as I discovered how easy-going he is and what a good listener. Because he was so attentive, I just spilled my guts, telling him everything. He must have been thinking, What the fuck? Get her out of my house ASAP! But he never showed it. After three hours or so he stopped me: 'I've got to sleep soon because I've got training in the morning. You can stay the night, or would you rather go home?'

'I'd better go home,' I said. 'Or my dad will go nuts.'

Even though I was so independent, my dad had dinned it into my head that I'd better make sure I went back to their house rather than my flat. That was his subtle way of saying, Don't sleep with him on your first date. So we climbed into Gav's midnight-blue Audi TT convertible. As soon as I saw it, I thought, Whoa, I've arrived! By then I was feeling much more comfortable and we chatted all the way home. We stopped outside my mum's house, Lionel Richie's 'Hello' playing, and we got to that awkward moment when you have to say goodbye. We hadn't touched or kissed at all, but as I was getting out, he said, 'Aren't you going to give me a kiss?' Of course I was dying to give him a snog, so I didn't need much encouragement. He was so lush in every single way.

As soon as he'd driven off, I texted him, and the minute I was indoors, I raced up to see my mum and dad, who were in bed. I woke them up and told them what had happened. My mum was excited for me, but my dad just said, 'I'm glad you came home!' A little bit of a subliminal message there – not very subtle, mind. I went to bed so happy, and sure that I was going to see Gavin again. But when?

CHAPTER 17

You're the One That I Want

TIP:

Be prepared to work your arse off, but also learn to be patient. The music business involves long periods of waiting for something to happen. Luck also plays an important part.

Gav was still in training for the Six Nations, so after our first date we couldn't see each other for another two weeks. When he's focused, he's really focused and there's no room for anything else in his life. Plus, he was hearing quite a lot of negative stuff about me from a couple of his team-mates and managers. His parents were advising him, too: 'Being a part of the Welsh team is so important, concentrate on that right now. Wait till the season is over and then you can do anything.' Although I had told him that the press exaggerated my lifestyle way beyond the truth, I don't think he really believed me. I think he thought I'd been doing what some celebrities, who shall remain nameless, do – i.e. ring the papers and set up stories to keep themselves in the public eye. 'Gav, they're obsessed with me,' I'd protested. 'I promise you they won't leave me alone.' I knew I'd have to wait until he saw it for himself, then he'd believe me.

Down at the Robin, I watched all the Welsh team games. Knowing Gavin made the games all the more amazing, and people would tease me, saying, 'Oh, your boy's playing.'

I'd just tell them to shut up, especially my mother, who told anyone who'd listen. 'My daughter's going out with Gavin Henson.'

'No, I'm not,' I'd insist. 'He's not my boyfriend. We're just seeing each other.'

Wales were flying, having beaten Scotland and the rest, but Wales v France in Paris was going to be a tough match. My dad and Paul, the co-landlord, were among the fans wearing 'I LOVE GAVIN' T-shirts, the 'I' decorated with Gavin's spiky hair. Never mind the Robin, the atmosphere in the whole of Wales was electric: people were going to work happy, people were polite in traffic jams, smiled and said hello in the street. There was a massive sense of anticipation and excitement. Come the Saturday, everyone was in their Welsh jerseys, Cardiff was buzzing and the pubs were packed. The first half of the game didn't go so well. France were winning, although we all kept our hopes high. I couldn't believe that with this atmosphere Wales would lose. A little voice inside me kept saying, 'No, it's not going to happen.' Then out they came for the second half, when the Welsh team upped their game and played amazingly well to beat France 24–18. What a fucking brilliant game, and what a result! We all went wild.

Gav always called me after the matches, but that night I was particularly star-struck when he called me from the lobby of the team's hotel at three in the morning. I was so glad to have found someone who didn't play games. He wanted to speak to me, so he phoned me to talk about how much he'd enjoyed the game and how he couldn't wait to see me. Some people might think it's not cool to be so upfront about your feelings, but neither of us wanted the other to do the chasing. We said what we felt without any subliminal messages going on. I haven't got the patience for all that and neither has he.

We arranged to meet in Creation just after my birthday. I took loads of trouble over my appearance, carefully curling my hair (honey-coloured at the time), and wearing a beautiful Arabian-style wraparound top that showed a bit of belly; a pair of jeans and lush Vivienne Westwood heels. I was definitely looking good. I knew he was going to be with all the rugby boys, so I took my friends along for moral support. As I walked over to him, about fifty camera phones lit up all around us, so I looked, waved and walked away. What was I going to do now? After a couple of drinks I felt more confident, so I took a couple of the girls with me and blagged my way into the VIP section that had been roped off for the Welsh rugby players. At last I got to talk to Gav, who was sitting with Jon Thomas (JT), another Ospreys player. Even though there were two bouncers on the rope and the lights were dim, people were still trying to take photos of us and I'd had enough. 'I'm going to go home now. So come back to my house?' I invited him.

'Yeah, OK.'

'No. Make sure you do.' I wasn't going to let him get away.

'OK. I will.'

'Promise me you'll come.' I was so worried that he wouldn't.

'I'll be there in about half an hour.'

'Don't stay here too long now.'

'OK.' He laughed. 'I'm coming. OK?'

By the time he and JT arrived, Beck, Sophie and I were stuck into something on the TV. They came in and we sat around drinking and talking together, having a laugh. All I wanted was to be alone with him, but I didn't want to be that obvious. There was a bit of a contest going on between Beck and Sophie as they flirted with JT, who was sitting between them looking knackered. Finally they left us to it, both Beck and Sophie dissatisfied because neither had won JT's affections.

The next day, my manager, Mark, came to Cardiff to take me to a fundraiser for the Noah's Ark Appeal. On the way, we drove past Gavin, who was walking along the street with a big smile on his face. Mark saw him first. Finally he could see what it was that I'd been going on about for weeks. Even though I'd hardly had a wink of sleep and had a shocking hangover, I spent the rest of the day grinning like the cat that got the cream. People kept trying to mention Gavin, but I kept on denying that anything was going on, that stupid grin plastered across my face.

Nothing was going to stop me supporting my new man or my country now. After that spectacular win against England in the first match of the Six Nations at the beginning of February, Gavin became a national hero. After that, everyone had a built-in belief that Wales could pull off the title. For the Wales–Scotland game a gang of us flew to Edinburgh: my mum, her friend, Abi, Kyla and Jaci Stephens, a journalist mate of ours, and me. We had 'Girls on Tour' sashes, red afro wigs, red hats and badges, and as usual, Kyla had a hipflask of vodka, just in case our spirits flagged. Put it away, Kyla, for fuck's sake. The first night, we ended up in the Grassmarket, where the pubs were full of Welsh supporters. The one we settled for seemed to have 'Delilah' and 'Donald, Where's Yer Troosers?' on a loop. Every time she heard 'Donald . . .' Abi went nuts because she remembered her dad singing it to her when she was a kid. Eventually I grabbed the mic from the DJ and led the whole pub in the Welsh national anthem. We were singing it till 2 a.m., in between dancing to 'Goldfinger', 'The Green, Green Grass of Home' and the like – we had a wicked night.

One guy apologised to Kyla, 'I'm sorry, but my friend has a tendency to get naked when he's drunk. Do excuse him.' The next time we turned round, his mate was fucking starkers. We moved swiftly away. What was in the water here? There were so many paparazzi out at the front that the bouncers tried to get Abi and me out the back way while Mum, her mate and Jaci acted as a decoy at the front. One of the bouncers had an ice-cream van, and when he offered us a lift, we accepted. We sat in front with 'Greensleeves' blaring out through the night until we pulled up at the back entrance to our hotel. That was my most unusual trip home and we didn't even get an ice cream. Probably too pissed to think of it.

I was completely KO'd and oblivious to the fire alarm that ripped through the hotel that night. The others were evacuated in their pyjamas to a church next door, but I slept on while Kyla stayed with me, unable to wake me up, but able to stand on the balcony having a bit of a *Braveheart* moment as she yelled at the firemen, 'You'll never take my freedom!' Fortunately it was a false alarm, so everyone crawled back to their beds to catch a few hours' sleep before the match.

The next day was Sunday, and it was freezing but fantastic.

The Welsh seemed to have taken over the city, driving the poor Scots into hiding. On the way to the game, we passed crowds of people making their way to Murrayfield, carrying inflatable daffodils, Welsh dragons, flags and banners. We had on our 'Girls on Tour' sashes again with our Welsh jumpers and I had a red glitter cowboy hat. Another wicked game ended with a Welsh victory, 46–22.

That night everyone was out celebrating again. We spent it dancing, dancing, dancing in a club where, as usual, I was trying to copy Beyoncé, even if I did end up looking like a stripper, shaking my arse all over the shop. I didn't care because the night had been spoiled with the news that the Welsh team weren't staying over after all. I was gutted. I'd been so looking forward to celebrating with Gavin.

The following Saturday I was due to join Katherine Jenkins and Max Boyce to sing the national anthem at the Wales–Ireland game at the Millennium Stadium for the last match of the series. Gavin wasn't too happy when he heard about it, because his dedication to rugby means that he prefers to keep that side of his life quite separate from his family and friends. He doesn't talk about it much and the only one who can wish him luck is his mum. I wasn't going to say no to this opportunity, though. It was going to be a huge game. The whole of Wales was in a state of excited anticipation. If Wales won, they would become Grand Slam champions for the first time in twenty-seven years. Would they complete their winning streak?

I knew I would have to sing operatically, so I went back to Lulu for four or five lessons. She was disgusted that I'd started smoking, especially when I stopped the lesson to have a cigarette. I was so pleased to see her again, though. My voice was much better than it had been before, simply because I'd grown up. Despite the smoking, I had better breath capacity, better control and my tone was much richer and more rounded. She made sure my Welsh national anthem was absolutely perfect by coaching me to sing it phonetically. I find the Welsh language difficult and was frightened I'd get a word wrong. One day I mean to take proper lessons, and I love the idea of my kids going to a dual-language school, but that's a long way off yet!

On the morning of the match – a gorgeous, crisp spring day – I woke up at home with the sun streaming through the window. I was so excited about the day ahead that I gave myself plenty of time to get ready, getting up at 7.30 a.m., which is unheard of for me. I was a lazy bitch back then and would stay in bed until twelve if I could. Not this day, though. I was looking forward to the match and to singing with Katherine and Max. I'd met Max a couple of times before. To my ears, he's the greatest baritone in the world, a wonderful man and the only singer I know who can eat a steak before going on stage to sing a full-length opera. As I got ready, I had the music up loud and was dancing around the house in my Welsh jumper and specially customised jeans with crystal Welsh dragons on the back pockets. I took ages putting on my make-up before I was ready to leave for the stadium.

Katherine came into our dressing room – a sports changing room, really – looking Cindy perfect in a pink Chanel suit with a pencil skirt, matching Chanel bag and little white high heels. Her face is utterly stunning, with completely symmetrical features and flawless skin. We hadn't met before, although we'd talked on the phone about what we were going to wear. I had wanted to customise a Welsh jersey, perhaps wearing it off one shoulder – quite cool but nothing too tacky – but the Welsh Rugby Union wouldn't let us. Instead, we decided to buy a couple of kids' sized, so they'd be tight and look fabulous. Warming up with her was hilarious. The first ten minutes were fine, but then it became a bit of a competition, unspoken of course. She went higher, so I went higher and she went higher still. She went louder, I went louder and so it went on. I was giggling to myself, but wouldn't give up until I was the highest and loudest. She's the sweetest woman I've ever met and probably wasn't thinking competitively at all, but I definitely was!

We were called through to the players' tunnel, where we had to wait with Max until the players had gone past us onto the pitch. Katherine started warming up again. Fuck this, I thought. If Gavin hears anyone's voice, he's going to hear mine, so off I went again.

Suddenly all the players were running past us. Gav smiled at me, so I gave him one of those really low waves that no one else would see. Once they'd warmed up, they lined up for the anthem and Katherine, Max and I went out to join them. I hoped Gavin had his eye on the sparkling dragons on my bum. There's nothing like singing the anthem in that stadium with 74,000 people singing along with you, all anticipating the game. What a wicked atmosphere. I was so relieved when I got everything right and was pitch perfect. As, of course, were Katherine and Max.

Afterwards, I joined Mum and Caroline, who were in the stadium, to watch the match. It was another great, great game and a brilliant win by Wales, 32–20. Wales had done it! The whole of the country must have erupted. Everyone on and off the pitch was ecstatic.

Mum decided to go back to the Robin, where she knew she'd be in for an excellent night, leaving me on my own in the stadium with thousands of people and no idea where I was going. I knew I had to get back to the changing rooms somehow. People were crowding round, calling out, 'Hey, Charlotte. Tell Gavin he's a god.' 'Charlotte, we love Gavin.' Tell Gavin this. Tell Gavin that. I was getting so swamped that I had to find a policeman to help me.

Normally, I'm nervous of the police because I always think they'll find me guilty of something. I don't know why. But this one was lovely and took me back to the dressing room where I found Katherine. I was meant to be joining Gavin at the after-match dinner, so I dolled myself up in a beautiful black satin D&G dress (there's a recurring pattern here!) with a bronze diamanté bow, pointy high-heeled bronze shoes and matching bag. I had my hair in a bob and was wearing minimal make-up, nothing too over the top, with a bit of black liquid liner for a tiny cat's-eye effect, lots of mascara and neutral lip gloss. I looked fucking chocolate. I know it sounds like I think a lot of myself, but I really don't. It's more because, on most days, I just don't bother. On the few occasions when I do make an effort, I really make an effort. Then I feel good about myself.

Katherine said she'd take me to the family room, where all the players were, but I hadn't been invited and the idea of meeting Gavin's family for the first time frightened the daylights out of me. Instead, I went to wait in one of the production offices on my own, in all my finery, drinking a Carling and eating chocolate footballs. After about an hour, Gavin called to say he was going on the team bus, so I would have to find my own way to the Hilton. Thank God for

Katherine and her mother, who came to find me, even though they weren't going to the dinner. All the streets around the stadium were blocked off and there wasn't a taxi in sight, so we had to walk. Katherine was still in her rugby gear, but I was in this skimpy little evening dress in the freezing cold, surrounded by thousands of ecstatic supporters. A group staggered towards us carrying a big banner saying something like CHARLOTTE LOVES HENSON'S TACKLE. As soon as they saw us, it was, 'Charlotte, Charlotte, look at the banner.' As if I could ignore it. 'Sign the banner.'

'Sorry, folks. Gotta go.'

We ended up running through the crowds, even me in my high heels. As we ran, people were shouting best wishes to Gavin. Finally we found him at the Hilton, looking gorgeous in his suit. I couldn't sit with him at the dinner because all the players were on their own table, so I sat by Ceri Sweeney's missus, Helen, who was lovely. Because I was meeting everyone for the first time, I felt a bit outside the clique. Afterwards, though, we all piled into the team bus and went to a Brains pub, where the drink was free and we had a brilliant night. There had been so much press speculation as to whether we were or weren't a couple that the Welsh Rugby Union had organised a *Hello!* photographer to take one photo of Gavin and me to avoid a paparazzi free-for-all. That picture flew down the wires and appeared all over the world. Gavin was looking forward to the Lions' tour of New Zealand in June, while the releases of my first single, 'Crazy Chick', and *Tissues and Issues* were imminent, together with all the promotion.

Vaughan Arnell is a proper Cockney, tall and well built, who reminded me of Ray Winston, and he wrote a treatment for the video of 'Crazy Chick' that I quite liked. When we met for the first time to talk about it, I was surprised that he seemed nervous, given that he's a massive director who these days concentrates more on commercials than music videos. In the past he's worked with everyone, including Robbie Williams, the Spice Girls and Take That, so it was an honour to be able to work with him. I soon discovered that he's a great guy who's 100 per cent passionate about his work and a fucking brilliant director. His wife, Carol, is an amazing stylist who wears some crazy clothes herself and picked out some great ones for me on the video. I agreed with Vaughan about almost everything, except one shot where he wanted me to be all over some guy. To be honest, I'm a bit of a prude and don't really like that sort of thing. I'm no actress and I don't want to pretend to lick some guy's armpit or whatever. I have my man and that's it. That was the only time I put my foot down.

We filmed in a couple of different locations: in a crazy Russian hotel in London and at Pinewood Studios. Even the paparazzi got into my first video! We filmed some shots where they were hanging around outside. I wouldn't have minded if they'd been young, good-looking guys, but they were all ugly, fat forty-year-olds who looked like train-spotting stalkers! Sorry, train-spotters, but you do have a certain look. On set at Pinewood, Carol had me wearing a cool embroidered cropped jacket that was almost backless and masses of funky jewellery. Vaughan wanted me to dance sexily around the band, but I felt incredibly awkward. I'm not that reserved when I'm out drunk and dancing with friends, but here I was stone-cold sober and I hardly knew these guys. I did the best I could, but wasn't too happy. When I saw the finished result, I thought we'd done a good job, except that it must be the only popstar's video where their belly wobbles. My mum and my nan didn't stop taking the piss out of me for that for ages.

'Crazy Chick' was the first single to be released from the album in June and it went straight to number two in the charts, so I was well pleased. I worked my arse off doing every TV and radio programme, photoshoots and interviews with so many magazines, giving the same old answers to the same old questions. Sony insisted that I must never be negative, so I had to make a nice fluffy little package for the media, explaining how exciting it was to be doing pop music now, how the audience was much more responsive and that at least I got to dance. Package it up nicely and they swallow it, because that's what they want to hear. The writing and recording process is one thing – I love that – but promotion is something else. The only thing that was exciting about it was being able to pick out clothes with a stylist, so that for once I looked halfway decent, and then wearing them back home on the weekend. Otherwise it was just the same old stuff.

Because this album was going down such a different route, I had to promote it as if I was starting all over again. We were all aware that I was going to lose a lot of my old fans, so I had to work hard to make new ones. I was kept extremely busy going back and forth to London, as well as travelling all over the country. I'd be stuck in the car for hours on boiling-hot days, going somewhere to perform a ten-minute set for audiences of twelve-year-olds who loved 'Crazy Chick', but who were really waiting for fucking McFly to come on. I know everyone thinks being on the road is glamorous and exciting, but it really isn't. I hate promotion. You bump into the same people, doing the rounds, every one of them as exhausted as you. You spend hours and hours travelling because some local radio stations won't play your single unless you go there to do a personal interview. Singing the same song fifty times during the promotion kills the passion you have for your art, however much you love the music. I guess that's what commercialism does to most things, but there you go. That's what you have to do to make money. What was especially daunting was that this was only the beginning of a rolling programme of releases that was to continue until the end of the year, with 'Call My Name' coming in September and 'Even God' in December. There seemed to be no end in sight.

One thing that completely surprised me was my so-called feud with Cheryl Tweedy. During an interview, she apparently accused me of ripping off the Girls Aloud sound. Not that they cared because they were going in a new direction by then anyway. When a journalist asked me about this, I replied in jest, 'When she can sing "Ave Maria", then she can have a go.' I should have known better. The next thing, she's reported in the *Sun* saying Gavin's 'scabby' and a 'posing idiot' and that I'm a 'nasty little piece of work with a fat head'. Instead of hitting back, I tried to douse the flames when we all appeared on *CD:UK* together. Inevitably I was asked about it, so I just replied that I was hurt and that I didn't think we should get that personal. The whole thing got blown out of all proportion. I think Girls Aloud can all sing and they come out with good strong songs. They go their way and I go mine. As for Cheryl? We've never met face to face, but we've reached a truce and that's an end to it.

What made the whole promotion bearable was having Holly Goodchild, Mark's assistant and my new PA, there with me.

She's the most super-organised person I've ever met. If you mess her about, she can be aloof and tough, but really she's outgoing, friendly and one hell of a party girl! Tall, dark and slim, she stands like the dancer she is. She was good for me because we're about the same age, so we were going through similar experiences and could talk about them together. But we could also go clubbing together, although, like Sarah before her, she was meant to stay sober so she could bundle me into a car if necessary. If I wanted to do anything – see a show or a gig, go to a restaurant or a club – she would organise it seamlessly. She's been in the business since she was sixteen, when she did work experience for a record label and they immediately offered her a job. As a result, she knows everyone! Wherever we were doing promotion, from Liverpool to Leeds to Brighton, we'd always bump into someone she knew. We've even been on my patch, walking down a Cardiff street, when we heard, 'Hi, Holly! How are you?' We have a wicked time together and I know I can trust her 100 per cent, and we've worked together ever since.

Gavin was in New Zealand for the whole of June and I was missing him so much. Although I was still renting, I'd practically moved in with him as soon as I could. I didn't even ask him! Luckily, the ceiling of my flat falling in gave me a ready-made excuse. To begin with we stayed at each other's houses, but the twenty-minute drive between us – and I couldn't even drive until recently – seemed like a lifetime away. Another reason I liked being in his house was because even when he wasn't there, it was far enough away from everyone so that they couldn't easily bother me. Before the promotion got underway, I'd spend my days just sitting in his house. I didn't even clean for him because his mum did that. I dread to think what she must have thought of me as I chilled out in my skanky pyjamas with my hair all over the place, smoking, smoking, smoking and watching daytime TV. If Gavin had been my son, I'd have got me right out of there. Instead, she just cleaned up around me. Gavin would make me go outside if I wanted to smoke, though sometimes I'd have a sneaky one indoors with the door open. He'd always be able to smell it when he came in, though. Being there was so calm and quiet; I loved every second of it. But while he was away, I couldn't bear to be at home alone, so I stayed with my nan and bampy, who looked after me.

At last, the first round of promotion was over and Gavin was back from New Zealand. He was able to take a couple of weeks' holiday, so we flew to Antigua. Not that we could escape the paparazzi, of course. Although we were staying on a private island, some of them booked into the hotel as guests and took pictures of us on the beach every day. Reports came out about us having a row when Gavin was seen alone in the sun while I was lying eight feet away from him in the shade. Nothing could have been further from the truth. The day before, I'd been sitting on a sun lounger at the edge of the sea, reading the latest Harry Potter for eight hours straight, and my sunscreen had washed off and I burned quite badly. I couldn't go in the sun without my skin feeling as if it was going to come off. Other than that, we had a fabulous time together and got on so well. He was kind, patient if I was being a pain in the arse, made me laugh and I realised I trusted him completely. And he couldn't beat me at Scrabble! If anything, the holiday confirmed one thing to me: I was wild about the boy.

CHAPTER 18

New Directions

TIP:

All the better if you can stand out from the crowd. When my first album came out, there were no other twelve-year-old opera singers around. Being in a market of one is invaluable.

A couple of weeks before the *Royal Variety Show* in December 2005, I met Will Young on *CD:UK*. He was going to be appearing on the show as well and asked me what there was to do in Cardiff, where it was being recorded. I said he should come to the Robin on the Sunday night before the show. You can imagine the regulars' faces when he strolled in. All my dancers from the show were there, as well as my family. We had a wicked evening and he and I sang a few numbers together. I'm as happy singing there as I am in front of thousands of people. Will is a brilliant musician and singer, but shit at remembering lyrics. I was trying to think of the most famous songs I knew for us to sing, but he didn't have a fucking clue. Not even 'Hopelessly Devoted to You'! We sang a bit of 'Crazy Chick' together and we made him sing 'Evergreen', which he hadn't sung since his *X-Factor* days. He said he enjoyed performing it that night more than any other. Someone snapped us on their mobile and sold it to the *Sun*, provoking the headline WILL IN THE HOOD.

The *Variety Show* was made much more fun by him being there. We chatted a lot as we hung around waiting our turn. I complimented him on his performance in *Mrs Henderson Presents*. 'Yeah, thanks,' he said. 'Did you see my cock?'

'Can't say I did.' I was rather taken aback.

'If you pause the video in the scene where we all get naked, there is one point where you can see it.'

'Oh. Er, OK . . .'

'It's worth a look. It's really big.' He was absolutely serious. I thought it was a bit strange, but he's a really nice, funny guy, if a bit eccentric.

He kept trying to make me laugh while Shirley Bassey was singing, but I wouldn't because I so admired her. In rehearsal she hadn't sounded like much, and I thought that, like Tom Jones, she should start enjoying her money and chill out. She'd been mean about my drinking, saying I was a bad role model, so I was quite happy that things weren't going so well for her any more. But come the night, when she went out on stage, her voice was as clear as a bell and she turned in an outstanding performance. I took everything back – almost.

Although Gavin owned his house, I wanted one of my own as well. I'd had it with renting and having to rely on the goodwill of the landlord if anything needed repairing. I also thought it was important to have my own bolt-hole. I'd made two mistakes in the Valentine's department before, and although I knew Gavin was 'the one', I wanted to have somewhere of my own as well until we knew what we wanted to do. I had begun looking earlier in the year when my ceiling fell in, but I didn't find the perfect house for months. I wanted something in Cardiff that was detached, quite private and with a nice garden that wasn't overlooked. At last I found what I wanted in Llandaff: a three-bedroomed family house with, as the agents always say, potential. The old lady who lived there was finding it too hard to cope on her own, so her daughter was encouraging her to move even though it broke her heart to leave all those memories behind.

The interior of the house was in a time warp, with some seriously dodgy décor: nothing looked as if it had been touched since the Seventies. Over three or four months, I had the whole place done out, although I was always going back and forth to London and never seemed to be in Cardiff for more than four hours at a time. My dad co-ordinated everything for me and kept landing me with all these decisions that had to be made in a split second. 'Come on, Charlotte. We need to know what tiles you're having.'

'Er. All right.'

So I'd hit the tile shop, and then it was a question of, 'We'll have those for the kitchen, and those for the bathroom, and those for the toilet and those for the other bathroom' and hope for the best. I did have a vision for every room, but when you have to make all those decisions in a matter of days, it's a bit hit and miss. I really enjoyed discovering my inner interior designer and chose new wallpaper, flooring, paint, furniture, curtains and cushions. I was slightly worried because all my choices were very instinctive and rushed, but in the end everything came together really well.

It was at this time that my family life fell apart. I was still promoting 'Call My Name' and 'Even God' when one of my mother's friends broke the news that she thought my dad was having an affair. I don't know why this woman chose to tell me rather than Mum, except that when there's bad news in our family, people always tend to tell me first. Although that can be hard, I prefer things to rest on my shoulders rather than on anybody else's. I'm young and I can usually deal with whatever the problem is, and I think I generally make the right decision. This time, though, the situation was too difficult for me. The rumours were that my dad had been having an affair with a woman who was one of my mum's friends. I had never trusted her and wasn't afraid to tell her so, especially after a few drinks. I tend to make snap decisions on people, guided by instinct, and so far I've rarely been wrong. To her, I was just a little girl, so she'd simply walk away.

When confronted, Dad denied everything. Then she went to the press with her story and it was open house on the Church family once again. Of course the story was horrible, but once these things get into print it assumes a truth in people's minds. My mother has always told me everything, rightly or wrongly, whether I want to hear or not, so I was horrified to read what that woman claimed.

During all of this my dad kept a low profile, and stayed with friends. Of course my mum was ridiculously hurt, and her distress showed in her behaviour. She'd go out on the weekends, get riled up, then go home and cut herself. For the rest of the week she'd be sober and quiet, not wanting to speak to anyone, imagining everyone was against her. In short, she was a pain in the fucking arse! She stopped eating and lost a lot of weight, so one evening, a couple of weeks before Christmas, her friend Abi and I took her to dinner at Mamma Mia's. After a bit, she said, 'Look, Charl. I'm sorry, but I'm in a fucking state and I haven't got you any Christmas presents.' I had gone all out on her that Christmas to try and make it better for her, so I was really pissed off. I absolutely understood how she felt and I was trying to be there for her as much as I could, but no presents?! Fall apart in your own time, love! Not in my fucking Christmas presents' time, OK? 'You're taking the piss!' was all I could say. We started to laugh until we were hysterical. I hadn't seen her smile for ages, so at least that was something.

As for me? I hated seeing Mum in such a state and not being able to help her. She'd always been so strong and decisive. I did what I could by keeping in touch, listening and talking whenever she needed me. If I was away promoting 'Even God', I was still at the end of a phone, and if I was at home, I'd go round to her.

That woman persisted in trying to sell her stories, which didn't help any of us. I couldn't understand why she wanted to do this. No doubt she had her side of the story, but that never interested me. My family is all that matters and she was helping to rip it apart. If I saw her today, I'd poke her eyes out because she was the cause of so much pain to my mother. Mum had already suffered from bouts of depression and had massive self-esteem issues, so this was a huge blow to her.

Everything came to a head one Thursday in the early afternoon. I hadn't heard from Mum and, untypically, her phone was switched off. I felt uneasy all day, and by lunchtime I was sure something was wrong, so I called Bampy and asked him to come round to her house with me. He let us in with his key and we found her upstairs in bed, out for the count in her pyjamas, with the curtains closed. Her three dogs, Queenie, Maddie and Sasha, were racing round the room. To begin with I thought she must be sleeping off a heavy night. I shook her, but she took ages coming to, so I slapped her face. 'Come on, Mum. Get up.' Every movement she made seemed to be taking all her effort, and although she was just about conscious, she was talking gibberish. 'Get dressed and come downstairs,' I encouraged her. 'I'll make you a cup of coffee.'

I went downstairs with Bampy, put the kettle on and worried, 'What d'you think's wrong? She's being all slow and stupid. She's like a rag doll.'

After a while she still hadn't come down, so I went back up again, furious. 'Come on, Mum. We've got things to do today. Get up. You're fine.' She struggled to get out of bed and I helped her to the bathroom, where she was sick in the toilet. I brought her a glass of water, beginning to feel really anxious. 'What have you done, Mum?'

'Oh, I just took some pills . . .' she muttered.

Now, my mum can be quite melodramatic. I've never seen her self-harm, because she knows how angry I'd be if she were to do it in front of me, but when she's been drunk, she's shown me the scars and they're not pretty. If she was capable of that, I could easily believe she'd taken something. I felt so many different emotions – worry, disgust, upset – but I didn't have time to dwell on them because I had to deal with the situation.

'What have you taken?' I yelled.

She gave me a couple of empty bottles of sleeping pills and a pack of paracetamol.

'God, Mum. How many did you take?'

Thank God the bottles hadn't been full when she started, but even though she'd been sick, I could see she still wasn't right. I rushed down to Bampy to see if he knew how serious it was and whether the pills could really harm her, and as we were discussing what to do, Mum came downstairs and slumped on the sofa.

I was overwhelmed by anger and gave it to her straight. 'Did you want to fucking kill yourself? Was that it? Did you want to leave me and your family? How could you? We love you.'

'No, no. It wasn't that,' she insisted. 'I just wanted to sleep. I wanted to forget about everything for a couple of days. Just to have some dreamless sleep.' She took the water I kept giving her in the hope that it would dilute whatever she'd taken, but she kept dozing off and coming to, and when she slept it was really hard to wake her, which made me panic.

Of course, Bampy was devastated. Neither of us knew what to do except phone NHS Direct. I gave my name, but I told them that I was phoning about my auntie, Caroline Cooper. I read them the names of what she'd taken from the bottles, half-expecting them to say, 'Oh, that's all right then. She'll be fine. Just let her sleep it off.' Instead they said, 'Take her straight to hospital.' That put the fear of God in me.

Dad met us at the hospital, because all Mum wanted was to see him, and that really upset me. I thought your love for your kids is meant to surpass everything, and after all, Bampy and I had saved her, but at the same time I could understand where she was coming from. If anything happened to me, I would want her there, but ultimately I would want Gavin. Luckily, she hadn't done herself too much damage. She was put on a drip to prevent liver failure and kept in under observation for a couple of days.

Unfortunately, someone at the hospital spilled the story to the press. That made me really angry. What the fuck's the matter with people these days? Weren't we having to deal with a difficult enough situation already? The speculation and

misinformation was an additional problem. Do you keep a dignified silence or exert your right to reply? It's a difficult choice
when all your friends and neighbours are reading about it in
the papers, and a reply can be taken out of context and mis-
quoted, so silence is usually golden. Nobody has the right to
make money out of my family's troubles. They have never
asked to be in the public spotlight. The paparazzi sat on my
nana's doorstep and rang her up for news until she told them
to piss off. And for her to say that is really something.

When Mum came home, she couldn't stop talking about
how depressed she felt, about the issues she was having to
confront. Within a couple of months Mum and Dad were back
together again: they couldn't bear to be apart. Dad and I
talked and came to the conclusion that we had to do something
because she couldn't go on like this. Although she was slowly
getting stronger, we insisted she went into rehab; she was
going even if I had to drag her there myself. The deal we
agreed was that she would go to the Priory, but only after we'd
had her fortieth-birthday party on 28 January.

I had put a lot of pressure on Dad to get my new house hab-
itable before Christmas, and he pulled out all the stops so that
Gav and I could move in with a few days to spare. We had
meant to divide our time between our houses, but in the end it
didn't work out that way – we loved mine so much that we
ended up staying there, although I had to agree to one condi-
tion. Gav has to travel to Swansea to train with the Ospreys,
so he said, 'If I'm going to move to Cardiff for you, it's going
to take me much longer to drive there than before, so you're
going to have to make me lunch when I get back. That's all I
ask.' He's so dedicated to his fitness that he's obsessive about
his diet and eats every two and a half hours. I guess that was

the moment when I shook off the 'Crazy Chick' tag and exchanged it for 'Domestic Goddess'!

With a bit of persuasion from him, I fell into the Nigella Lawson mould and took it one step further. I've always got something cooking when he comes in and the house is always spotless. I can't bear to have anything even the slightest bit dirty. It's not that I love cleaning, although I do find it quite therapeutic. It's as if the clutter in my house is the clutter in my mind, and while I'm cleaning, I get rid of both. The two things I really fucking hate doing are cleaning the oven and washing the floor. Otherwise, give me a duster and some polish and I'm off.

Once I settled down a bit, I did put on some weight, as the press were only too happy to point out to the world. But they can say what they like, I'm happy with the way I am, and when I'm not, I'll do something about it. The pressures on young women to be super-skinny are ridiculous. I love food and hate the gym and that makes for a pretty curvy combination. I did try working out in Gavin's gym at home, but please . . . it's not for me. When I feel like it, I put in the effort to wear the clothes that make the best of my figure, emphasising my best bits (boobs and waist) and disguising the worst (legs) and I do my best with my hair and make-up. That's enough. You don't have to look like Posh to be happy and have a nice fella.

Just before Christmas, Gavin had to go to Ireland to stand in front of the European Rugby Cup's disciplinary committee because he'd been cited for elbowing a Leicester player. While he was away, I got all the decorations up – something I love doing – so the place would look really welcoming when he got back. I was up till four in the morning doing the Christmas trees. I go over the top every Christmas and had loads of presents for him and my family under the main one.

When he came back, he was gutted about being given a ten-week ban, but he loved the house. On Christmas Eve we went to a party thrown by a friend of Gavin's in Bridgend. I knew my nana expected me at midnight Mass, but there were a couple of girls there who got me on the karaoke with them. I don't know how it happened, but I got really drunk. I didn't mean to but I suddenly noticed it was 11.45 p.m. 'Oh God! We're late, Gavin. I've got to go to Midnight Mass.'

'You're smashed,' he pointed out unnecessarily. 'Are you sure?'

'My nan will kill me if I don't go.'

I was hanging when I turned up at the church. My nana said afterwards that she was really embarrassed because when I knelt down, my knickers and love handles were hanging over the top of my jeans. She was furious with me, even though everyone in our family has done it. Caroline even puked outside the church once. Going drunk to Midnight Mass is something we've all done once but would never do again. I'm never really embarrassed by my drunken behaviour, but I was mortified by that.

On Christmas Day I had a stinking hangover. I had six or seven presents for Gavin that I'd thought long and hard over, and he produced a massive bag of presents for me: beautiful green (my favourite colour) jewellery, a handbag, a belt and so on. In the last box was a set of keys. He'd only given me the purply-blue, custom-built Mini I'd been dreaming of.

'But I can't drive,' I pointed out.

'Yeah. But I had to get you a car or you'd never learn.'

He was probably right. As it was I couldn't wait to start, and within months I'd passed my test and was legally behind the wheel.

Gavin and I went round to Nana and Bampy's for Christmas dinner with the rest of my family, then his parents and sister and my whole family came back to ours in the evening. We had a brilliant night and it felt like old times again.

On her birthday, Mum looked lush. She'd lost weight, was wearing a beautiful black dress and had had her hair done. We'd hired the hall of the Canton Liberal Club and I'd gone all out on the balloons – £800 worth of them! I wanted everything to be perfect for her. There was a huge arc of red and cream ones over the stage, where everyone was going to sing, with two huge flashing balloons on either side. I'd ordered a banner with her photograph on and 'HAPPY 40TH, MARIA'. The small dance floor was surrounded by loads of tables that we sprinkled with tiny coloured paper hearts and 40s. And I put glass bowls in the middle of each table, filled them with water and floated red and cream candles and rose petals. At the opposite end of the hall to the stage was the bar, which was cheap as chips. I'm talking 85p for a double vodka and mixer! The scene was set for another wicked Church family bash.

Mum had invited H from Steps, an old friend from our court-case days when he had phoned out of the blue to commiserate with and support Mum. They'd stayed in touch ever since and he phoned me and said, 'I know your mum's having a party tonight, but I'm down with my boyfriend, who manages Journey South. They're doing a gig down here, so would you mind if we all came?' Mind? Having watched that year's *X-Factor*, we were over the moon. So Journey South were guests of honour and did a couple of songs, which gave the evening something extra special.

Afterwards, about half the party, including Journey South, crowded into Mum's house, a semi-detached number right by Victoria Park. Everyone was on tenterhooks about Mum going off to the Priory in a couple of days, so we all got absolutely bolloxed as a way of dealing with it. All sorts of drunken arguments kicked off. I had a go at one of Mum's friends, telling her I didn't agree with her lifestyle, and she retaliated by saying that no one wanted me in my mum's house. What a cheek! I've never really liked her, so I didn't hold back with my reply.

She got so upset that she ran out of the house. Mum shot after her, but only to catch the dogs, then she brought them back in and slammed the door. I thought that was genius. Mum's friend was banging on the outside, wanting to come back in, but I wouldn't open it.

Another mutual friend stepped in and got right in my face, yelling, 'No one wants you here. You're just a stupid little girl.'

'If you're going to get that close to me, love,' I came back, 'at least shave off your moustache.'

Then my nana got involved, sticking up for me. Meanwhile Caroline was in the kitchen with the Journey South boys, who were looking increasingly bewildered by the mayhem taking place around them. Somehow Caroline managed to slip and pour her port and brandy all over her head. As she picked herself up, she said with a flourish, 'Welcome to fame, boys!' It was a legendary moment.

Two days later, Mum went off to the Priory. They sorted her out so that she looked better, slept better, ate, had vitamin injections and seemed a lot happier in herself. I wish I could say that going there solved all her problems, but I guess life-long patterns of behaviour are hard to break, because in a weird way, they give you a crutch that supports you when things go wrong. When I first found out about Mum's self-harming, I cried and begged her not to and asked her to call me when she felt like doing it. Then I made myself harden up. If she called me to tell me what she'd done, I'd say, 'That's your fault, Mum. There are different ways of dealing with problems, but I don't want to know.' I'm sure that doesn't help her, but it's the only way I can deal with it. We both have to get through in our own ways and you live and learn. We've talked about it a lot and she's explained that it was just her way of dealing with things. It gave her release from all the pressures of trying to balance her family life with being on the road.

She has since been diagnosed as bi-polar, so at least she can be monitored and medicated as she does her best to deal with it. It's been a very strange time for both of us. When she was in the Priory and I visited her, I hated saying goodbye and leaving her there, because it felt so odd. Perhaps I was lucky in that my out-of-the-ordinary childhood had made me stronger and more able to take the knocks life throws at you. I certainly feel that I'm quite strong in myself and am able to cope with whatever life chucks at me.

People say that time is a great healer, and it's true. We've put those bad old days behind us and are getting on with our lives. Apart from running their two hotels, Mum has opened a boutique in Cardiff. She's back in business and doing what she loves, with Dad's practical help and backing. They've even bought a holiday home in the south of France. Everything is rock solid between them. Life has a funny way of working itself out.

CHAPTER 19

Welcome to My Show

TIP:

*Don't be afraid of new challenges. It's
better to fail than not to try at all. You
only become a better performer by
constantly stretching yourself.*

I thought 'Call My Name' was a really strong song with a
good video, so I was surprised when it did less well than
'Crazy Chick', only reaching number ten in the charts. I really
sexed it up in the video in a Moulin Rouge way with thigh-
high boots and a red and black basque. Pretty cool, I thought.
I had wanted to follow up 'Call My Name' with 'Confessional
Song'. I thought it was quirky enough to follow in the footsteps of Gary Jules's cover of 'Mad World', which had hit the
number one spot in 2003. I would have gone with my instincts,
but all the businessmen went, 'No! We know best. It's got to
be "Even God".' I thought 'Even God' was a sophisticated,
subtle song with beautiful words that worked well on an
album, but not as a single. I had fight after fight with Nick
Raphael over it, but he kept insisting, 'This is going to be a
much bigger hit than "Confessional Song".' Then he delivered
the final fucking punch to the solar plexus: 'Trust me. I know.

I do this for a living.' I knew he was wrong, and by then he knew that's what I thought, but I just said, 'Fine. You just fucking do it and let's see how right you are.' When it climbed to the giddy heights of number seventeen, all I heard was, 'Oh, yeah. Well, perhaps it was the wrong decision.'

I fucking love having arguments with high-powered, arrogant men, because I come into my own and can give every bit as good as I get. My most productive arguments were with Nick. However opinionated he may be, he's a nice man who is passionate about what he does. I respected that and the fact that his opinion was based on my track record.

By this time, I'd been promoting the album 24/7 for months. After such a heavy schedule, you get tired of talking about yourself and need a month of quiet time – longer if possible. I desperately wanted a break from all the work.

While working on the album, I'd been approached with offers to do TV shows such as *I'm a Celebrity, Big Brother* and all that shit, but they're not for me. It's enough that people form opinions about me based on a couple of snippets I'm supposed to have said. I don't like the idea of people seeing the real me: I'd rather not put myself out there like that. It's not a question of being liked or disliked, I just find the idea of being observed 24/7 and picked to pieces wholly unappealing. I toyed with the idea of *An Audience with Charlotte Church* or an hour's TV special, but I felt they were a bit too cheesy: good in the late Eighties and Nineties, but the only good one recently was the one done by Take That. Presenting and acting have never had much appeal for me either. Let's face it, work in any shape or form doesn't have that much appeal!

When you're famous in one field, new opportunities are always being thrown your way. Everyone around me had been saying that I should have my own TV show, but I wasn't sure I'd be competent enough. One evening, when I was on *Friday Night with Jonathan Ross*, his producer, Suzi Aplin, was chatting with Nick Fiveash. She offered to introduce me to the boys from Monkey Kingdom, a TV production company. I agreed to meet them, not because I wanted to do any particular type of show, but just to see if they could say anything that would make me go, 'Wow!' That hadn't happened since I was twelve.

Mark, Nick and I met them for lunch in the Oxo Tower. Will MacDonald reminded me of a forty-year-old Harry Potter with messy hair and funky trainers, which he reckons draw attention away from his pot belly. Dave Granger looks as cool as a cucumber but reminds me of a giraffe at the same time. They are both really posh, though they fight it a little bit, as well as being funny, clever and full of energy. I immediately liked their vibe. They had both been part of Chris Evans's team when he did *TFI Friday* and *Don't Forget Your Toothbrush* – Will was his trusty sidekick on the show.

Nothing really came out of that first meeting except the realisation that these would be great people to work with if we could come up with the right idea. We went on to have several more meetings, but key was the one we had sitting round a snooker table in the Groucho, a London club, eating terrible sandwiches with the crusts cut off. Will and Dave were trying to gauge what sort of show I'd like to do, and as I hadn't a clue we used a weird process of elimination.

'What about an Ant and Dec-type family show?'

'No. I'd like it to be on a Friday because that's my favourite day of the week. And I'd like it to be funny and different.'

'A chat show, then?'

'No. I don't think so. But I loved *TFI Friday*, so something more like that, with loads of guests, comedy and music.'

We talked around that really simple brief before they went off to see which of the channels would be interested. Fabulously, they all were. Channel 4 are a bit more risqué than the rest, though, and we thought we'd be able to retain more control over the format and content if we went with them as well as be a bit ruder. Decision made. Time for the church-hall pilot.

Picture a typical church hall: parquet flooring, white walls, not too run down and absolutely freezing. The set was made up of black boxes that made a platform with a bit of a bar set up. Four members of the band shivered in the corner; Tara Palmer-Tomkinson and the comedian Alan Carr were my guests, but there was no audience. Then, at the very last minute, we heard Andrew Newman, Head of Entertainment and Comedy at Channel 4, was on his way to check us out. Monkey had wanted me to sing, but I couldn't see how that would work in a comedy show. I don't mind taking the piss out of myself, but not out of my singing, because that's the one thing I know I'm good at. I have got a bit of pride, like. They wanted me to open and close singing Luther Vandross's 'Never Too Much', but it seemed too cheesy to me and didn't work with the rest of the show.

'Couldn't I sing some sort of theme tune instead?' I suggested, with only two hours to go.

There was a tune going round my head that I sang to the band, and then Dominic English, the scriptwriter, Will, Dave and I put some words together, basically taking the piss out of the type of show it was aiming to be. We got it right just as the door opened and Andrew Newman walked in.

The show was a raving success with the twenty people in the hall, and I think everyone was surprised, and relieved, including me. I'd never done anything like it before, so I'd been anxious about putting my hand in the fire. Loads of presenters have no inhibitions, but I have. This was like putting my cock on the block – so to speak! – but I managed to carry it off without anything too bad happening.

I was lucky that Dom involved me in writing the script so that I could edit out anything I thought wasn't funny or felt uncomfortable saying. He has worked with all sorts of people, including Sacha Baron Cohen and Ricky Gervais in the early stages of their careers, and he's the funniest man I've ever met. He's my Ian Shaw of the comedy world. Like Will, he's got a uniform, only his is a short-sleeved khaki shirt with combats and trainers. He always looks well ironed! When we watched the church-hall pilot back on screen, he pointed out that I always try to justify a joke after the punch line. 'You can't do that. You have to deliver it with confidence,' he insisted. He showed me how to deliver jokes, and which words to stress in what order. I thought nothing went into telling a joke, but it's much more complicated than I'd realised. Fortunately, I've got quite good timing, just like my aunt Caroline and Bampy, so at least I didn't have to work too hard on that.

We had to go back and forth, sharpening the script and deciding on the set before the proper pilot was recorded in July. We rewrote the theme song so it was less negative about the show. Originally Monkey had thought we might film on location, maybe even in my mum's pub, but in the end they went for a three-part glam studio set in the London Television Centre on the South Bank, which I loved. All my family and

Gavin's mates came up on a bus to be part of the live audience. They'd been drinking all the way and then found a pub opposite the studios, but they still managed to be quite well behaved and left me alone to get on with it.

Dom and I had been through the script, but he still fed me questions through an earpiece to ask my guests, Sally Lindsay and Trisha Goddard. I'd already vetoed quite a few because I've been on the receiving end of so many interviews and know what it's like. I want to ask the questions people want to know the answers to, but I won't be rude to my guests. Sometimes I've asked for certain subjects to be off-limits for good reason, but the interviewer has gone ahead and asked them anyway. Parky once asked me, 'How's your sex life?' What a question for a man in his seventies to ask a teenager! What would he have said if I'd replied, 'How's yours, Parky?' I always tell the guests that I'll make sure that anything that embarrasses them isn't used, and I really would see that through.

In the end, the poor audience had to sit through four hours of filming. I hadn't expected it to stop and start nearly so much, as we had to redo a couple of links and sort out camera angles and stuff like that. Sally was a great guest, very funny, while Trisha was a bit more difficult for me to interview because she wasn't giving anything away, though I sympathised with that completely. Although the pilot show was never seen by the public, a journalist sneaked in and the press went nuts about a nun sketch we tried out. We had specifically said we didn't want press there, so they had no right to make the content of the pilot public knowledge. The whole point of a pilot is to test things out. I was horrified that we caused offence over a couple of bad-taste jokes that never got beyond the cutting-room floor.

Despite the fuss, Channel 4 really loved the show and commissioned a series of seven, plus a Christmas show. I was made-up, but at the same time quite apprehensive. Would we be able to think up enough material for a whole series? Every Tuesday, I'd go up to London, do a script read-through, make any changes, be briefed on the guests for that week, rehearse with the guest artist and do a band rehearsal for the theme tune, which changed every week: rock, pop, dance, blues, whatever.

My trusty band has been with me since the *Tissues and Issues* tour: JBoy the bassist, Adam the guitarist, Jim, Nicol and Dom on horns, Rob on keys, and Lucy and Shena on backing vocals. Bob Knight's the drummer and MD, who does the arrangements and makes everything easy for me. We work brilliantly together, always cracking jokes and having a laugh. After we'd finish, I'd take a car back to Cardiff, arriving at about ten at night, then leaving again at six the following morning. I don't like staying the night in London on my own and would much rather get back to my own bed, my dogs and Gavin – not necessarily in that order, mind! – even if it means an early start the next day.

Wednesday was a whole day of rehearsal, make-up and hair at 2 p.m., then a dress rehearsal. That much fucking rehearsal was a pain in the arse, but it was for the cameras and directors, so they could all be a bit funny about whatever I was wearing. I never took any notice of what clothes they liked or disliked. It was a great environment to work in and I loved all the people. At the end of the week I'd have to film the video clips (VTs), where I went on location to play tricks on the public.

Some guests were easier than others. If they were promoting a book, I tried to read as much as I could by the time I met them, even though I was usually only told a day or two before. As soon as Rupert Everett arrived at the studio, all the researchers and production people kept bursting into my room. 'Charlotte, it's Rupert. He's in a really bad mood. Go and say hi to him.' Come on, he's a fucking grown man. He's here to do work that he's being paid for. Grow up.

I'd been looking forward to meeting him because I think he's quite cool and, from his autobiography, he seemed like an interesting man, but when we finally did meet, he looked as if he'd rather be anywhere than sitting in the studio. Fair enough, but no one was forcing him to be there, and he did have his book to promote. He was wearing Adidas tracksuit bottoms, some dodgy-arse zip-up fleece and he hadn't even brushed his hair. The interview kicked off slowly, but eventually Rupert relaxed and was very funny, although he made me uncomfortable when he was talking about filming sex scenes. 'You know, they're constantly measuring from the camera to your pussy,' he explained, demonstrating at the same time. I was like, Fuck off! But he's gay, so it was fine. He had the whole audience in stitches, and by the time he left he'd charmed the pants off us all.

Johnny Vegas was a complete pain in the arse because he wouldn't stop talking. I know he plays the part of a sad, lonely drunk, but I couldn't tell whether he was being himself or whether it was all part of the joke. He seemed really tragic and made it quite difficult for me, interrupting even when the interview was finished, talking to the audience while I was doing the link. In the end I had to slap him just to shut him up. He kept saying, 'Oh, sorry, sorry. You must hate me. I'm a fucking nightmare.'

Yeah, you are. Just shut up. 'No, you're not. Just be quiet now.'

He'd stop for a second and then he'd start off again. It took forty minutes to record the five minutes of interview that was finally aired. The funny thing is that everyone who saw it thought it was really good, so I take it all back, Johnny!

The only other real embarrassment was Amy Winehouse. She was absolutely fucking hammered on the night. She's an amazing singer with a wicked talent, so I'd been looking forward to having her on the show. She'd seemed a bit odd when I'd met her the day before, but I'd put her down as one of those kooky artists, hair all over the place in a proper backcomb. We were due to sing 'Beat It' together, but she kept jazzing it up in a not very good way. I hoped she'd do it better the next day. Out of the blue she said to me, 'See my friend over there? He really fancies you.'

'Yeah, OK, but I'm with somebody.' I took another look. 'Anyway, he's a fucking girl, isn't he? Are you sure?'

'Yeah.' She smiled. 'He'd like to see me put my tongue down your throat.'

'Yeuch!' I turned away. 'Bob, let's do the song again.'

Afterwards I thought I'd been really rude saying 'Yeuch' to her face when she'd just offered to snog me, but that's life.

When we did the next rehearsal at midday on the day of the show, she stank of champagne and was a bit all over the place, but I thought, She'll sober up by tonight. She's got to. Come the show, she was even more hammered than before and wouldn't read a joke off the autocue: 'I can't fucking do it. It ain't even funny.' The audience were beginning to laugh by then, and when one of the other guests did a joke about Temazepam, she piped up, 'I love that.' The audience were roaring with laughter. I thought Temazepam was something like marzipan that you put on cakes, so I didn't get what was going on at all.

When we got to the song, she was shit and we had to do it four times. Every time, the cameras had to be reset and the director was tearing out what was left of his hair. Sometimes she'd forget to come in, sometimes she'd come in at the wrong place and sometimes she'd just stop singing and put her hands over her mouth. I was trying to be encouraging, but she kept laughing and the audience was hysterical. Some of them called out, 'Sing it on your own, Charlotte.' At one point, during the instrumental, she turned to the drummer and said, 'I'm fucking hammered.' As if we didn't know. By the final take, I'd had enough, so I put my hand behind her back and poked her hard when she had to sing. Even then she was doing some kind of weird-arse harmony that wasn't working. Whenever she tried to walk away or turn her back, I just held her so she couldn't move. 'Ladies and gentlemen, Amy Winehouse.' Fucking stay there. Don't move till we've finished. But she's won a Brit and had a massively successful album, so I'm sure it was just a temporary hitch.

All the other guests I sang with were brilliant. I loved singing with the Brand New Heavies, Nelly Furtado, The Feeling, Sugababes and Orson. Jamelia is one of the most beautiful women I've ever seen and lovely to work with. In rehearsal she kept apologising if she got something wrong, but I was like, 'Shuddup. It's fine.' I was messing everything up as well.

The bad was far outweighed by the good. A lot of guests are just not interested. You can see they're thinking, Just get me in and out – I know. I've been there myself – but not Liza Minnelli. She was a little bit of a diva, keeping us waiting, but never a nasty one. She's a legend and she was just showing her status, which is fair enough. I'd have waited all day if I'd had to. Sometimes she'd ask for a change, so we couldn't make fun of someone she knew who was dead, and she refused to throw a ruby slipper across the set because she didn't want to disrespect Judy Garland's red slippers in *The Wizard of Oz*. Every second that she wasn't talking, she was smoking; and after the show she wanted to stay and talk some more, but was very sweet when I told her I had to get back for one of Gavin's games. I thought she was fabulous: a friendly, lovely woman who made a real effort.

When Billie Piper came on, she reminded me that she had been my upstairs neighbour in St David's when she was filming *Dr Who* in Cardiff. On the show she said she was jealous because it sounded as if I was having amazing parties downstairs while she was sitting all on her own, watching re-runs of *Sex and the City* or whatever. If only I'd known, I'd have asked her down.

My memory of the same time was of me and the girls coming back from town, completely bolloxed, and hearing she was having a bit of a rave upstairs. We stood outside shouting up at her open window, 'Let us in. Let us in.' And singing 'Because we want to . . .' over and over again. But she never heard us. In the end we only met for half a second when she came down to borrow some sugar, so it was great to meet her properly on the show. I gelled with her instantly because she's open and honest, charming and funny – all the qualities I most appreciate in a guest.

This business is full of tortured souls, which, to be honest, gets a bit boring after a while. One person who doesn't fit into that niche is Davina McCall, who was honest, warm and, in a word, fabulous – an absolutely brilliant guest. Some guests are more reserved, though, and don't want to give anything away. They tend to answer yes or no and not much more, which makes it harder to keep the conversation going, to make it funny and to make them look good too. I think that's an important part of my job. That wasn't a problem with Davina, though. She's very comfortable with herself and we really clicked.

Being an interviewer didn't come easily to me at all. After the first two pilots, everyone said I'd have to work on being more relaxed, but it was Gavin who nailed it. He said, 'You're just not listening to what they're saying. They say something funny, but you cut them off with the next question. You don't even laugh.' I could see he was right. I was racing ahead because I was nervous that I'd go blank or not have the next question ready. I also had Dom talking in my ear, so having a conversation with someone while that was going on took a bit of getting used to, and if he misjudged when they were going to finish and came in too late, I'd be stuck.

The worst thing, though, was wearing the prosthetic make-up for the VTs. To make a cast, plaster that feels about a foot thick was spread all over my face, leaving two holes for my nose. Being under it felt like how I imagine death feels: absolute blackness. Then, using the cast, the prosthetics were made to fit my face perfectly. Looking at myself in the mirror when I was the boy, Charlie Chapel, was weird because the face was so realistic. I kept repeating to myself, 'Keep in touch. Keep in touch with yourself. I'm Charlotte Church.'

What I like most about the show is that I'm working with a great group of people behind the scenes who are all good at their jobs. Duffy does my hair, Amanda does my make-up and

Kate or Faye do my styling. Kate is the wonder woman who found the wicked corset that knocks pounds off me without my having to diet. Usually I do my own hair and make-up, because I'm not that interested and I can be quite quick, but when I'm knackered after rehearsals, it's quite nice to sit down and have it all done for me. Working with people you really like makes such a difference; we just have a scream.

On the day we record the show, I haven't got a second to spit. I only have time to eat something like a sausage sandwich because there's no time to stop. Everything would probably be easier if I spent more time in London rehearsing, but I don't.

I was really happy with the first series. I thought the shows were well put together, fast-paced and entertaining. I did get some letters about my swearing from the old ladies who used to be my fans when I was younger. What can I say? I'm sorry, but I grew up. I understand where they're coming from, but this is a different era and different things are acceptable. It's not like I'm killing people, I just swear a bit too much, so cut me some slack. Having said that, when two more series were commissioned by Channel 4, I did make a New Year's resolution to try and stop swearing so much. I think I've been quite successful . . . sometimes.

What was especially fabulous was winning the award for Best Female Newcomer at the 2006 British Comedy Awards. I'd already been given the 2005 *GQ* Woman of the Year Award and the 2006 *Glamour* Award for Best Female Artist of the Year, and an extra award, the Editor's Choice, thrown in for good measure, so this was the icing on the cake. Jonathan Ross hosted the awards, and everyone from the comedy world was there, from Sacha Baron Cohen to Catherine Tate, Russell Brand to Ant and Dec, and the boys from *Little Britain*.

Being there felt a bit odd because I'd spent the day at the funeral of a friend, Phil Piercy, who used to lodge with my mum. Mum, the hostess with the mostest, would invite us round to dinner and get Phil to cook. He made the most fabulous chocolate cake I've ever tasted and was a sweetheart of a man. He was very funny, a great friend of the family and did a lot of the carpentry work in my house. Caroline and I sang 'Wind Beneath My Wings' for him at the funeral. On the way up to London, I'd decided that if I did win the award, I'd thank everyone, but dedicate it to him. I was so pleased to be able to do that.

I completely love my show and the way it's developed. Once we got to the second series, we tightened up the format, doing more of the stuff that people liked from the first and cutting what they didn't. I was much more comfortable with the interviews, too, and less frightened that I was going to run out of questions, so I threw away the earpiece. I was even hoping we'd do the third series live. Not having the safety net of being a recorded show, when you can re-record things if it goes wrong, would be a real challenge and I like the idea of pushing myself a bit more every time. However, I didn't think that appearing on a Channel 4 Friday night TV show and telling crude jokes with a massive pregnant belly was appropriate. I didn't like the idea of doing that at all, so we had to postpone the series. People ask me how I think the show will change my career and what I think I'll be doing in five years' time, but I haven't a clue. Watch this space!

However much I love the show, singing will always be my first love. I'm going to go back to Lulu for lessons in piano and singing. Gav gave me a beautiful grand piano for Christmas, so the least I can do is learn how to play it! I will continue to take lessons with Ian Shaw, but I want to see whether I can still sing classical: not because I'm harbouring a secret ambition to appear at La Scala any more, but for my own pride and personal curiosity, to see whether I can still do it.

I have absolutely no idea what musical direction I'm going to take next. I used to joke with Mark that my next album would be Ukrainian folk, so I wouldn't have to do any promotion. Seriously, though, the sound of the acoustic guitar hits me in the guts more than any other instrument, so perhaps I'll do something a bit Damien Ricey. I love 'The Blower's Daughter' and other tracks like that. I thought a lot of *Tissues and Issues* was trodden on by production, making it unnecessarily complicated. Instead, I like the idea of stripping the music back and writing some beautiful soulful lyrics with lovely melodies that will sound perfect with the guitar. But maybe I'll get into the studio and discover that my voice doesn't suit that sort of thing and that I need a slightly whiny voice, like Chris Martin from Coldplay, to pull it off. If that happens, then I'll have to take myself in another direction. I can't be sure about anything at the moment.

The one thing I can be sure of is that my relationship with Sony BMG is over. I owed them one more album after *Tissues and Issues* and we had talked about extending the contract for one more after that. We agreed a deal, but before it was signed Rob Stringer left for America. He was really the last person I knew at Sony. Most of the old greats, including Paul Burger, had gone by then and Sony had merged with BMG, so everything was changing. The guy who replaced Rob wanted me to take a cut in money, but having seen the success of my show he also wanted me to agree to develop some TV programmes with them. As far as I was concerned we'd already reached an agreement that I was happy with, and I felt they were changing the goalposts at the last minute, while they felt I was unreasonable in refusing to renegotiate and take a cut in money, so they threatened to drop me if I refused. I was like, 'So fucking drop me then!' And they did.

CHAPTER 20

What Next?

TIP:

Try to be flexible and remain open to new opportunities. If life throws something unexpected at you, take it on the chin and roll with it. Who knows where it may lead.

Being dropped by Sony felt a bit weird at first, since they had been part of my life since I was twelve, but I wasn't heartbroken. For me it was more a question of moving on. Since then I've had a lot of interest from all of their competitors, but I'm not in a position to make a new album right this minute, what with the baby and all, so rather than signing me immediately, giving me shitloads of money up front and then piling on the pressure, they have indicated that they're willing to wait until I'm ready. I've been really heartened by their cool attitude.

I want time to adjust to having a baby with Gavin. I never thought I'd be pregnant at twenty-one, but I definitely don't think having a child this young is a bad thing. I've already had an amazing career so it's not as if I'm making difficulties for myself just as I'm starting out, and I'm in a stable relationship with a fabulous man. Gav's so dedicated to his career and I'll do everything I can to support him, just as he supports me. We're so comfortable together now that it's a given that we're going to be together. Our relationship isn't the volatile kind. If we do have an argument, we're over it in five minutes. If I ever get really pissed off about something, I go to my nana's for half an hour to cool off before I come back home to talk things through. Gav's very calm and takes things in his stride without getting all riled up.

Maybe we'll get married one day, but I don't need a wedding ring to make me feel secure or complete in this relationship, and I don't think that it's necessary to be married before you have a baby in this day and age. I know that my nan would have liked one of the women in her family to do it all properly – get married and then have a baby – but I've fucked that up as well now.

Another cool thing to come out of our relationship is getting to know Gav's family. I liked them as soon as I met them. They're a rarity in that his mum and dad work as a complete team, doing everything together and usually for everyone else. Alan is a bit of an entertainer, ruddy-cheeked and a really funny guy. Gav has his strong nose and Walt Disney eyes, while he's inherited his mother's cheekbones and good skin. Audrey is a lovely auburn-haired woman who usually looks quite country casual in jeans, a vest top and cashmere jumper. She's a real mother hen who does everything for her kids. Nothing's too much trouble. She's also a brilliant cook, so there's always food on the go in their house: delicious desserts, fairy cakes and cookies. If they look after our dogs when we're away, the dogs hate coming home because they've been fed with great leftovers and been on long walks every day. I can only imagine that our baby will be the same!

Gav's sister, Sarah, is just as special. She's a natural beauty who looks like the rest of her family but also reminds me a bit of Kyla, in that they're always well presented and are very friendly and easy-going. We've become firm friends, and got on brilliantly when we went for a week in Thailand together after I'd finished the last TV series.

I've no idea what Gav and I will be like as parents. He's like, 'It's going to be lovely.' He hasn't a clue! I have no romantic ideas at all. In fact I'm shitting myself because I know having a baby is hard work. I'll be so tired and that will put a massive strain on us. When I've asked him how he'll feel when I'm giving so much time to the baby that I won't be able to look after him as much, he just says, 'That's what I want. That's what it's supposed to be like.' I can't ask for more than that.

One thing I'm sure of, if Gav's anything like his parents, is that he'll be a great father. He makes his childhood sound idyllic, full of long walks with the dogs, camping with his parents at the weekends and always a hearty meal on the table, complete with extra helpings and desserts. I love the idea of bringing up our kids in the country, surrounded by fields and animals, rather than in a street full of traffic like I was. We're moving out of Cardiff to somewhere near Merthyr Mawr in Bridgend, where we often walk the dogs in the sand dunes.

Saying that, I wouldn't change my upbringing for the world. I know our baby will get so much self-confidence from being one of my family, and it's bound to inherit the performing gene that's in every one of us. Me, my mum and my dad have always been close and I hope that I'll have the same sort of relationship with my child, though perhaps a bit less excitable! If our child turns out to be particularly talented, then I would do exactly what my parents did: make them go to school, give them the choice of what they want to do and encourage them. I'm immensely proud of my parents and how they handled everything as I grew up. I wouldn't be the person I am today if they hadn't been there every step of the way.

I'm reasonably level-headed and think I'm aware of all the possibilities ahead. People say that having children is a life-changing experience, but that it's also life-enriching. I expect my perspective on life will change, but I'm looking forward to that. Since I've been living with Gav, I've happily said goodbye to my party days. Been there, done that. The only time I get all dolled up and go out these days is if we're invited to awards ceremonies or charity events. I'd rather stay in with Gav and a good DVD or go out quietly with my good friends.

I feel totally happy with the new chapter of my life that's opening up. I have no idea how having a child will affect me on the work front. I may want to take a good long time off to be with our baby or I may want to dash straight back to recording a new album or making another series of the show. Who knows? I'm lucky that I've got enough money to be able to make that choice. I'm just going to wait and see, knowing that Gav and both our families will support me, whatever I decide.

I'm so blessed to have lived a full life so far. I wouldn't change a thing. It's been full of ups and downs, but at least it's been exciting and different. So far, I've managed to deal with pretty much everything life has chucked at me, so I hope I'll be able to deal with whatever else comes my way. On the other hand, I've discovered that routine suits me well, too. Having a steady relationship with Gav and my family means everything to me. I'm immensely proud of my achievements so far, even though when I look back at what I've done, all the places I've been to and the people I've met, I can't quite believe that person was me.

Most of all, I'm grateful for how happy I am at the moment. I wake up every morning and look forward to the day ahead. I'm getting more and more excited about having our first baby. I know everything will be fine because Gavin's such an amazing man and will take such a hands-on role. The baby may change our life, but I feel confident that it's also going to make us even happier. Should times get tough in the future, I know I'll get through them somehow if I keep on following Bampy's sound advice and keep smiling.

Index